Shot All to Hell

ALSO BY MARK LEE GARDNER

To Hell on a Fast Horse: The Untold Story
of Billy the Kid and Pat Garrett

Shot All to Hell

Jesse James, the Northfield Raid,
and the Wild West's Greatest Escape

Mark Lee Gardner

HARPER **LUXE**

An Imprint of HarperCollinsPublishers

Maps on pages 105 and 188 courtesy of Chris Erichsen

Grateful acknowledgment is made to the following for use of photographs that appear throughout the text: collection of the author (pp. 33, 109, 110, 114, 119, 123, 307, 315, 322); Library of Congress (pp. 43, 46, 95, 313, 324, 330, 343); Northfield Historical Society (pp. 98, 100, 101, 131, 140, 158, 159, 225, 242: images of Jim Younger and Bob Younger, 244); Robert G. McCubbin Collection (pp. 125, 242: images of Cole Younger and Charlie Pitts, 317, 342, 344); courtesy of Leona Hardwicke Mustion (p. 297).

HarperCollins books may be purchased for educational, business, or sales promotional use. For information, please e-mail the Special Markets Department at SPsales@harpercollins.com.

FIRST HARPERLUXE EDITION

HarperLuxe™ is a trademark of HarperCollins Publishers

Library of Congress Cataloging-in-Publication Data is available upon request.

ISBN: 978-0-06-220151-5

13 14 ID/RRD 10 9 8 7 6 5 4 3 2 1

To Duane and Joan Olson
Northfield, Minnesota

A man who is a damned enough fool
to refuse to open a safe or a vault when
he is covered with a pistol ought to die.

—Jesse James

These men are bad citizens, but they are bad
because they live out of their time.

—John Newman Edwards

Contents

Contents

Shot All to Hell

Prologue

Nerves hard as blackjack oak, the ability to ride like blazes, and the latest six-gun all played a role in the James and Younger boys' special brand of mayhem. Equally important to their astounding success was the art of the lie. They excelled at deception—they had to.

During the Civil War, as Missouri bushwhackers, they often wore bluecoat jackets to deceive Union troops and Northern sympathizers. Later, as outlaws, they took on aliases and were able to stop trains or empty bank vaults while moving about freely in public, telling people they were livestock dealers, businessmen, or land speculators. On those occasions when they were accused of brazen robbery, they would write letters to the press denying their involvement and offering up alibis to show they had been far, far away from the scene of the crime. Powerful friends lied for them—and so did their kin.

This tendency to deception creates an incredible challenge for the historian in telling the story of the Northfield Raid. The words of the three Younger brothers, from the first interviews given following their bloody capture to Cole Younger's deathbed narration related in 1916, are a minefield of lies and half truths. The outlaws' calculated statements were designed not only to protect themselves but to protect their brothers-in-arms, Jesse and Frank James, who famously got away. The Youngers steadfastly refused, at least under oath, to say the James boys were ever part of the fiasco. And thirty-nine years later, Frank James went to his grave still claiming he had never set foot in Minnesota.

Fortunately, there are a number of eyewitness accounts from the men who defeated the James-Younger gang in 1876, including the surviving bank employees, the deadeye Northfield citizens, and the several posses that pursued the bandits. But these eyewitnesses don't always agree, as is common after any event marked by excitement, great confusion, and tragedy. Some participants told and retold their stories over a span of years; others did not share their stories until decades later. Newspaper reports are another significant source of information about the raid and the manhunt, but in their craze to publish any piece of news about the robbers, these papers often ran items that were nothing more than rumors and speculation.

Still, my efforts to uncover the true story of the raid and its aftermath have led to new discoveries—and new answers to old questions—that are published here for the first time. The following narrative is the most accurate account of the nineteenth century's most famous robbery and manhunt. All dialogue within quotes comes directly from primary sources and has not been made up or altered.

My personal pursuit of the James-Younger gang naturally led me to the reading rooms of aged archives and libraries, to which I made multiple visits. But I spent just as much time out in the open, following the winding blacktops of Missouri and Minnesota. Along with thousands of others, I witnessed the smoke-filled reenactments of the Northfield bank robbery and the capture of the Younger brothers. I sought out fellow historians, writers, curators, James-Younger gang buffs, and reenactors. I retraced the escape route the robbers took out of Northfield. I visited the rural home of Jesse and Frank near Kearney, Missouri; the modest house where Jesse was killed by the coward Robert Ford in St. Joseph; and the graves of Cole, Bob, and Jim Younger in Lee's Summit.

Some of these historic places were like old friends because I grew up in the heart of Missouri's Jesse James country. Like most boys my age, I was fascinated by Jesse and pretended to rob banks and trains during school recess, all the while doing my very best imitation of the notorious outlaw. I taped wanted posters on my bedroom wall in the small town of Breckenridge. In more ways than one, this book has truly been a journey home for me.

Jesse, Frank, Cole, Bob, Jim, Clell, Charlie, Bill—eight men at the top of their game. No gang of criminals was more feared, more wanted, more hated, and more celebrated. They were the quintessential horseback outlaws. Before September 7, 1876, the James-Younger gang had never been challenged, denied, or defeated. On that fateful day, the people of Northfield had little idea who these well-mounted strangers were.

And that is just the way the gang wanted it.

One
Rocky Cut

They were no common thieves or vulgar robbers, but had an ambition to make themselves famous, in, as they termed it, "a fair, square and honorable" way of doing such things.

—KANSAS CITY WEEKLY JOURNAL OF COMMERCE

Friday, July 7, 1876
Two months to the day before the Northfield Raid

Henry Lewis Chouteau, the bridge watchman for the Missouri Pacific Railroad, sat smoking on a bench outside the pump house on the bank of the Lamine River. It was approximately 9:00 P.M., and express train number four was about an hour down the tracks to the west. When its puffing locomotive, baggage car, express-baggage car, three coaches, and two sleepers approached the bridge, a loud whistle would blow.

The express-baggage car held two locked safes, which were the property of the Adams Express Company and the United States Express Company. Those safes had enough hard cash inside to operate a small bank.

Chouteau was waiting there by himself. The closest town, Otterville, was a good mile away. And it was hot. At that time of evening, in the middle of a typical Missouri summer, the river bottom's sticky stillness made a man's sweat come easily. Suddenly, Chouteau tensed and gazed at something moving across the bridge. Four men were walking along the tracks toward him. Chouteau, a forty-six-year-old native of Switzerland, had been on the job only two weeks, and though he might not have been surprised to see a fisherman near the bridge, these four men were suspicious. The moon was bright that night, and as the strangers got closer, he could see that they were well dressed, their pants tucked into heavy, high-topped boots. He could hear the clinking sounds their spurs made as they walked. Three of the men sat down next to him without saying a word. The fourth, a tall man, stood out in front.

"What are you doing here?" the man said.

"I am here watching the bridge," Chouteau answered.

Then the man asked Chouteau how he halted the train if there was danger. Chouteau thought this was puzzling but explained that he would stand on the tracks with his red-glass lantern. If all was safe with the bridge, he used his white lantern.

The tall man turned to one of his companions on the bench. "What time is it?"

That man reached into his trousers and pulled out a pocket watch. He tilted the watch's face into the moonlight. "Ten minutes after nine."

"It is about time," the tall man said.

Another man on the bench stood up and asked Chouteau where he could get a drink of water. Chouteau told him there was a good, clear spring nearby, and he got up and walked with the stranger to where they could see it. Then Chouteau went to get a drinking cup from the pump house. He didn't see the man's three companions but still he stepped inside the small building, where the three men jumped him, grabbed his arms, and pointed a shiny, nickel-plated revolver at his chest. Chouteau stared at the pistol, trembling and speechless. He watched as the three strangers pulled masks from their pockets and put them on their faces.

"Old man, come along with us," one of the men ordered. "We have work for you to do."

Chouteau pleaded with the men that the Missouri Pacific would fire him if he left his post. "They laughed at me," he later recalled, "and said the company would not mind that, as I had to go."

The men told Chouteau to hammer a large nail into the west side of the bridge and hang the lit white lantern there. The lantern would be clearly visible to train number four and the engineer would proceed across the bridge at normal speed. The men then walked Chouteau to the pump house to get the red lantern, after which they blindfolded him. With one of them holding on to each side of Chouteau, they crossed the bridge and followed the rails east for three-quarters of a mile. Along the way, Chouteau could hear them whispering to more men who had joined them. They eventually stopped where the rails entered a long, deep cut through the side of a limestone bluff and told Chouteau to sit down off to the side of the tracks.

"You ain't going to hurt me?" asked Chouteau.

"What do we want to hurt you for?" a man said. "We want that money. That is all we care for."

One of the bandits began digging a hole between the wooden ties of the railroad bed so that a post could be sunk there in the ground, but it was exhausting, time-consuming work. The robbers decided it would be easier to block the tracks with some railroad ties they discovered stacked nearby.

Chouteau, still guarded by two men, heard the robbers' groans as they lifted and piled the ties on the rails. "The mosquitoes were thick there," he remembered, "and every time I would brush them from my face with my hand, [the robbers] would put their hands on me and say, 'Hands off your face.'"

Once they finished, the robbers grilled Chouteau about those on the train: the express men, conductors, and engineer. They particularly wondered if any of those men carried firearms. Chouteau had no way of knowing that and told them so.

Rocky Cut, as that remote place was known, was on one end of a long, broad curve in the Missouri Pacific line, which meant the robbers would hear the train before they saw it. A few minutes after 10:00 P.M., right on schedule, they heard the clear blast of the locomotive's steam whistle from across the river bottom.

Someone lit the watchman's red lantern, handed it to him, and then led him to the middle of the tracks, some twenty feet behind the stack of ties. Finally, in the distance, they saw the beam from the locomotive's oil lamp as it threw a traveling glow upon the leaves of the nearby cottonwoods and sycamores and the brush and vines growing near the rail bed. The robbers sharply ordered Chouteau to flag the train, and he passionately swung his lantern in big arcs from side to side.

The moonlight was bright enough that the train's engineer had trouble making out the red light, but the minute he recognized the warning signal ahead, he immediately grabbed the air brake lever and reversed his engine. There was a piercing squeal of metal on metal while the engineer did his best to halt the train. But the distance was too short. Chouteau, still blind-folded, prayed like never before as the locomotive's cowcatcher hit the stacked ties and slid up on top of them before finally coming to a stop.

That's when the robbers fired off their pistols and started letting out triumphant whoops from both sides of the train. Some of these desperadoes had stationed themselves on the bluff overlooking the cut, and they were carefully watching to make a move. The locomotive's own weight caused it to ease backward and down again upon the rails, a burst of steam hissing from the engine as if it were angry at how rudely it was being treated. An emotionally spent Chouteau was led away from the tracks and warned to stay put.

Two robbers clambered up into the locomotive's cab and pointed their revolvers at the engineer and fire-man. "Better keep quiet, you know," they said. At the back of the train, the other men threw ties and any-thing else handy on the rails to stop the engineer from trying to back away.

At the sound of the first gunshots, John B. Bushnell, the twenty-seven-year-old express messenger, who had the key to one of the safes, headed to the rear of the train. As Bushnell rushed down the aisle, a passenger asked him what was the matter. Without stopping, a visibly distressed Bushnell blurted out, "The train is being robbed, that's what's the matter!"

Bushnell's words electrified the passengers, who frantically began looking for places to hide their valuables. Gold watches, breastpins, and greenbacks were shoved down boot tops and socks. Diamond rings were slid under the carpet. Some found hiding places in the cars' dirty coal bins. One traveler climbed up and pushed his wallet through the ventilator in the ceiling so it rested on the roof of the car. All the while, the gunshots and yelling continued outside, causing more than a few terrified passengers to drop down and curl up beneath their seats.

When a woman began to cry, one man exclaimed, for the entire car to hear, "Madam, I'll protect you at the risk of my life." This led another to say, "Why, then, don't you go and fight those fellows in the front?" No one said another word.

The Reverend Jonathan S. Holmes of Bedford, New York, began to sing the hymn "I'm Going Home (to Die No More)." Someone stopped him from singing and told him he should forget the camp meeting and find a way to hide his money. But the minister went back and finished his song in a quavering voice. Then he stood up and testified to his fellow passengers. He said that "if he was doomed to be murdered, he wanted his remains forwarded to his family . . . and to write them that he had died true to his faith and in the hope of glorious resurrection."

Bushnell made his way to the rear sleeper, where he saw a brakeman and quickly pressed the key into his hand, telling the man to hide it in his shoe, which the brakeman did. Bushnell then moved back to the nearest coach and took a seat, hopeful that he would be mistaken for a passenger.

The baggage master, twenty-one-year-old Pete Conklin, was alone in the express car. The front and rear doors of the car were closed and locked, but the sliding side doors were open to let in air during the summer heat. As soon as the train came to a stop, three of the robbers climbed up on their companions' shoulders and came through the side of the car. They immediately spotted the safes—and Conklin—and pointed their revolvers at him and demanded the keys. When Conklin said he did not have the keys, they began roughly feeling over his body, cursing the whole time. The men's faces were covered with bandannas up above their noses, but he could not miss the fierce, blue eyes of the man who was the leader. His eyes seemed to blink more than normal. This man shoved his six-shooter into Conklin's rib cage and demanded that he tell them who had the keys.

"I suppose the messenger has 'em," Conklin said.

"Where's the express messenger, then?"

"He's back in the train somewhere."

"Come with me and find him."

With Conklin leading the way, the outlaw chief and one confederate headed to the rear of the train. As they worked their way through the cars, some of the passengers sat up and were completely still and looking straight ahead, scared they might be shot if they made even a slight move.

It did not take long for Conklin to find Bushnell.

"You're the man I want," said the leader. "Come forward now and unlock that safe without any nonsense."

Bushnell said he didn't have a key to the safe.

"You want to find it damned quick," the leader said, raising the barrel of his pistol up to Bushnell's face, "or I will kill you."

Bushnell didn't need any more convincing. He led the robbers into the sleeper car and straight to the brakeman.

"Give us the keys, my Christian friend, and be damned quick about it," said the outlaw. With that the brakeman took off his shoe and handed over the key.

The robbers now started back for the express car with Bushnell and Conklin. In the smoking car, a lanky man from Indiana was having a hard time squeezing his entire body beneath his seat, and one of his boots was sticking out in the aisle. The robber leader tripped over the boot and, after catching his balance, turned and looked down at the man.

"Oh, Mister," screamed the Hoosier, "*please* don't shoot me! I didn't mean to trip you up, Mister! I swear I didn't! I wouldn't a did it for anything! I beg ten thousand pardons, Mister!"

The outlaw laughed and walked on.

After the men had all passed through the coaches, the passengers started chattering excitedly back and forth. Someone said the robbers had to be the James boys. But they were even more worried about a freight train expected to come through very soon that could ram the rear of this train. A crash would send jagged wooden splinters, glass, and bone-crunching steel through the air, not to mention the danger of fire and scalding steam from a ruptured locomotive boiler. What the passengers did not know was that the robbers had already sent a man down the track with a lantern to stop the freighter.

To intimidate the passengers and keep them from fighting back, the robbers kept up their firing and yelling outside. Anyone brave enough to poke a head out a window or door was greeted with a pointed gun and "Pull in your head you son of a bitch!" or "Go back you son of a bitch!"

The passengers and crew did as they were told—except for one. Louis Bales, a twenty-two-year-old black newsboy from St. Louis, carried a pocket-size, small-caliber pistol that could perhaps hurt someone, if that someone happened to be standing directly in front of the gun's muzzle when it went off. Bales and another gentleman were out on the platform of one of the coaches when Bales spotted a man on the bluff. He pointed his little weapon at the bandit and squeezed the trigger. The pistol made a pop like a cap gun.

Several of the robbers started laughing. "Hear that little son of a bitch bark!" one of them roared. A return shot that struck between Bales and the passenger sent the two scurrying for the safety of the car's interior. Bales "was game," recalled Pete Conklin years later, but he "probably had more courage than discretion."

The engineer and fireman were now waiting in the express car. As soon as the robbers entered with Conklin and Bushnell, they put a gun to the latter's head and ordered him to open the safe. Bushnell slid the key into the United States Express Company safe and pulled open the heavy door. The robbers began to fill a long wheat sack with the safe's contents, all except the waybills. But one of the outlaws seemed disappointed.

"Where are the remittances from the Kansas City, Sedalia and Atchison railroad?" he asked Bushnell.

The messenger did not know, but he said they might be on the earlier train. That was true, and although this was an extremely good haul for the outlaws, the previous train was carrying about four times the funds as this one.

After cleaning out the first safe, the robbers ordered Bushnell to open the Adams Express Company safe, but Bushnell nervously told them it was a "through safe," and there was no key on board that would open it. The robbers let loose with a long string of profanity and threats and insisted on trying several keys in the lock, their frustration mounting as none of them worked. Bushnell explained that the through safe had been sealed and loaded in Sedalia, fifteen miles back, and the key was left there. A second key was waiting in St. Louis, 170 miles down the tracks to the east. To Bushnell's great relief, the robbers finally accepted his story, but there was no way in hell they were leaving without the safe's contents. One of the robbers went to the engine tender and came back with a coal pick. First he slammed the pick's pointed end against the safe's hinges, several times, but nothing happened. Then he furiously swung the pick against the door. Nothing.

Another outlaw, this one a brawny fellow with a "fist like a ham," stepped forward and took the pick. Everyone gave the man plenty of room as he reared back and delivered a mighty blow against one of the safe's panels, which had only a single thickness of iron. After a dozen or so such swings, he was able to bust a small hole in the safe, but when he forced his large hand through the ragged opening, a good bit of his skin was taken off, and he couldn't pull out any of the safe's contents. He screamed out in pain as he withdrew his hand, cursing the safe as he did so. The leader could only laugh.

"Let me get at it," he said. "I wear a number seven glove, and both my hands will go where one of your mauleys won't."

He reached in nearly to his shoulder and grabbed hold of a big leather pouch, but it was too large to get through the hole, so he took a knife and slit open the pouch and brought out the money, a fistful at a time. He dropped it into the wheat sack, which was getting bigger and bigger.

The outlaws scavenged about the car for more booty, breaking into the newsboy's chest, which was loaded with candies, apples, even homemade pies and cakes.

The robbers gorged themselves as if they were a bunch of unsupervised seven-year-olds. The big outlaw who had conquered the safe acted like he was in a pie-eating contest, taking giant bites and "smearing his face till he looked ridiculous." The men also broke open the car's letter box and carelessly scattered the letters and documents all over the floor but found nothing of value.

The robber who was leading the shouts about blowing the heads off nosy and uncooperative passengers suddenly became hoarse and thirsty. He asked the other outlaws in the express car if there was any water. Conklin pointed to the water bucket and its drinking cup, but the leader, who had thought nothing of eating the goodies in the locked newsboy's chest, was suspicious of the open pail and asked if anyone had put anything in the water. Conklin said no, but the outlaw demanded that someone had to sample it before his men did.

"Here, you son of a bitch," he said to Conklin, "take a drink out of that. I don't propose to run any chances in any of this water business."

Conklin gladly swallowed two big gulps because his mouth had gone bone-dry almost an hour before when the first revolvers had been pointed at his face. When Conklin seemed okay, the robbers took turns dipping the cup in the bucket and finally sent a full cup out to the man outside who had requested it in the first place. He drank it quickly, water dripping from the corners of his mouth and down his neck, and then flung the cup into the bushes.

Next the leader insisted that Conklin unlock the other baggage car that had been added in Sedalia, but a quick look inside confirmed there was nothing worth bothering with. The leader then asked a curious question. He wanted to know if there were any detectives on board. He was not asking out of caution or concern; it was too late for that. The crew was aware of no detectives. The leader's deep blue eyes became even more intense and cold-blooded. That's a good thing, he told them, because if there had been any detectives on the train, he would have made "the train men point them out, and it would be goodbye for the detectives."

One of the men said he wanted a nice pocket watch and suggested holding up the passengers in the coaches and sleepers. The outlaw chief harshly vetoed the idea. "We've been an hour here already," he said, "and can't waste any more time, as trains are coming up. Must get away." He then turned to the conductor and said, "Now Cap, you can take your damned old machine and go ahead."

The outlaw told Conklin it would be wise to gather some men and remove the ties from the tracks so the next train would not be derailed. Then, with a "Goodbye, boys," the robbers jumped to the ground at the side of the car. They mounted their horses, and as they disappeared down the tracks, one of them fired a parting shot in the air, and Conklin heard the leader shout back, "Tell Allan Pinkerton and all his detectives to look for us in hell!"

The engineer and fireman hurried to their locomotive. Conklin wasted no time getting some others to help him roll the ties off the tracks. With all the noise and commotion now passed, Conklin and the others could plainly hear the jubilant robbers laughing and talking as they rode over a hill a half mile away.

The engineer engaged the locomotive's throttle, and with a slight jolt from the engine, they began pulling ahead, the passengers and crew looking out the windows and seeing, to their immense joy, the train was moving. Those passengers still hiding crawled back into their seats and put money and valuables back where they belonged. There was a sense of excitement, relief, and stunned disbelief. Many thanked God they had not been shot or otherwise harmed. And they all had a story they would tell and retell for the rest of their lives.

The robbery had taken approximately one hour and ten minutes. It would be another half an hour, though, before anyone else knew what had happened at Rocky Cut. When number four pulled into the station at Tipton, the conductor leaped off the train and headed straight for the telegraph office. First to be alerted was Missouri Pacific headquarters in St. Louis, and from there messages and orders burned up the lines for the next several hours. By 4:00 A.M., the first posse was in the woods, searching for the bandits.

The holdup was sensational copy for Missouri's newspapers as well as many others across the nation. The *Kansas City Daily Journal of Commerce* said the robbery equaled "in all respects, and exceeding in many, any other one on record." The *Weekly Sedalia Times* called it "audacious," "astonishing," and "the very supremacy of daring." Incredibly, some Missouri papers wrote glowingly about the robbers, who had managed "a dangerous task without shedding blood." The perpetrators were "cool and courageous," "bold banditti," and, in what must have struck the express companies as especially outrageous: "dashing knights of the road." The *Boonville Daily Advertiser* even seemed to downplay the seriousness of the crime: "No one was hurt, and no one loses anything save the express company."

The robbers' take was estimated at $17,000, although some of that amount was made up of drafts and other paper useless to the bandits. But the express companies still lost big, in the neighborhood of $10,000 in cash. The two express companies and the Missouri Pacific offered $700 for the arrest and conviction of each outlaw. Governor Charles Hardin posted a reward of $300 each. A thousand dollars a man was a healthy incentive for the posses, but no one could say for sure exactly how many were involved in the robbery and, most important, exactly who they were.

Estimates on the size of the gang ranged from twelve to twenty. With all the shooting and yelling around the train, many of the passengers thought they had been attacked by an entire army. And the robbers had done a good job of concealing their faces and making sure not to call each other by name. Still, the James and Younger boys were immediately suspected, particularly because of the bandit chief's remarks about killing detectives, especially his singling out of Allan Pinkerton.

Pinkerton was no longer pursuing the gang, but the Jameses and the Youngers still had plenty of reasons to despise Pinkerton and his famed Chicago detective agency. A year and a half earlier, at about half past midnight on January 26, 1875, approximately eight heavily armed Pinkerton men crept up to the rural home of Jesse and Frank's mother, Zerelda Samuel. Jesse had been born and raised in this house, situated three miles from Kearney, Missouri, and he and Frank were known to visit the old homeplace on a regular basis.

Pinkerton had been planning this raid for months, and after he received word from a local informant that the James boys had returned, he wired his men the go-ahead. The plan was to burn the boys out. To accomplish that, they brought an evil-looking metal sphere, seven and a half inches in diameter, filled with a highly flammable liquid that, once lit, was designed both to illuminate and start a deadly conflagration.

As silently as possible, some of the Pinkertons set a fire outside of the kitchen while others lit the fuse or wick on the metal ball. Busting in one of the windows, they tossed the sphere inside. The racket and bright light quickly raised the Samuels and their black servants. Dr. Reuben Samuel, the James boys' stepfather, raced outside and easily extinguished the flames on the house's clapboard siding. Returning to the kitchen, he used a shovel to maneuver the heavy ball into the fireplace. Other than its fierce, licking flames, the ball did not seem dangerous. They could not know, nor could the Pinkertons, that something was not right with the device. It suddenly exploded like a grenade, sending jagged pieces of shrapnel across the kitchen. One piece ripped through Zerelda's right arm, just above the wrist. Another lodged in the stomach of eight-year-old

Archie Samuel, the James boys' half brother, who died two hours later. Zerelda's arm had to be amputated below the elbow.

Waiting in the darkness and the cold, the Pinkertons were stunned to discover that Frank and Jesse were not in the house as reported—they would learn later that they had missed the notorious pair by one day. Worse, though, the raiders saw and heard the horrible explosion followed by the shrieks of terror. The detectives fled, firing a few shots from their pistols to discourage anyone from following. At a rendezvous point on the Hannibal & St. Joseph tracks, a little more than two miles away, they boarded a special train that whisked them back to Chicago, empty-handed and humiliated. The news of their disastrous raid outraged Missourians; a Clay County grand jury indicted Allan Pinkerton, among others, for the murder of little Archie.

The Youngers had also lost family to the Pinkertons. It happened deep in the Missouri Ozarks, near the village of Roscoe, on March 17, 1874. On Chalk Level Road, a crooked path barely wide enough for two men to ride abreast, Jim and John Younger confronted three well-armed men whom they believed to be detectives. Their suspicions were right because two of the men were Pinkertons, and the other was a local guide. One of the detectives spurred his horse and raced away when the Youngers first ordered them to stop, but the brothers detained the other Pinkerton and his guide.

But as the Youngers attempted to disarm the men, a vicious gun battle broke out, flame and smoke belching from an assortment of weapons at point-blank range. John received a fatal wound to the neck, but the brothers shot the guide dead and inflicted a mortal wound upon the detective. A black man who witnessed the melee from across a fence watched Jim calmly bend over his brother's body and search his clothing, retrieving John's money, pocket watch, and his four revolvers. Jim threw one of the pistols over the fence to the man, saying, "See that John has a decent burial." He then mounted his horse and galloped down the road and out of sight. Jim and his brothers Cole and Bob would like nothing better than to reap deadly revenge for John's death.

The Rocky Cut robbery also seemed like the work of the James-Younger gang because of its fearless efficiency. "The scoundrels laughed and joked as coolly as though they had been at a picnic," reported one newspaper. These bandits were clearly the best, and the James-Younger gang was the best at robbing banks and trains in 1876. The gang was also the best at not getting caught, but the local posses—no less than three were in the field right after Rocky Cut—were bragging that the bandits would be captured within twenty-four hours. "The whole country is aroused," wrote the captain of the manhunt, "and it looks as though it would be impossible for them to escape."

The first arrest actually came just forty-eight hours after the holdup, and it caused a lot of excitement. The man arrested, Edmund Graves, had arrived in the Otterville area from Texas a week before the robbery, and he had been living in a house that was situated just three hundred yards from Rocky Cut. Locals described Graves's conduct since the robbery as "very suspicious," so a deputy sheriff took an agitated Graves to Sedalia for questioning. Standing in front of Missouri's adjutant general, Graves explained that he was a native of the area but had been working as a stockman in Texas for the last five years. He said he had nothing to do with the holdup, nor did he know anyone who had been involved. The house he had been staying in belonged to his mother. It soon became obvious that Graves was telling the truth, and he was released later that same day.

"I want you to state to the public," Graves said rather testily to a newspaperman, "that there are lots of men in Texas who do not rob railroad trains, and pass for honest men."

There were more false arrests and bumbling missteps by the posses in the weeks to come—and one inexcusable tragedy. At about 2:00 A.M. on July 25, a special train pulled out of Sedalia carrying a posse of eight well-armed men and their horses. They were responding to an urgent dispatch that one of the Rocky Cut bandits, a young man named Samuel McKeehan, was believed to be at an isolated farmhouse near La Monte, Missouri. The train stopped at La Monte, twelve miles west of Sedalia, and the posse unloaded its horses, procured a guide, and mounted up for the ride of approximately five miles to the home of Albert Harris.

McKeehan was part owner of the farm where Harris, his wife, Margaret, and their six children lived. Just before daybreak, the posse quietly surrounded the Harris cabin. Deputy Sheriff Steve Homans and posse member Emmett Harris walked up to the front of the house and knocked on the door. A sleepy and confused Albert Harris called out to see who it was. Homans identified himself and demanded that Albert open up; they needed to talk.

A rustling came from inside the house as Albert and his wife got out of bed, and soon the front and back doors, separated only by a short hallway, were unbolted and opened. Margaret Harris was blocking the front doorway, facing posseman Harris and the deputy sheriff. Standing next to her, Albert peered around the door.

"Madam, you need not be at all alarmed," spoke up posseman Harris. "We do not come here to hurt you or your family in the slightest manner. We came after Sam McKeehan, to take him to Sedalia. Is he here?"

"No, he is not here," Margaret answered. "He was here last Saturday night. He was here trying to sell my husband a piece of land."

"Ain't this man in your house now?"

"No, he is not."

Posseman Harris continued to assure the woman that no harm would come to her when he was suddenly cut off by a blinding flash and a deafening blast from the back door. Margaret stiffened. "I am shot. I am a dead woman," she gasped. She fell limp, her head rapping loudly against the floor's hardwood planks, her body penetrated by six heavy buckshot. Posseman Harris was on his knees, wood splinters from the surprise shotgun blast having struck his face, stunning him.

An unknown man burst from the house and "ran like a deer" for a nearby cornfield. Two of the posse got off shots before the man disappeared down the crop rows. Posseman Harris struggled to his feet and rushed around to the back of the house, toward the sound of the gunshots. Still dazed, he tripped and fell, his gun going off as he slammed into the ground, but causing no injury.

A doctor who had spent the night at the Harris home to tend a sick child rushed to Margaret's side as her distraught family and the posse members gathered. She was dead in five minutes. The gunshot that killed the thirty-six-year-old woman came from a double-barreled shotgun of one of the posse, a railroad employee, who had been guarding the back door. He claimed his gun went off accidentally.

No one ever found out who fled the Harris home, but that didn't matter much because the tip implicating Sam McKeehan, like so many others about the outlaws, was false. McKeehan's reputation was less than stellar, but he'd had nothing to do with Rocky Cut. Now, six children were without their mother, and the real robbers were long gone.

Hobbs Kerry had been blowing lots of money—more than a thousand dollars—and he was not the type of fellow who was flush with cash. The twenty-three-year-old son of a schoolteacher was somewhat of a local tough around Granby, Missouri, a lead-mining boomtown in the extreme southwestern part of the state. The brown-eyed Kerry was of slight build, not weighing more than one hundred twenty pounds, and he stood five feet, eight inches tall. Probably the most noticeable things about him were his large, sharp nose and the way he moved: he was quick and wiry. And he was a pitiful gambler. He lost most of a wad of greenbacks in a matter of days at the faro and poker tables in Granby and nearby Joplin.

On July 31, two undercover St. Louis police officers surprised Kerry in Granby, arresting him at gunpoint. Heavily ironed, he was quickly ushered onto an eastbound train before any friends could come to his aid. An associate of Kerry's, Bruce Younger, uncle of the infamous Younger brothers, was arrested the same day in Joplin. Both men were accused of participating in the Rocky Cut robbery.

In St. Louis, Chief of Police James McDonough and Larry Hazen, a well-known Cincinnati private detective who worked for the express companies, interrogated Kerry and Younger. The accused men said they knew nothing about Rocky Cut, with Kerry claiming that several "respectable citizens" of Granby would vouch for his whereabouts at the time of the holdup. But Kerry could not explain where he had gotten all the cash he had blown on his recent drinking and gambling spree—he only had $20 in his pockets when he was arrested.

Chief McDonough ordered a special train to transport Kerry and Younger to Sedalia, where he had witnesses waiting to view his prisoners. Express messenger

Bushnell did not recognize either Kerry or Younger, but a Mr. and Mrs. Duvall, living twelve miles southeast of Sedalia, positively identified Kerry as one of four strangers who had shown up at their home the Sunday before the robbery. With this identification in hand, McDonough and Hazen pressured Kerry to talk, but he continued to claim he was innocent. At this point, McDonough pulled a letter from his pocket and began slowly reading it out loud. Kerry's face turned pale as he recognized his own words. The letter had been written to a Granby saloonkeeper, a friend of Kerry's, and it described Kerry's efforts to get in the James-Younger gang and also his attempts to persuade the gang to rob the office of the Granby Mining & Smelting Company.

McDonough told Kerry that his officers had intercepted the letter several weeks ago after receiving a tip about the planned Granby holdup. He had hoped to set a trap for the James-Younger gang in Granby, but for reasons unknown, the robbery attempt never happened. However, McDonough had quickly concluded that the Rocky Cut holdup was the work of the same gang, and Kerry's absence from the Granby area for several days, coupled with his recent return and newfound wealth, confirmed the chief's suspicions.

Kerry broke down. He admitted that he had been involved in the Rocky Cut robbery and offered to tell everything he knew in exchange for a promise of a reduced sentence. He was not really a bad person, he pleaded; it was Bruce Younger who had "led him into bad ways." But McDonough refused to make promises. Kerry thought for a moment, the room going silent as McDonough, Hazen, and an Adams Express Company agent anxiously awaited Kerry's decision. Finally, Kerry said he would take his chances and make a full confession. He revealed that a total of eight men had robbed train number four of the Missouri Pacific. Bruce Younger had not participated, Kerry said, although he knew about the holdup.

Then came what everyone desperately wanted to hear: the names of the men Kerry had ridden with to the Lamine River the night of July 7. Kerry spilled it all. The robbers were Bill Chadwell, Charlie Pitts, Clell Miller, Cole Younger, Bob Younger, Frank James, and Jesse James.

The press aptly nicknamed Hobbs Kerry "the squealer," and he was the James-Younger gang's first big mistake. Not only did he tell McDonough all about the Rocky Cut robbery, but he furnished details he had picked up about the gang's involvement in other hold-ups: the train robbery at Gads Hill, Missouri, in January

JAMES McDONOUGH, CHIEF OF POLICE.

St. Louis Chief of Police
James McDonough.

1874, which netted more than $6,000, and the September 1875 robbery of the bank in Huntington, West Virginia, of more than $10,000. Kerry cautioned that the gang was very well organized and extremely wary, employing secret "grips, signs, passwords, [and] signals of danger." The easiest part of a robbery, he offered, was the getaway, because the bandits had "numerous followers and friends throughout the State."

Kerry's confession was an incredible coup for the rotund, sixty-nine-year-old Chief McDonough, who was in his third stint as head of St. Louis's metropolitan police department (he had been selected as the city's first chief in 1861). McDonough sported a bushy white mustache and had a reputation for being a little too fond of his liquor, but no one could complain that the chief was inactive; he, or at least his men, had proven themselves to be determined manhunters. They were exactly the type of force the Missouri legislature had in mind when it passed the Suppression of Outlawry Act in 1874 that set aside a "state secret service fund" to finance a special force to capture the robber band.

But McDonough completely squandered his advantage over the James-Younger gang, and his undoing was failing to keep the lid on his investigation. News of the arrests of Kerry and Younger splashed across newspaper pages on August 4, and the names of the men Kerry fingered were published just four days later. Despite a promise to withhold Kerry's full confession until all the robbers were apprehended, McDonough released it to the press on the evening of August 12, with several newspapers publishing it in its entirety the following day. Some of the detectives complained to the press that McDonough's indiscretions only served to give "the robbers notice, and will result in driving them out of the country."

Those detectives were dead right. It was plain to the James-Younger gang that they needed to get away from Missouri for a time. Money was not a problem; they just had to decide where they wanted to go.

Two
Band of Brothers

*The Younger boys, and the James boys,
are as much a terror to the honest people
of the southwest as was Captain Kidd in
his day to the merchantmen on sea.*

—*THE EXPRESSMAN'S MONTHLY,* 1876

They were all young men. Not one of them was older than thirty-five, and half of them were still single. People thought of them as courteous and good-natured, even jolly. And their Missouri drawls added to their charm. This "twang" sound, with the *r*'s barely audible, was not as harsh as a Texan's, or as southern as a Georgian's. But it stuck out, especially to folks from the North.

Nobody had the slightest inkling these affable men were stone-cold killers. Yet the men of the James-Younger gang were hardened to violence and bloodshed. Many of them had been baptized by fire as guerrilla fighters (better known as "bushwhackers") in the most savage theater of the Civil War. These outlaws wouldn't hesitate to pull a trigger and snuff out a man's life. But they had not always been that way.

At the outbreak of the Civil War, Henry Washington Younger was a farmer, merchant, and mail contractor with extensive properties in Jackson and Cass Counties. The family was wealthy enough to have house slaves to tend to the chores and meals for the large Younger family—nine girls and five boys. Thomas Coleman Younger, known as Cole, and his siblings were well-schooled, churchgoing Missourians living in what he fondly remembered as a "garden spot."

Henry Younger was against the South's secession but he was also pro-slavery. He feared secession would cause upheaval and unrest, which he thought would lead to the end of slavery.

"He was for the Union," Cole recalled, "in spite of his natural inclinations to sympathy with the South."

But Henry Younger's particular stance didn't matter to the Kansas jayhawkers who rode across the border to punish and plunder Southerners. Their relentless raiding in the war's first year alone cost Henry Younger several thousand dollars in stolen and destroyed property. Cole was seventeen years old at the time, and he left home to join the pro-Confederate Quantrill Raiders. His punching of a much older Missouri State Militia officer at a recent dance party helped this decision along.

"I happened to be rather more popular with the girls," Cole explained.

Cole learned how to hide out in the brush as a member of Quantrill's band, and he learned how to fight like a man possessed. But, as with many of his fellow bushwhackers, his fierceness was born of personal tragedy, bitterness, and a fire for revenge.

Now that Cole was a known guerrilla, Henry Younger and his family were even more of a target. In July 1862, militia soldiers waylaid Henry just outside of Westport and put three bullets in his back. The murderers were never prosecuted; after all, it was just one more atrocity among countless others committed by both sides during Missouri's war years. Seven months later, militia soldiers showed up at the Younger home. Cole's mother, Bursheba, had been providing food and clothing to her sons, and the soldiers were there to put an end to that.

"They pillaged the house," Cole recalled angrily, "and forced my mother to set it on fire with her own hands."

Then in the summer of 1863, three of Cole's sisters and two of his female cousins were arrested and confined in a three-story brick store building in Kansas City, along with several other young women suspected of spying for the bushwhackers. On August 13, the building suddenly collapsed amid shrieks of terror and a boiling cloud of dust. Four of the women inside were crushed to death, including one of the Younger cousins. Cole always believed that Union soldiers had caused the building to be "secretly undermined . . . with the [intended] murder of my sisters and cousins and the other unfortunate women in mind." He was not the only one who thought that, and he wouldn't wait long for vengeance.

Early on August 21, a column of more than four hundred heavily armed horsemen appeared on the outskirts of Lawrence, Kansas, a jayhawker hotbed a good forty miles west of the Missouri border. The enigmatic William Clarke Quantrill rode at the column's head, and close by rode a young man who had quickly become one of his best and most loyal fighters: Cole Younger. What followed was, in Cole's words, "a day of butchery."

"Kill! Kill and make no mistake!" Quantrill shouted to his men that morning. "Lawrence should be thoroughly cleansed, and the only way to cleanse it is to kill! Kill!"

By 9:00 A.M., the guerrillas had massacred more than 150 men and boys, most of them civilians. Many were gunned down in front of their wives and families. One hundred homes were torched, as were dozens of businesses. As the raiders escaped, their pockets and haversacks stuffed with booty, black plumes of smoke rose high into the sky. There was not even the gentlest breeze that mild day, and for hours the smoke could be seen for miles.

One writer later claimed that Cole saved at least a dozen Lawrence citizens from slaughter that day, and there may be some truth in this. In other incidents from his bushwhacker days, he was known as a man who could show mercy to his enemies. But Cole never denied he did his fair share of the killing in Lawrence, and he never expressed a bit of remorse for the attack.

That fall, Cole rode south to Texas with a company of bushwhackers. He later wrote of fighting here and there in Texas, Arkansas, and Louisiana. He also said he'd been part of an astonishing expedition across the plains in 1864 to cut a transcontinental telegraph line in Colorado and, following that, a "secret mission" escorting a Confederate agent to Victoria, British Columbia. These latter exploits were some of Cole's whoppers (he even said he'd gotten into scrapes with Comanches and Apaches). Whatever Cole's wartime adventures might truly have been, at the end of the Civil War, he was living in California, at the home of an uncle.

Cole's brother James joined a small band under Quantrill in 1864. The "brave, dauntless, high-spirited boy," whom everyone called Jim, was only sixteen years old at the time. In January 1865, when Quantrill slipped into Kentucky with fewer than forty men, Jim Younger was with him. Before the month was out, though, Jim and several companions had been captured by Kentucky Federals at a farmhouse near Harrodsburg and were in jail in Lexington. The bushwhackers were threatened with hanging—on three separate occasions—but nothing happened to them. Jim was lucky; had he been caught back in Missouri, the Federals could not have gotten the noose around his neck fast enough.

Jim was eventually transferred to a Louisville prison, escaped (or was released), and made his way back to Missouri.

Quantrill never made it out of Kentucky. He took a rifle ball to the spine in a surprise attack on May 10. Paralyzed below the shoulders, the once-feared guerrilla chieftain died from his wound four weeks later. On July 26, the last of Quantrill's bushwhacker followers, just sixteen men, surrendered at Samuels Depot, Kentucky. Among the ragtag group was a twenty-two-year-old veteran fighter from Clay County, Missouri, by the name of Frank James.

Alexander Franklin James and Jesse Woodson James spurred their horses and worked their Navy Colts with a ferociousness equal to any of their fellow guerrillas. On September 27, 1864, they were part of "Bloody Bill" Anderson's band of eighty men as they thundered into the small town of Centralia, situated on the line of the North Missouri Railroad. Bloody Bill's nickname was well-earned. He and his followers were famous for scalping and mutilating dead enemy soldiers, not to mention murdering pro-Union civilians. Bloody Bill had turned especially sadistic after one of his sisters was killed and another seriously injured in the Kansas City prison collapse.

On this day, a steam train had the misfortune of arriving at the Centralia depot just as the bushwhackers were finishing sacking the town. Twenty-five Federals on furlough, most of them unarmed, were passengers on the train. Bloody Bill marched the soldiers onto the station platform, forced them to strip, and then joined his men in a cold-blooded execution, sparing only one sergeant for a possible prisoner exchange.

A few hours later, 115 Federals tracked the bushwhackers to their camp three miles away. Instead of finding the eighty culprits, they ran face-to-face into more than two hundred long-haired, revolver-packing guerrillas. Bloody Bill led the single, devastating charge. Many of the Federals were shot down running away in terror—others while begging for mercy. Jesse James, his seventeen-year-old boyish face without a single whisker, galloped straight for the Federal commander and shot him dead.

"We never took prisoners," Frank James explained years later. "How could we carry them around with us? We either killed them or turned them loose."

The bushwhackers never had a problem with the killings, but the Federals weren't troubled by it either. Frank was likely right when he said the Federals would have killed all of Anderson's men if they'd had the chance. The war in Missouri was a deeply personal one. It made no difference whether you wore a uniform or not. The violence was unforgiving, and, like the Youngers, the James boys had their own reasons for shedding Union blood.

Frank and Jesse's father was a cultured, college-educated Baptist minister named Robert James. A well-liked "doer" in Clay County, Robert was instrumental in the founding of William Jewell College at Liberty—which thrives to this day. The boys, born in 1843 and 1847, respectively, grew up on a small farm

Jesse's birthplace, the James farm, from an 1877 photograph.

nestled in rolling hills and scattered patches of woods. The James family was not as well off as the Youngers, but they had enough to own a family of slaves and were typically "Southern" in their feeling about that.

In 1850, Robert James left Clay County for the California gold fields. Some say the Reverend James went to find the famed riches that were talked about in blacksmith shops, post offices, taverns, and other places. Others claim he left to preach the gospel. But the Jameses' neighbors said he left to get away from his wife, Zerelda. She was a tall, strong-willed, and deeply outspoken woman; one acquaintance called her "Captain Zerelda." If it was to flee his marriage, he succeeded; Robert James died in a California mining camp from an unknown illness just five months later.

Zerelda and the boys stayed on in Clay County, where they grew tobacco and other crops on their two-hundred-acre farm. In 1855, Zerelda married

Dr. Reuben Samuel, her third husband, and continued to reign supreme in the family. She made sure the farm and slaves would remain her property through a prenuptial agreement. The remarkable mother of the James boys, as everyone knew, was a force as unbending as a hickory rail.

The outbreak of the Civil War brought both excitement and apprehension to the citizens of Clay County—not to mention suspicion of one another.

"The people were all mixed up and everybody was a spy for his side," Frank James recalled. "You were for the South and your neighbor was for Lincoln."

Frank joined a local company in May 1861 and was part of the Southern victories at Wilson's Creek and Lexington. But he contracted measles and was captured that winter while recovering in a military hospital. The Federals paroled Frank and sent him home, but he could not stay out of the fight—no one could. By spring 1863, he had joined up with the bushwhackers. He rode with Quantrill, Cole Younger, and the other guerrillas to Lawrence. There is no evidence that Frank James spared anyone's life on that bloody August day.

Jesse was too young to join up, but, as Frank would claim later, the Federals "drove him to it." Frank had been riding with the bushwhackers for a few weeks when a local militia detachment arrived at the James farm looking for Frank and his comrades. When Jesse refused to give away his brother, the soldiers whipped him until the boy couldn't speak. The militiamen next found Dr. Samuel, put a noose around his neck, and, as his family watched in horror, strung the man up. They released the rope before Samuel passed out, and he fell to the ground in a lump, tears streaming from his eyes as he gasped for breath. That was enough for the doctor to lead the soldiers to the bushwhacker camp. Upon their arrival, a surprised Frank James ran like the devil, narrowly escaping as bullets whizzed through the brush near him.

The James family would tell this story for years with the same anger they recounted the murderous Pinkerton raid on their farm in 1875.

"After that day," Frank said, "Jesse was out for blood."

Jesse did not actually join the bushwhackers until June 1864, a full year later. In only a few months' time, though, the sixteen-year-old saw plenty of blood, both the enemy's and his own. His first wound was self-inflicted: while practicing with one of his revolvers—every respectable bushwhacker carried no less than four—he shot off the tip of the middle finger on his left hand. Jesse had to hide this in later years because it was a sure way of identifying him. One account says

Jesse James, teenage guerrilla fighter, 1864.

this was how Jesse got the nickname his close associates would call him for the rest of his life. With blood squirting from the stump of his finger, Jesse cried, "O, ding it! ding it! How it hurts!" The boys started calling Jesse James "Dingus."

Another more serious wound would come in August 1864 when Jesse was trying to steal a saddle from the farm of an old German Unionist living in Ray County. The German, who had a bit more gumption than smarts, poked a rifle out of his doorway and took a potshot at Jesse, after which the old farmer fled his house and darted into a cornfield. The lead slug tore into the right side of Jesse's chest, passing through his lung. It was a close call but, after a few weeks, Jesse was back in the saddle alongside Frank.

Jesse kept company with the worst, most-feared of the bushwhackers: Bloody Bill Anderson, Arch Clement, Dave Pool. It was a hell of a life for a teenager, but Jesse took to it well; indeed, there was little choice if one wished to survive such embattled times. Fittingly, his bushwhacker career would end violently, with more of his own blood spilled. In May 1865, with Frank off in Kentucky, Jesse and several bushwhackers ran into a Federal patrol in Lafayette County, Missouri. Lead started flying back and forth immediately. A pistol ball punctured Jesse's side, entering the same lung that had been wounded previously, and in nearly the exact same place. But this hit was more dangerous than the first; every time he breathed, "air and blood matter" passed from the hole in his chest. One week later, as Jesse lay in a hotel bed in Lexington, Missouri, convalescing, he formally surrendered and swore an allegiance to the United States. It would take months for him to fully recover.

But he would never recover from the war.

We were outlaws the moment the South lost," Frank James recalled. "Why, we had as much chance of settling down, tilling our farms and being decent as a tallow dog chasin' an asbestos cat through hell."

Frank may have been overstating but not by much. The fighting may have ended, but the war's horrors in Missouri were still fresh in people's minds. Bitterness and personal grudges still smoldered. Former bushwhackers, isolated on their farms and no longer protected by their comrades, became easy pickings for anyone bent on revenge. After returning to Missouri from California, Cole Younger came face-to-face with what he described as "so-called vigilant committees."

"They were hunting out Confederates," Cole asserted, "accusing them falsely of crime and adopting any excuse to take their lives. Neither I nor my brother Jim could remain at home. . . . Everywhere we went armed, everywhere we were on the lookout for enemies."

And former Confederates were "outlawed" politically as well. A new Missouri constitution instituted the infamous "Ironclad Oath," which said that before you could hold public office or even vote, you had to swear you hadn't fought for the South, nor ever "given aid, comfort, countenance, or support to persons engaged in any such hostility." Any past or present sympathy with the South was enough to put you in political exile. This meant the bushwhackers and their families and supporters had no voice or place in postwar Missouri. Still, a few found other means to make themselves heard.

On the afternoon of February 13, 1866, ten or twelve men rode into Liberty, Missouri, and robbed the Clay County Savings Association of nearly $60,000 in U.S. bonds and gold, most of which belonged to the Unionists (now the Radical Republicans) who controlled the state and local government. This was the first daylight bank robbery in American history, and it was pulled off by the kind of men who had experience conducting daylight raids on unsuspecting towns. As the *Liberty Tribune* reported, most everyone believed that the robbers were "a gang of old bushwhacking desperadoes."

And it was fairly easy to guess who'd done the job—it was Clay County, after all. But producing hard evidence was another matter. Solid identification was always the tricky part. This continued to be difficult in the bank raids, train robberies, and assorted hold-ups that followed the Liberty heist. The first robbery in which Jesse James can, with absolute certainty, be named as a participant was three years later, at the holdup of the Daviess County Savings Association in Gallatin, Missouri. In this robbery, Jesse murdered the cashier, John W. Sheets, whom he mistook for Samuel P. Cox, the commander of the Federals who had killed Bloody Bill Anderson. While no eyewitnesses could positively identify the two robbers at the time, they did recognize the fine mare the bandits were forced to abandon in their escape. The champion racehorse named Kate belonged to Jesse James.

With each brazen holdup that followed, from Kentucky to Iowa to West Virginia, suspicion centered more and more on the Jameses and Youngers. Still, the boys never failed to elude the posses and the detectives. Jesse invariably wrote a letter to the newspapers claiming he was miles away from the outrage in question, a claim that could be corroborated, he said, "by some of the best men in Missouri." If he and Frank could be guaranteed a fair trial and protection from mobs—one of Jesse and Frank's favorite lines—they were more than willing to turn themselves in and face all charges.

This was all fired up by the popular newspaper editor and former Confederate John Newman Edwards, a champion of the Jameses and Youngers. "They are outlaws, but they are not criminals," he wrote. He praised them and embellished their daring exploits while railing against the law enforcement and detectives who hunted them. Countless Missourians joined Edwards in sympathizing with the bandits, especially after the Pinkerton raid. This even led to an amnesty bill for the brothers being introduced in the state legislature in March 1875—and it almost passed.

Then came the sensational capture and confession of Hobbs Kerry following the 1876 Rocky Cut robbery. He named the Jameses and Youngers, though no one was surprised by this. Still, it was an important confirmation by an actual gang member. Kerry also identified other gang members, including Clell Miller,

Charlie Pitts, and Bill Chadwell. These men were not the prizes the Jameses and Youngers were, but two of them had even enjoyed a degree of anonymity. That was over now.

Clell Miller grew up in a prosperous slave-owning family in Clay County, not far from the James farm. At five feet, eight inches tall, he was the shortest of the outlaws. His hair, cut short, was light and curly, and he had modest sideburns. Clell had joined Bloody Bill Anderson's guerrilla band at the tender age of fourteen, but his introduction to bushwhacker life was short-lived; in his first fight, a disastrous skirmish in Ray County on October 27, 1864, Bloody Bill was shot dead. As Miller rushed to the corpse, a bullet knocked him from his saddle.

Wounded but alive, Miller was recognized by the Federal commander, Colonel Cox, who was an old friend of Clell's father. This coincidence saved Clell's life because one of Cox's men had already decided to execute the boy. Clell spun a tale for the colonel about how he had been "kidnapped" by Anderson's men, but Cox knew better, and the boy remained a prisoner of war. Later, Miller's father lied for the boy, as did several neighbors, who vouched for him as a loyal citizen. Clell was eventually released from a St. Louis prison, by which time the war had ended—at least officially.

Clell, who sometimes used the alias Jim Hines, was not a drinking man, but he certainly liked to have a good time. He deeply admired Jesse and would follow him anywhere.

On June 3, 1871, he joined Jesse, Frank, and Cole and robbed the Ocobock Brothers Bank in Corydon, Iowa. The boys rode out of town that day with $6,000, but the Pinkerton National Detective Agency was hot on their trail. Clell was captured a year later by a Pinkerton operative who whisked him off to Iowa, to be put on trial. A host of friends and relatives made the trek north to testify on Clell's behalf, some swearing that they had been with him in Missouri on the day of the heist. These alibis got Clell acquitted, and the court even paid $150 to cover the costs of his witnesses.

As the bank and train robberies continued, Clell became a favorite suspect, along with his pals the Jameses and Youngers. On December 8, 1874, during a train robbery a few miles west of Kansas City, Miller helped empty out $27,000 from a Wells, Fargo & Company safe. On a still night four months later, a local sheriff and several Wells Fargo men surrounded Miller in a house near Carrollton, Missouri. The outlaw asked the sheriff to come into the house *unarmed* for a parley. The sheriff agreed, thinking to himself this little talk would end with Clell's surrender. But the young bandit had something else in mind. He grabbed the officer by the throat, pushed a Navy Colt to the terrified man's head, and threatened to blow his brains out if he did not cooperate. The sheriff cooperated.

Clell then jumped on the back of a horse, politely shouted, "Goodbye, gentlemen," and galloped away. The stunned Wells Fargo men got off a few shots but missed their target in the darkness. Clell could be heard laughing in the distance. The *Carrollton Journal*'s comment on the affair was succinct and to the point: "Missouri outlaws are not to be trifled with."

Charlie Pitts, whose real name was Samuel Wells, had grown up near Lee's Summit in Jackson County, Missouri. The Wells family were neighbors and good friends of the Younger family. Charlie and his mother had discovered the body of Henry Younger after he was murdered by Missouri State Militia soldiers. Charlie, fourteen years old, raced to notify the closest Federal command post while his mother remained to watch over the body. Two months later, Charlie's own father, a civilian, was shot and killed while cheering for the Confederates at the Battle of White Oak Creek.

Charlie and a brother joined the guerrillas (virtually nothing is known of their early bushwhacking days). After the war, Charlie married and moved to Kansas, where he worked as a wagon teamster for the Missouri-Kansas-Texas Railroad. For a year or more before Rocky Cut, he and Bill Chadwell were frequently seen in the coal, lead, and zinc mining towns of southeastern Kansas and southwestern Missouri, where there was plenty of action and money.

Strongly built, Pitts stood nearly five feet, ten inches tall. He had noticeably short, thick feet (he wore a size 6 boot, quite petite for his body size), and his hands were small and fat, though calloused from hard work. His impressively broad forehead was topped by thick, black hair, and he had a short beard and dark mustache. His knowledge of horses was so respected that, when looking to rob a bank or train, the gang had him take care of their entire stock.

In the summer of 1875, Charlie became smitten by a Mrs. Lillie Beemer, a Cherokee, Kansas, woman described by a newspaper reporter as a "sprightly young grass widow who has a history." And Mrs. Beemer, too, seemed taken with Charlie—or at least with the money he always seemed to have. Even though he was already married with a family, Charlie continued to pursue Lillie, and they became engaged.

Wanting to impress Lillie, Charlie began making thinly veiled references to his daring robber exploits. Lillie later said Charlie gave her so many details about an April 19 robbery of a Baxter Springs, Kansas, bank she became convinced he was one of the two bandits. She didn't need any more proof after Rocky Cut, when he handed her a package containing nearly $2,000 in greenbacks and asked her to hold it for him while he was away. Lillie used part of the money to buy a wedding dress. But during Charlie's absence, Lillie began to have second thoughts about marrying the outlaw.

He returned to Cherokee on July 29 anxious to get married that very night, but the widow refused. The wedding was off, she told him, placing the money back in his hands. Charlie became enraged, and Lillie trembled as he threatened to shoot her down on sight if she married another man. Charlie "carried two large revolvers," the widow recalled, "and appeared very nervous and restless."

Charlie apparently rebounded quickly because he reportedly married another gal just three days after the breakup, which may explain why Lillie was so forthcoming with information when the detectives came to question her. In addition to Lillie, the detectives tracked down two of Pitts's brothers. One broke down under questioning, confessing that Charlie had admitted using part of his Rocky Cut share to purchase mules, harnesses, a brand-new Studebaker freight wagon, and a spring wagon. The widow Beemer also remembered Charlie saying he'd bought a fine team of mules in Missouri. This property was promptly attached and auctioned for the benefit of the Adams Express Company.

With the law closing in, Charlie could not return to his Kansas haunts—especially not after Lillie Beemer gave the authorities a recent photograph of the outlaw. Perhaps worst of all, though, was that Charlie's dalliances were published in the region's biggest newspapers. This provided some very interesting reading for his wife, Jennie Wells, as well as her friends and family.

William "Bill" Chadwell fled Kansas with Pitts. Standing six feet, four inches tall and clean shaven, Chadwell was such a robust man that he naturally attracted attention. Born twenty-three years earlier in Greene County, Illinois, he had been named for his father, a farmer. But the senior Chadwell died when Bill was a small boy, and in the 1860s the family migrated to southeastern Kansas. Bill was not a particularly bright teenager, but friends and neighbors thought he was hardworking and inoffensive. He did have a troubling flaw, though, according to a woman who boarded Chadwell for several months in 1871 while he worked on her husband's farm: the young man could be "easily influenced by the society in which he was thrown."

The society Chadwell entered a short time later, Missouri's tin and lead mines, was rough, and only then did he become known as a "desperate character." One incident from 1874 even made him a local legend. Chadwell and a fellow miner were having a rousing good time around a campfire when his intoxicated pal inexplicably picked up a small keg of blasting powder and tossed it into the flames. Quick as a flash, Chadwell knocked his friend senseless, coolly reaching into the fire for the smoldering keg and heaving it into a ditch. Folks would tell that story for a long time to come.

By 1876, Chadwell's best buddy was Charlie Pitts. On April 19 of that year, he and Pitts strode into the bank in Baxter Springs, Kansas, and shoved their pistols into the face of the cashier. They walked out with an easy $3,000. Rocky Cut would be another good haul for the pair less than three months later, but, like the other gang members, Chadwell had given Hobbs Kerry a little too much of his personal information. Lawmen easily traced Chadwell to Cherokee County, and, according to one newspaper account, had him surrounded in a cornfield. Incredibly, the outlaw escaped his pursuers.

A later report described how the posses made a surprise appearance at the home of Chadwell's father-in-law, "old man Robinson," just south of Fort Scott,

Kansas. They found Chadwell's and Pitts's wives, but the robbers had ridden away days earlier. One thing was sure: if Chadwell tried to come home anytime soon, the detectives would be all over him.

Most of the time, the James-Younger gang acted like a bunch of good ol' boys. They liked to have their fun, and they got along relatively well. But there could also be tension and arguments and, most notably, a jostling for leadership. Cole Younger and Frank James, close in age, were good friends, but Cole and Jesse simply tolerated each other. Jesse's strong personality and sizable ego—not to mention that he was younger— grated on Cole, who had a considerable ego of his own. Cole later said that Frank "would bear acquaintance," while Jesse "was inclined to be quarrelsome." In later years, Cole loved to tell the story—over and over—of how he and Jesse nearly "shot it out" once, only to have Frank and others intervene.

Jesse and Frank were as different as night and day. Frank, slightly taller than his brother, was also con- siderably slimmer, almost effeminate looking, with a small neck and a long, narrow face flanked by rather large ears. One journalist described him as "spare but sinewy." He inherited his distinctive hawklike nose from his mother, who nicknamed her boy "Buck"—a name his friends and gang members called him. Usually quiet and serious, Frank wasn't interested in being well known. He had two great pleasures. One was reading, and he often spouted lines from Shakespeare and the Bible. The other was tobacco, which he chewed constantly.

A newspaper reporter claimed that Frank never touched liquor, but a former gang member said the outlaw was one of the few in the band who "would get dead drunk." Frank was "a bad man in a fight," commented future gang members Bob and Charley Ford, and "he was a great deal more cunning than Jesse."

Jesse, more handsome than Frank, had an oval face and a slightly turned-up, or "pug," nose. Easily the most striking thing about his appearance was his stunning blue eyes, which seemed to move constantly— almost nervously. Strong and sturdily built, he sat a saddle like no one else, riding so erect "that he almost leaned backward."

Jesse was "light-hearted, reckless, devil-may-care," wrote John Newman Edwards, and he "laughs at everything." "He had a keen sense of humor," recalled Charley Ford, "and delighted to humbug people with whom he came in contact." One of Jesse's pleasures was striking up a conversation with a stranger and then, ever so deftly, changing the subject to the James gang and seeing what the person happened to think about the outlaws.

Jesse did not quote the classics like his brother, but instead liked to boast of his own exploits. "He liked some reckless expedition, and was a wonderful horseman," stated Jesse's brother-in-law, Thomas Mimms. He loved to read the newspapers. And he had a flare for letter writing. "He would dash off a letter without pausing once," said Mimms, "and would never read it over." Frank, on the other hand, "never wrote a letter and did not unnecessarily expose himself."

Jesse was said to be liberal with the other gang members, whereas Frank could be stingy. But while Jesse was more excitable than his brother, he was no less fearless. "If you hear they've captured me alive," Jesse once said to a cousin, "say it's a lie; they may kill me, but they will never get me otherwise."

Strangely, Jesse believed in the supernatural. Charley Ford described a late-night incident where a "ball of fire" (probably ball lightning) rolled across the road and underneath the horses he and Jesse were riding. Ford had never seen anything like this, and it frightened him. But Jesse told Ford he had been visited by these "balls" before, and each incident was followed by "serious trouble." They were meant to be warnings, he said, and he took them seriously. A Liberty newspaper editor perhaps summed up the outlaw best when he said, "Jesse James was a queer combination."

Perhaps so, but the man was so unquestionably charismatic it made sense for him to assert himself as the gang's leader. But Jesse was forced to share this role with Frank and Cole. A half brother of Jesse and Frank, John Samuel, once told a reporter that "Frank planned and Jesse executed." This was said years after Jesse's death while Frank was still living, so the older James brother may have had a hand in shaping that assessment. Jesse's many letters to the press show that he saw himself as a top leader of the gang.

Standing six feet tall, Cole Younger may not have been the tallest gang member, but he was by far the most impressive in size. A powerful man with large hands, he weighed a good two hundred pounds, was nearly bald, and had a sandy mustache and chin whiskers. "He looks anything but a villain," wrote one journalist, "but every feature and expression indicates caution, shrewdness, and a high order of intellect." Cole could quote the Bible as well as Frank, and he was known to toss out a line or two of Byron. He was quite amiable, liked to talk, and could spin a damned good yarn.

Jim Younger, something of the darling of the Younger clan, was an inch shorter than Cole and weighed a good thirty pounds less. He had dark hair, large eyes, and, according to one observer, "a changing, peculiar expression." Cole once said that Jim was "either in the garret or way down in the cellar," referring to his brother's tremendous mood swings. "He was either as chipper as a bird or else he was very melancholy."

Bob Younger, the youngest of the three brothers (he was only twenty-two years old in 1876), was, by all accounts, the most handsome. He stood an impressive six feet, two inches tall with brawny arms and a thick neck. No one could miss his deep blue eyes, which had a "cold, searching look." In addition, his heavy brow reminded one reporter of those that "phrenologists would give men of wonderful mathematical ability." His face was clean shaven save for a neatly trimmed, sandy mustache. Bob had been too young to fight with his brothers in the Civil War, but the terrible ordeal had impacted his life just the same.

"Circumstances sometimes make men what they are," Bob once said. "If it had not been for the war, I might have been something, but as it is, I am what I am."

On a Kansas City street, on the evening of August 17, 1876, a young man on horseback rode up to a reporter of the *Kansas City Times* and handed him a letter. Without saying a word, the man turned his horse and rode away. The reporter unfolded the letter and read the dateline: Oak Grove, Kansas, August 14. Skipping quickly down the page to the signature—"J. W. James."—the reporter realized that Jesse had written a direct response to the recent publication of Hobbs Kerry's confession, and its naming of the Jameses and Youngers as accomplices in the Rocky Cut affair.

"If there was only one side to be told," Jesse wrote, "it would probably be believed by a good many people that Kerry has told the truth. But his so-called confession is a well-built pack of lies from beginning to end. I never heard of Hobbs Kerry, Charles Pitts and Wm. Chadwell until Kerry's arrest. I can prove my innocence by eight good and well known men of Jackson County, and show conclusively that I was not at the train robbery. . . . Kerry knows that the Jameses and Youngers can't be taken alive, and that is why he has put it on us."

The defiant taunting did not stop there. Only four days later Jesse wrote an even longer letter, again to the *Times,* a newspaper noted for its sympathy to the outlaws. While the letter contained a point-by-point rebuttal of Kerry's account—calling him "a notorious liar and poltroon"—it also ranted against state and railroad officials, the leader of the Sedalia posse, and, of course, the Pinkertons.

"If we (the Jameses and Youngers) had been granted full amnesty," Jesse wrote, in an obvious appeal to his pro-Southern supporters, "I am sure we would of been at work, trying to be good, law-abiding citizens."

As to the express companies that continued to help bankroll the manhunt, the outlaw advised that they "give [their] extra money to the suffering poor and don't let thieving Detectives beat you out of it." This letter was datelined "Safe Retreat," and there was little question now that Jesse and Frank and the Youngers were safe from capture. They "have disappeared as they always do," the *Times* commented in another column, "leaving no trail, and they will not be heard from again till they have robbed another train or another bank in some remote locality."

Three
Tigers on the Loose

*None but a very daring and a very cunning man
can be a successful criminal nowadays.*

—WEEKLY SEDALIA TIMES, 1876

They had been to Minnesota before, but they didn't get there on the roads or rivers, or the train rails. They came on the wind, millions of them, darkening the sky and falling to earth like snowflakes in a storm. The biggest locust swarms hit in July and August. Someone said they'd seen one that was seventeen miles wide. Minnesota farmers couldn't do anything but watch helplessly as their wheat, corn, oats, and barley were completely devoured. It was another bad summer in a string of bad summers. Over the past four years, ending in 1876, crop losses to grasshoppers totaled no less than $8 million.

There was more bad news that summer. Some eight hundred miles to the west, on the banks of the Little

Bighorn River in Montana Territory, General George Armstrong Custer and more than two hundred men of his vaunted Seventh Cavalry were wiped out by an overwhelming force of Lakota and Cheyenne warriors. The July 7 *Winona Daily Republican* said that Custer, a bona fide Civil War hero and experienced Indian fighter, "was either betrayed and led into an ambuscade by his Indian scouts, or he was guilty of inexcusable rashness in attacking a large body of savages strongly posted." One thing this did mean: more bluecoats would be marching into Indian country.

More depressing to most Americans were the effects of the Panic of 1873, which caused high unemployment, a downward spiral for crop prices, and the failure of thousands of businesses. And President U. S. Grant, whose floundering administration was littered with corrupt officials, was incapable of doing anything constructive.

Yet amid all these hard times and bad news, the biggest birthday party in the nation's history was taking place in Philadelphia. The Centennial International Exposition was many things: World's Fair, gaudy architectural and artistic showpiece, but, most of all, a chest-thumping display of everything American. More than two hundred buildings showcased exhibits with countless mechanical wonders and inventions, not the least of which was the typewriter and the telephone. Fairgoers *ooh*ed and *ahh*ed over steam locomotives, gleaming brass telescopes, ominous Gatling guns, a foot-powered drilling machine for dentists, and the latest lifesaving devices for seafarers.

In one corner of the main building was a faux post office lobby fabricated by the Yale Lock Manufacturing Company of Stamford, Connecticut. The elaborate exhibit featured the firm's latest invention: a chronometer, or time lock, for bank safes and vaults. Mounted on the inside of a safe door, Yale's patented lock with its two time mechanisms (which had to be periodically wound with a key) regulated the hour when a safe could be both unlocked and locked.

Bankers would set the device to lock at the end of the business day and open the next morning. It was impossible to open the safe or vault until the chronometer reached the preset time. The time lock completely thwarted the dangerous tactic used by some robbers of showing up at a banker's home in the middle of the night, rousting him from bed, dragging him off to the bank at gunpoint, and forcing him to open the safe. This method of robbery was known as "bulldozing."

By the end of 1876, nearly a thousand banks used the celebrated Yale chronometer lock. First National Bank in Northfield, Minnesota, got its Yale time lock in late August. The *Rice County Journal* joked that the Northfield bank would be able to avoid "the annoyance of having burglars pull the cashier's hair to make him open the safe."

The bank's cashier was George M. Phillips, and on September 4 he boarded a train bound for Philadelphia, where he would tour the Yale exhibit and many others. The First National Bank's bookkeeper, Joseph Lee Heywood, planned to take his wife to see the exposition upon Phillips's return. Indeed, the Americans converged on Philadelphia that summer like the grasshopper swarms that struck Minnesota. Tens of thousands walked through the exposition gates daily. The railroads offered special trains and rates to those wanting to travel there.

But while countless midwesterners sped eastward in the August heat, eight strapping and somewhat mysterious men boarded a train in Missouri that would take them north. They were bound for no exposition or fair, but it was to be a pleasure trip of sorts. The destination for these eight men, the infamous James-Younger gang, was the last place police and detectives would expect to find them.

Minnesota was also the last place attorney Samuel Hardwicke expected to find the Missouri desperadoes.

So much so that he was betting his life on it. Hardwicke had secretly played a singular role in organizing the disastrous raid on the James farm in January 1875, in which little Archie Samuel was mortally wounded and Zerelda maimed after an incendiary device tossed into the house exploded. Hardwicke was Allan Pinkerton's right-hand man in Clay County. The forty-two-year-old Hardwicke had even gone with the Pinkerton men on their scorched-earth mission.

"Above everything," a seething Allan Pinkerton had instructed the attorney, "destroy the [James] house, blot it from the face of the earth."

It's hard to figure out what drove the bookish Hardwicke to take on the James boys. He was born of pioneer stock—his father had been a California argonaut and his uncle a famous Santa Fe trader—but Hardwicke was content to practice the law and start a family in his native Clay County, where he put together one of the region's finest private libraries. A pro-Union Democrat, he was, for the most part, quiet and unassuming, though he could sometimes exhibit a "nervous temperament."

Hardwicke's alliance with Allan Pinkerton was nothing short of courageous; some would say a fool's errand. His involvement in a plan to destroy a home he knew housed innocent family members, however, made him the worst sort of vigilante. And with the tragic death of Archie Samuel, Hardwicke and the Pinkertons became murderers. Jesse and Frank had killed men, yes, but they had never killed a child.

Just seven days after the raid, the *Chicago Tribune* ran a story naming Hardwicke as a Pinkerton operative. Missouri papers copied the story, and Hardwicke had to pack up his family and move from his rural farmstead to quarters on Liberty's town square. The attorney was in such a hurry to get into town he paid the former tenant a month's rent to move out.

Hardwicke sent two letters to Jesse via Jesse's friend, newspaperman John Newman Edwards. Hardwicke admitted that he had corresponded with Allan Pinkerton, but it was only as Pinkerton's local attorney. Hardwicke also reached out to Zerelda Samuel, promising to come out to see her as soon as court was out of session.

An enraged Jesse James would have none of this. His own sources in Clay County had told him all he needed to know about Sam Hardwicke. On March 23, as a grand jury in Liberty heard testimony on the Pinkerton raid, Jesse wrote his stepfather, Dr. Samuel: "They [There] can not be a doubt but Hardwicke is the instigator of the brutal murder and he knows every mane [man] that was there & I am convinced Hardwick[e] was with the murder[er]s when poor little Archie was so cruelly murdered."

Jesse sent Dr. Samuel the two letters he had received from the attorney and instructed his stepfather to present them to the grand jury. "D[o] have this horrible vlian [villain] thoroughly investigated," he wrote. "For I want the Law to take its course and spair Clay Co[unty] of a mob that will be bloody and desperate. I have pledged my self to let the law take its course but my friends will be forced to mob the murder[er]s of poor Archie if the grand Jury don['t] have the guilty party indicted. They [There] cannot be a doubt but H[ardwicke] is guilty. . . . Strain every nerve to have the midnight assassins punished."

Hardwicke did testify before the grand jury, but, in the end, he was not one of the men indicted. Neither was the Samuels' closest neighbor, Daniel Askew, who had also been working with the Pinkertons. For weeks prior to the attack, Askew had boarded one of Pinkerton's detectives, passing the man off as a hired hand. Jesse figured that out, too.

At approximately 7:30 P.M. on Monday, April 12, Jesse and Clell Miller surprised Dan Askew at his front gate, toting a bucket of spring water. Askew realized it was too late to run, and he stared at the two revolvers pointed at his face while slowly setting down his pail.

Quiet words were exchanged. Perhaps Askew begged for his life, but as he looked into Jesse's eyes, he saw the anger and the finality. Three pistol shots in rapid succession shattered the night's silence, and Askew collapsed to the ground, blood bubbling out of three bullet holes in his skull.

Askew's murder sent chills through Clay County and much of western Missouri. Everyone knew it was a revenge killing. "There is a tiger loose in Clay County," commented the *Kansas City Times,* "and no man can say who will be the next victim." It was not that hard to guess, though. One newspaper named five men who had supposedly been warned that they were next to follow Askew to an early grave.

Sam Hardwicke was one of the five, but he had known for a long time he was at the top of Jesse's list, which was why he had moved into town. But he still had to be on the lookout. The James boys were bold and ruthless, and they just might ride straight into the square one day and gun him down. Hardwicke armed himself, but as the weeks and months passed, he and his family felt like they were living in a prison.

Finally, in May 1876, Hardwicke and family hurried to the train station under cover of night. As the locomotive hissed and their train lurched forward, Hardwicke breathed a sigh of relief. Within forty-eight hours, they would safely arrive at their new home: St. Paul, Minnesota, far from the stomping grounds of the James brothers.

Three months after Sam Hardwicke fled Missouri, most, if not all, of the James-Younger gang got together to discuss their future plans. Despite the gang's incredible ability to stay one step ahead of the authorities after each bank or train robbery, their former gang member Hobbs Kerry, who ratted out so many of them, had made it much hotter for the boys than usual. Private detectives, police officers, and citizen posses traipsed all over western Missouri, southeast Kansas, and even northeast Texas. Kerry sat alone in a jail in Boonville, Missouri, where he received letters from his old pals. Each one had a cross of blood at the head and told Kerry he would be a dead man the minute he got out of prison. In the meantime, the James-Younger gang needed a change of scenery.

Jesse told the boys they should go to Minnesota. Everyone knew this involved a personal vendetta, but Jesse likely argued that the gang would have freedom of movement in Minnesota. The gang had never before operated that far north and no one would suspect they were who they were. And no one there would be on the lookout for them. Plus, there were the bustling, wide open towns of Minneapolis and St. Paul with their brothels and casinos and places where the boys could have a damn good time spending their Rocky Cut loot.

Minnesota also offered lots of fat banks, many of them easy marks, with the potential for a big haul from a *Northern* bank. Additionally, a bank robbery conducted with the coolness and daring with which they were so often associated—their signature, so to speak—would likely pull the detectives and police away from their favorite hideouts in Missouri.

And then there was Sam Hardwicke. Jesse's brilliant blue eyes seemed to catch on fire when he spoke his name. Hardwicke had evidently believed he was so safe he could write a letter to the *Liberty Tribune* and give his St. Paul address. That was helpful for Jesse, who had every intention of looking up the murderer of little Archie and sending him to hell.

Bob Younger and Jesse were close, so Bob was all for Jesse's plan. He relished the idea of a strike against the North—it was bold and exciting—and the chance to empty a bank vault of thousands of dollars was always appealing. Cole, though, argued against the plan. He later said he had a "terrible urge" not to make the Minnesota trip, which made a wonderful tale for newspaper reporters. Cole did have an urge; however, that urge was to disagree with anything Jesse suggested.

Jim Younger, who had been summoned from California to join in the expedition, bringing the gang back up to eight men, also was not keen on the idea, or at least that is what he claimed afterward. Cole would say that his opposition to the northern jaunt was "over-ruled," suggesting that he was bound by the decision of the gang. Perhaps so, but Cole always seemed to do what Cole wanted to do. If anything, Cole and Jim were not about to let their little brother go off without them: "kinsfolk are born to share adversity."

They packed light. No extra change of clothes; one could always get a garment laundered, and new clothes could be purchased when needed. Revolvers, their side-arms of choice, were cleaned and oiled, leather ammunition belts filled. Some of the gang carried as many as four revolvers, and they were the best killing hardware to be had. The Colt Single Action Army and Smith & Wesson Model #3 Russian (notable for its break-open design and automatic cartridge ejector) were favorites. And they preferred them with nickel plating, which gave a mirror finish, and ivory grips. In other words, they liked fancy guns, even if most people never caught the slightest glimpse of their weapons.

The train station or stations the gang departed from are not known, but at St. Joseph, Missouri, the outlaws were all together. From that point, their passenger train rolled north to Sioux City, Iowa, the shiny tracks hugging the Missouri River Valley. At Sioux City, the outlaws transferred to the St. Paul & Sioux City Railroad for the 280 miles to the Minnesota capital. Their train sped northeast through prime Iowa farm-land, but soon after crossing the Minnesota border, the boys began noticing the sloughs and lakes the state was noted for.

East of Mankato was the famed Big Woods, a heavy forest of elms, sugar maples, oaks, and thick shrubs one hundred miles long and forty-five miles wide. There were roads through the Big Woods, but they were poor, and, when muddy, nearly impassable. But more awful than the roads were the swarms of mos-quitoes and the impressively large deerflies. And one could forget about any kind of breeze; the woods kept the air still and sticky. The James-Younger gang was used to the brush, but that was Missouri, where most of them had been born and raised. This was altogether different. To get the lay of the land was no easy feat for a newcomer, especially when the forest all looked the same and a horizon was nowhere to be seen.

But the boys had no plans for the Big Woods. For now, it was the Twin Cities that occupied their attention.

On August 23, a Wednesday, a J. C. Horton and H. L. Nest, both of Nashville, Tennessee, checked into the Nicollet House, an upscale hotel on Minneapolis's busy Washington Avenue. The next day, three more men, W. G. Huddleson, J. C. King, and John Wood, scrawled their names in the register. Huddleson said he was from Maryland, and King and Wood identified themselves as Virginians. But everything these men wrote was a lie. The James-Younger gang was cautiously moving about Minneapolis in small groups.

But other than changing their names at the hotel, these outlaws did not seem to care that just about everything about them drew attention. It started with their striking physiques and the confident way they carried themselves. And their dress was different from most anyone you would find in Minnesota. They tucked their pants into knee-high boots, brandished long spurs, and wore ulster dusters. These unbleached linen dusters did exactly what the name implied: they kept the dust and dirt of the road off one's clothes. But the boys preferred dusters for another reason: the light, loose-fitting garments concealed their heavy six-shooters and ammunition belts.

Locals also picked up on the gang's Missouri drawl and quaint speech. The outlaws told people they were "grangers," meaning farmers, but their uncalloused, white hands said otherwise. As did their vest pockets flush with cash, which they spent freely. One afternoon they threw money to a poor organ grinder from the hotel's second-floor balcony. The grinder eventually walked away with $8 (a week's board cost $5).

If all this was not enough, the Missouri outlaws didn't remove their wide-brimmed hats when they entered the hotel's dining room, and they committed several other social faux pas. The hotel managers thought this was all an act and were convinced the "grangers" were actually "roughs." But they still took the men's money and kept the suspicions to themselves.

Some of the boys spent their leisure time gambling, poker being a favorite game—saving for a rainy day had never been the gang's strong suit. Others sought out the female offerings of Minneapolis. One night, Jesse and two others stepped into a horse-drawn hack outside the Nicollet and told the driver to take them to the nearest bordello. That was Mollie Ellsworth's establishment, just two blocks away.

Twenty-seven-year-old Mollie was dressing for the evening when Jesse walked into her room. He stared at the madam for some time as she finished dressing. Finally, he asked her if she had not operated a brothel in St. Louis. And was her name not Kitty Traverse? Surprised, Mollie turned to face the man, suddenly recognizing him.

"What are you doing up here?" she blurted out.

"Oh," Jesse said, "nothing. I am going out into the country for a few days and will be back soon; then you and I will go to the Centennial."

Mollie had known Jesse for years, or so she claimed, and she had a good idea there was something more to his presence in Minnesota than stopping by her establishment.

"You don't want to drop onto any 'cases' around here," she said, meaning the outlaw should be careful to stay out of trouble.

"Oh," Jesse replied, "you know I never get left [caught]."

She couldn't help but notice the several revolvers he was carrying and asked what he was going to do with them. He told her he needed them for "a man that he knew up town."

Mollie again began to warn Jesse, but he cut her off with one of those peculiar Missouri phrases: "I shall die like a dog or eat the hatchet."

Mollie also saw the big wad of cash Jesse carried— she was a working girl, after all—and she said she could tell he was doing very well.

Jesse, with a bit of a wry smile, said "he generally had everything he wanted."

Mollie never said the two of them had sex that night; it was not the kind of thing one would make public.

But Jesse and the boys hadn't come there that night for pleasant conversation. Later, Mollie did share with a reporter an interesting detail about Jesse's footwear that would have been difficult to know unless his boots had been off. She said the boots weren't the same size. "He has a small foot," she added, "and could wear my shoe."

Just ten miles away, in St. Paul, some of the gang stayed at the Merchants Hotel and patronized a stylish gambling establishment on East Third that was owned by John P. Chinn and his brother-in-law George Morgan. Chinn, who everyone knew as Colonel Jack Chinn, was a large, dark-skinned, powerful man who dressed quite elegantly and was remembered for the flashy diamonds he wore. He had a well-deserved reputation as a master knife fighter (many compared him to the famed Jim Bowie). Chinn perfected a type of switchblade fighting knife that he loved to demonstrate.

The outlaws' visits to the Chinn & Morgan place may have been more than happenstance. Both Chinn and his brother-in-law were from the Harrodsburg, Kentucky, area, the same region Quantrill and his dwindling band of bushwhackers galloped over in the waning days of the Civil War. Chinn had joined the Confederate army as a teenager, and although little is known of his military service, it is possible that he and

Frank met sometime in 1865. If not then, the James boys made almost annual trips to Kentucky after the war, and they could very well have encountered Chinn on one of those excursions. If Chinn was indeed a friend or acquaintance to the Jameses, he would have been a most significant source of information about southern Minnesota.

One warm evening, two of the outlaws, probably Bob Younger and Bill Chadwell, created a stir when a floor manager, noting the stuffiness of the gambling hall, suggested that they remove their dusters. The outlaws readily obliged, but they did not stop with the dusters. They unbuckled their heavy cartridge belts and laid their guns and knives on the table. The arsenal suddenly on display took the manager's breath away, and there were plenty of stares and murmurs from the patrons. But the tension in the room lasted only for a moment. The doors were locked, the guns covered up, and the sounds of shuffling cards and roulette wheels resumed. The game went all night and into the next day, with the outlaws losing $200 to the house.

Jesse may have tried his luck at Chinn & Morgan's gaming tables, but the jackpot he was after was not a stack of chips—it was attorney Sam Hardwicke. He was referring to this when he told Mollie Ellsworth his pistols were for "a man that he knew up town." That man was not in Minneapolis, where Mollie ran her bordello, but in the neighboring city of St. Paul, but this was surely a deception on the outlaw's part. Jesse was far too smart to tell a prostitute what he was really up to.

Hardwicke lived at 43 St. Paul Street, which was in the far northwest corner of the city. That was the address published in the *Liberty Tribune*. His law office, which he shared with A. K. Barnum, was at 11 Wabasha Street, in the heart of the business district and just a few blocks from the Merchants Hotel. Jesse would have had no problem locating both addresses, but he wanted to kill Hardwicke without getting caught. Sending a slug through the attorney's brain in broad daylight in the heart of downtown St. Paul was the last thing he wanted to do.

Jesse probably started casing Hardwicke's home and his office. And Sam Hardwicke, his mind occupied with the normal thoughts of work and family, would have gone about his day without the slightest inkling that those burning blue eyes were on him, that the terrible menace he had fled just three months before had followed him to Minnesota. Yet, for whatever reason, Jesse failed to assassinate his quarry.

Perhaps Hardwicke was out of town and Jesse never saw him. But more than likely Jesse never felt he had the perfect opportunity to strike. The same thing happened when he traveled to Chicago to kill Allan Pinkerton. According to Jesse's cousin, George Hite Jr., Jesse spent four months in Chicago, "but he never had a chance to do it like he wanted to." Jesse wanted Pinkerton to know who his assassin was. "It would do no good if I couldn't tell him about it before he died," Jesse told Hite. "I had a dozen chances to shoot him when he didn't know it. I wanted to give him a fair chance, but the opportunity never came."

Maybe that's what happened with Hardwicke, although that does not mean that Jesse gave up entirely on his plans. The gang had no set date for leaving Minnesota, and Jesse always believed that God would deliver his enemies into his hands.

After some high-priced fun, the boys looked more and more to the next haul, and the sooner the better. They sent small detachments into the Minnesota countryside with two purposes. They needed good, fast horses, and that would take time to locate and buy, and they needed information: What towns had banks? How prosperous were the communities? Were there good escape routes?

On August 24, a Thursday, one of the gang walked into the express office in Red Wing, Minnesota, forty-five miles southeast of St. Paul. He carried a small box of cigars and gave his name as Kelly. He told the express clerk he wanted to ship the box to a Jefferson City, Missouri, address. The clerk's eyes bulged when that address turned out to be cell number eight in the Missouri State Penitentiary. But the outlaw was very matter-of-fact about this, telling the clerk the convict was a "pal" of his, and he was not ashamed to say so. The clerk didn't know how to respond, but he took the package and sent it off in care of the prison's warden.

Which member of the James-Younger gang shipped the package remains unknown, but he went back to his outlaw confederates, told them what he'd seen, and two days later, four men wearing linen dusters arrived in Red Wing on the noon train from St. Paul. These men—Jesse, Frank, Clell Miller, and Jim Younger— spent the weekend there, purchasing four fine horses (two sorrels and two bays), new saddles, bridles, and a map. At the local gun shop, Jesse and the boys surprised gunsmith Charles Witney when they asked for .44-caliber pistol cartridges. None of his regular customers shot such a large pistol.

The boys were a tight-lipped group, but Witney and more than a few of the townspeople could not stop themselves from asking the men their business. The outlaws gave conflicting answers, politely telling some they were cattle drovers on their way to St. Paul and others that they were Kentuckians bound for the Black Hills to search for gold. At their hotel, one of the men got the guests' attention when he said he'd bet $1,000 that Minnesota would go for Democrat Samuel J. Tilden over Rutherford B. Hayes in the presidential election. Someone should have taken the bet.

Jesse and the boys left Red Wing on Monday, August 28, three riding off in a northerly direction while the fourth boarded a stage.

On that same Monday and the Tuesday after, Bob Younger and Bill Chadwell went shopping in St. Paul. One of them stopped in William Burkhard's gun shop on East Third Street and bought a new Bowie knife, lightly gliding his thumb across the knife's edge several times before slipping it into his belt. Younger and Chadwell then went to at least three livery stables before deciding on two "splendid" mounts, a black and a bay. They then bought two nearly new saddles (McClellan style, one bearing a Masonic emblem) and bridles. One of the outlaws was seen trying out the black steed on Wabasha Street, his duster flapping in the wind as he spurred the horse, urging it into a lively canter.

The livery owner, Edward McKinney, later described Younger and Chadwell "as fully six feet high, with keen eyes, quick movements, good talkers, smart in dealing, liberal with their money, and paying prices asked without question." All in all, he said, they made "an appearance that was so remarkable and unusual that they at once attracted attention."

McKinney asked the boys where they hailed from. Missouri, they answered, and said they were in Minnesota "just to look around." Well, McKinney offered, they were doing the right thing by riding horseback, as riding was necessary to keep up one's health. That caused one of the outlaws to burst out laughing.

"Do I look like a man who was out of health?" he asked.

While Bob and Chadwell were shopping in St. Paul, Cole Younger and Charlie Pitts were at St. Peter, a town of three thousand that is seventy-five miles southwest of the Twin Cities on the St. Paul & Sioux City Railroad. Cole and Pitts spent most of the last week of August there, lodging at a hotel called the American House. The hotel employees and guests didn't know what to make of these guys—they claimed to be cattle dealers— and it was not just their dress and language. They had been awfully particular about the kind of horses they were after. And there had been a curious discussion between Cole and the hotel clerk. Cole asked if St. Peter was not a rather dead town. The clerk assured Cole it was not. The outlaw then said that maybe the reason it seemed so dead was the town had no bank. The clerk corrected Cole immediately. St. Peter had a fine bank, the First National, and it was just a half block from there. Cole thanked the clerk and said he felt like going for a drink at Evanson's saloon. But on his way to the saloon, Cole was seen pausing in the street and "closely scrutiniz[ing] the bank."

Children noticed these men as well. Cole and Pitts were enjoying a couple of cigars outside the American House one afternoon when some boys stopped in front of them, cocked their heads, and stared. Cole chomped down on his cigar, pulled a coin from his pocket, and flipped it to the ground. "It belongs to the first one who gets it," he said. The boys snapped out of their trance and dived for the coin. Pitts tossed the next coin, causing another mad scramble. The outlaws laughed and dug in their pockets for more coins, tossing all that they had, one at a time. It was a good show while it lasted.

Younger and Pitts eventually found the horses they wanted just across the Minnesota River in Kasota. They bought saddles in St. Peter and spent each day exercising and training the new mounts. During one of these sessions, Cole came upon a beaming young girl who ran up to his horse and told him she could ride horseback. Cole reached down, grabbed the surprised girl, and pulled her up and onto the saddle, in front of him. As they rode up and down for the next few minutes, the girl told Cole her name was Horace Greeley Perry. He thought that was a big name for such a little tot. "I won't always be little," she told the outlaw. "I'm going to be a great big girl, and be a newspaperman like my pa." Little Miss Perry's father had published a newspaper in St. Peter since 1866, and she would grow up to become an editor and publisher herself—and write about the outlaw Youngers.

Outwardly, Cole and Charlie were cool and relaxed, but they were more than a little worried because Bob Younger and Bill Chadwell were supposed to have met them in St. Peter. But as days passed without them showing up, Cole thought they might have been apprehended. He had been scanning the newspapers for any arrest reports that described his little brother and Chadwell. What Cole did not know was that Bob and Bill had missed their train, which had led to their purchase of horses in St. Paul. Two of the gang did show up in St. Peter on Friday, September 1, but they were not Bob and Chadwell; their identities remain unknown. These two strangers had been in St. Peter only a few hours and were seen buying a couple of rubber coats before riding out of town to the west. They'd had plenty of time to case the small town and its bank, though.

Cole and Pitts, finally having had enough of waiting, left St. Peter on Saturday, September 2, also heading west. That very evening, Bob and Chadwell rode into town, registering at St. Peter's Nicollet House (not to be confused with Minneapolis's Nicollet House) under the names G. H. King and B. T. Cooper. They passed themselves off as sportsmen hunters. Their fine horses and new-looking McClellan saddles, fringed saddle blankets, and new bridles caught the eyes of several townspeople. They were friendly and, as reported later, "made themselves familiar with everyone." That was how they found out what their other gang members had been doing before they got there. Bob and Chadwell then went straight to the American House and pumped the clerk for information about Cole and Pitts and found out they had just missed them. Yet Bob and Chadwell didn't appear to be in any hurry. They did not ride out of St. Peter until the next afternoon.

Of all the towns the gang members visited, Mankato seemed the best prospect for a holdup. Three railroads intersected in the prosperous city, which was situated on a bend of the Minnesota River, eighty-six miles southwest of St. Paul. The seat of Blue Earth County, one of the most fertile regions in the state, Mankato was twice the size of St. Peter—and it had three banks. It had several hotels, the Clifton House being the best with its "commodious billiard room" (lodging $2 per day). Equally appealing was the notorious brothel run by twenty-nine-year-old Irishman Jack O'Neil. The bane of Mankato's moral majority, it was located in the woods just across the river, which was outside the city limits.

As many as five of the outlaws rode into Mankato on Saturday, September 2. Two lodged at the Clifton House and another two at Gates Hotel, but unlike at other hotels, the men declined to put their names in the guest registers. They were frequently seen about town that weekend making small purchases and playing cards in the saloons. Again, their impressive horses and dress attracted attention, as did their expert riding skills. Some of the gang were more than pleased to discuss their horses with anyone who admired them.

The robbery was planned for Monday, September 4, but two of the outlaws spent Sunday night at O'Neil's brothel, which means they were probably not at their best Monday morning. But the daylight robbery was one of the gang's specialties, and they were confident they could take just about any bank, especially in a place like Minnesota, where such bold raids were unheard of.

Then on Monday morning, outside one of the hotels, a day laborer named Charles Robinson, who was working nearby, suddenly spoke up: "Hallo, Jesse, what are you doing up here?"

Jesse cocked his head and gave Robinson a curious look. Robinson was from Missouri, from James-Younger country. He even claimed to have once sat across a card table from Jesse.

A slow smile broke across Jesse's face, sending a shiver down Robinson's spine. "Hell, man, I don't know you," Jesse said, finally. And with that, he put his horse into a trot.

At about this same time, or shortly after, Cole Younger and another gang member walked into the First National Bank of Mankato, located on South Front Street. Cole went up to the counter and asked the assistant cashier, George Barr, to change a twenty-dollar bill. This was a favorite ploy of the gang that allowed them to get a better sense of the bank. Barr gave Cole his change in five-dollar bills, which the outlaw slowly counted one by one, making occasional glances toward the bank's vault.

While Cole was in the First National, another gang member visited the Citizens' National Bank, which was in the same block on South Front. The gang had decided to rob one or the other, and these visits were meant to help them choose between the two. The outlaws then gathered some blocks away and decided that the First National was their best bet. In the meantime, Charles Robinson walked into the First National and told assistant cashier Barr that the James boys were in town and they had best "guard their bank well." Barr looked at Robinson as if the man were crazy.

"Well, they are," Robinson exclaimed. He said he knew Frank and Jesse "as well as he did his own children." Barr thanked Robinson, telling him he would pass along the information to the cashier. This Barr did, but the cashier was just as incredulous as his assistant, and they promptly forgot the whole thing.

Sometime around noon, five or so of the gang rode toward the First National while the others hung back to watch their escape route, poised to rush in if things went wrong. But as the outlaws came in sight of the bank, situated on a corner of the block, they saw a number of people on the sidewalk, one of whom was pointing out the horsemen to a companion. Fearing they might have been found out, the outlaws casually turned their horses and rode back to the other gang members.

But Jesse and the boys were not about to give up just yet. The First National, with $120,000 in capital, was one ripe plum. They wanted that money. So the robbers again approached the bank about an hour later, but again the same crowd was on the sidewalk, and like before, they seemed to be paying close attention to the riders. This unsettled the outlaws. Jesse had been identified earlier in the day so this could be some kind of trap. The robbers turned their mounts and calmly retreated from Mankato.

In the James-Younger gang's line of work, suspicion was a constant companion, but there had been no trap. An unusually large number of people were on the street because of a weekly meeting of the Board of Trade and ongoing construction for an expansion of the bank. And although the gang had been right that these townspeople were watching them, the people were only doing what most others did in every town the Missourians visited: they were admiring the fine horses.

The boys headed east. Cole and Charlie Pitts had scouted Madelia, twenty-three miles southwest of Mankato. It was a pleasant town, but it had no bank. The St. Peter bank had struck them as a rather small operation, so they had no intention of returning there. The bank they now had in their sights was in Northfield, a town of about two thousand people on the Cannon River thirty-nine miles south of St. Paul. Jesse and Clell had spent a day or two poking around Northfield, pretending that they wanted to buy some land in the area. Northfield had only one bank, the

First National, which meant the town's money was all in one place and not divided up like in Mankato with its three banks. And they had come across an article in the local newspaper that said it had a new safe and time lock and that two heavy doors for the vault had been added as well. A bank would not invest in those kinds of improvements unless there was a substantial amount of money to protect.

Jesse and Clell had pumped one local fellow about the Northfield townspeople, as if they were considering whether or not to live there. Were they a peace-loving, law-abiding people? When the man answered yes, one of the outlaws commented, "Why, according to your statement of the Northfield people, a very few men so inclined could capture the town, couldn't they?"

"Of course they could," said the local.

It was exactly the kind of conversation Jesse found amusing.

But the next part was Jesse's favorite. One of the bank's large investors was Adelbert Ames, a Union Civil War general and Radical Republican who until only recently had been Mississippi's governor. Ames had been derided by Mississippi Democrats as a "carpetbagger" and despised by Southern whites for his pro-black Reconstruction policies. It did not help that Ames's father-in-law was General Benjamin Butler, the hated former military commander of New Orleans (Southerners knew him as "Beast Butler"). After the Democrats gained control of the Mississippi legislature in 1875, they initiated impeachment pro-ceedings against the governor for "high crimes and misde-

Adelbert Ames.

meanors." Unwilling to endure what would surely be a very public tar and feathering, Ames resigned and moved to Northfield in the spring to join his brother, an early town settler, and his father in the family flour-milling business.

Jesse was the ultimate Southern partisan, and he rel-ished the idea of striking a blow for revenge, be it per-sonal or political. He would hit the bank of Adelbert Ames and ride off with grain sacks stuffed with a notorious carpetbagger's money. He could envision the newspapers having a field day with the story, enhancing his notoriety and, of course, feeding his ravenous ego. Northfield had to be the bank they would rob next.

The gang traveled in two parties. On the evening of September 6, a Wednesday, Cole, Jim, Clell, and Pitts lodged at Millersburg, eleven miles west of Northfield. Jesse, Frank, Bob, and Chadwell spent the night at Cannon City, ten miles south. Jim nearly derailed the gang's plans when he began having second thoughts about the robbery. One farmer who saw him that day said Jim "did not act like the others, but seemed low spirited and homesick." Jim said he wanted to sell his horse and get on a train back to California. But after a long talk with Cole and the others, he decided to stick with the plan. They needed him.

On the morning of September 7, the outlaws carefully looked after their horses, pulling up the animals' hooves one by one to check for loose shoes. And they placed each saddle blanket and saddle just right, pushing a knee into the horse's belly so the animal would exhale and then drawing up the cinch good and snug. There would be hard riding in just a few hours, so nothing could be left to chance. But if everything came off well, as they fully expected, their steeds would carry them at a breakneck pace through the Minnesota woods, the boys laughing and whooping in the wind.

Four
The Hottest Day
Northfield Ever Saw

*It is true, we are robbers, but we always rob in the
glare of the day and in the teeth of the multitude.*

—JESSE JAMES

There was no way Joseph Lee Heywood hadn't heard
about it. People were talking about it at the bank,
and he must have seen the broadsides posted all over
town. It was Thursday, September 7, and Northfield
was going to have some excitement that night.

The "Great" Professor Lingard, an Australian illu-
sionist, was going to perform, and before his show the
public could watch him send up his two hot-air balloons
named Tilden and Hayes—free of charge. Admission
to the magic show was twenty-five cents, fifteen cents
for children under ten. Maybe Heywood would take
his five-year-old daughter, Lizzie May, and his wife,

Lizzie, at least to see the balloons. The ascension was not until 6:45 P.M., so he would have plenty of time to get home after work, have dinner, and then help get the family ready to go out.

That morning Heywood set off for the First National Bank, which was approximately six blocks from his home. He was a rather shy man, and at thirty-nine years old, the New Hampshire native had been the bank's bookkeeper since 1872. He had fought during the Civil War in the Deep South, though his service was plagued by chronic illness. He came to Northfield in 1867, and quickly gained a reputation as a steady and trustworthy man. In addition to his employment at the bank, he was also city treasurer and treasurer for the fledgling Carleton College, which had awarded its first bachelor's degrees—a total of two—in 1874.

Joseph Lee Heywood.

The First National Bank was in a stark, rectangular room in the rear of a two-story stone building called the Scriver Block. The front of the Scriver Block faced north onto the open and treeless Mill Square. But the bank's entrance was on the side of the Scriver Building on Division Street, a busy north-south avenue where most of Northfield's merchants were clustered: furniture, hardware, jewelry, drugs, grocery, cigar, saloon, you name it. Division Street was also the east boundary of Mill Square. The Cannon River and the millworks of Jesse Ames & Sons were across the square to the west, which explains the square's name. An iron bridge spanned the river, and Heywood crossed it and Mill Square twice a day because his home was on the west side of town. The tracks of the Milwaukee & St. Paul Railroad were also on the west side, and its locomotives made sharp whistles that could be clearly heard throughout Northfield.

The bank's cramped workspace and vault area were protected in the front by a curved wooden counter that was topped by a glass-paneled railing, except for an opening in the curve where the teller greeted customers. Heywood's desk was built into this counter, but the bank's cashier, George M. Phillips, was away attending the centennial, so Heywood was working at Phillips's small desk on the north side of the room and near the vault.

Northfield's iron bridge over the Cannon River, looking east onto Mill Square.

The vault faced the bank's large pane windows that looked out onto Division Street. The heavy vault door, manufactured by the Detroit Safe Company, screamed Gilded Age with its gaudy pediment, heavy gold trimming, and pastoral scene painted on the door.

A unique clock, popular at the time, called a "calendar clock" was hanging on the wall just to the left of the vault. It featured two circular faces. The top face, the larger of the two, gave the time, and the bottom face gave the date, the day of the week, and the month. The clock had no chime, but it was hard to miss its distinctive ticking in that small room. This clock, and the elaborate vault door, always caught the eyes of bank customers standing at the counter.

Interior of the First National Bank, 1876.

Also at the bank that morning were Frank Wilcox, assistant bookkeeper, who would turn twenty-eight years old the next day, and Alonzo E. Bunker, the teller, who was twenty-seven years old. Heywood greeted the men and told them what he needed them to do that morning. Then he opened the vault's outer door and walked inside to the steel safe, also a product of the Detroit Safe Company. The new chronometer lock would have automatically disengaged by the beginning of business hours, so Heywood worked the safe's combination and unlocked it, but he left the safe door closed, its bolts still in place. There was approximately $15,000 in the safe.

Just three days earlier, Heywood had stood in the vault with the president of Carleton College, James

Strong, who had read in the papers about the bank improvements and asked his friend Heywood about the new time lock. As they talked, Strong brought up the St. Albans Raid of October 19, 1864, in which twenty-one Confederate cavalrymen invaded the Vermont town and robbed its three banks of more than $200,000. Strong, a native of Vermont, had been told what happened during the raid by one of the bank cashiers.

After pausing to see how Heywood reacted to his story, Strong asked his friend a pointed question: "Do you think, under like circumstances, you would open the safe?"

"I do not think I should," Heywood answered.

Something in Heywood's response—his simple frankness, perhaps—left Strong convinced that Heywood would never bend to the demands of an armed robber. But, of course, the question was purely hypothetical, for such an attack would never happen in Northfield.

By 10:00 A.M., the first of the James-Younger gang began to ride into town. Four men came up Division Street from the south, two hitching their horses in front of the First National Bank while the others continued on past Mill Square and stopped in front of the Exchange Saloon. The two at the bank glanced up and down the street, opened the bank's door, and walked in. They were inside for only a moment before they came back out to the street.

The outlaws may have asked to have a twenty-dollar bill changed—or they may have asked the time and been shown the calendar clock on the wall. In any event, they got a good look inside the bank and noted how many employees were on duty. The outlaws next mounted their horses and rode around to the front of the Scriver Building and through Mill Square to the bridge. At the bridge they met three others, talked briefly, shook hands, and left.

The outlaws were spotted on the east and west side of town, usually in pairs and trios, over the next four hours. They occasionally exchanged pleasantries with folks on the street. Some visited the hardware stores and asked if they had any rifles for sale—which was their way of figuring out what might be available to the townspeople and what they might encounter in a fight.

They had never really raised much suspicion in the other Minnesota small towns they had visited, but for some reason, on this day, more than a few locals looked at these strangers with worry and concern. It started with Walter Lewis, a black man who was on his way to Northfield and saw four of the outlaws coming out of some woods. Lewis told Salma Trussell, the owner of an agricultural implements store, that something didn't seem right about these men. Trussell shadowed some of them along Division Street and became suspicious as well. He had half a mind to go to the bank and alert Heywood about the men in the dusters, but first he consulted Elias Hobbs. Hobbs, the former chief of police, knew all about these well-dressed fellows. They were cattle buyers, he told Trussell. Hobbs and others chastised him for being "too suspicious." Trussell decided to let it go; perhaps he *was* being a little silly.

Druggist George Bates also saw four of the strangers coming over the bridge that morning and marveled at the fine horses these impressive men were riding. Bates recalled later that he had never seen four "nobler looking fellows." The men had a "reckless, bold swagger about them that seemed to indicate that they would be rough and dangerous fellows to handle." He had a bad feeling about them.

Shortly after 11:00 A.M., two of the outlaws entered Gerden Jefts's restaurant, on the west side of the river and near the railroad depot. Jefts had nothing prepared, but he told the strangers he could whip up some ham and eggs. That sounded good to the boys, who requested four eggs each. They were in a jocular mood and turned to one of their favorite topics: politics. They

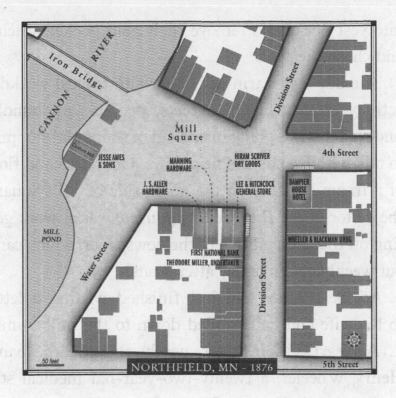

wanted to know what Jefts thought of Tilden's chances in the presidential election. Jefts said he had no interest in politics, which the boys just ignored. As in Red Wing, one of the outlaws grandly proffered a $1,000 wager that Tilden would carry the state.

Two more of the gang joined their pals at Jefts's and ordered the same eggs. The other half of the gang was split between John Tosney's saloon on Water Street (also on the west side of the river) and the Exchange Saloon on Division. They ordered wine and whiskey, lightly sipping their drinks and periodically digging into vest pockets to remove their gold pocket watches and check the time.

The day was warm and calm with typical weekday activity on Northfield's streets, people with bundles under their arms going in and out of shops and stopping to talk with friends and neighbors. On the second floor of a frame building on the north side of Mill Square, the editor of the *Rice County Journal* was at work getting off the latest edition of the newspaper, which came out weekly on Thursday afternoons.

Adelbert Ames had just finished writing a letter to his wife and had strolled down to the mill to mail it. Across Division Street, nearly opposite the bank, Henry Wheeler, a twenty-two-year-old medical student on break from the University of Michigan, killed time sitting in a chair under the awning of his father's drugstore, Wheeler & Blackman Drug.

A few minutes before 2:00 P.M., Frank James, Bob Younger, and Charlie Pitts slowly crossed the iron bridge, the roar of the water that rushed over the nearby mill dam momentarily drowning out the sound of their horses' hooves. The plan was for these three to be the inside men, to conduct the robbery. Cole and Clell Miller would post themselves on Division Street outside the bank, and Jesse, Jim Younger, and Bill Chadwell would wait in Mill Square to guard their escape route—if there was trouble, they would rush forward with a Rebel yell.

Frank, Bob, and Charlie were to proceed with the holdup only if there were just a few people on the street. They had to make this decision because there would be no way to consult the others without drawing unwanted attention. The boys were all quite confident; they had been pulling off these jobs for years. Clell Miller was so certain he fished out his pipe and lit it, telling Cole he planned to smoke it during the whole damned robbery.

Frank, Bob, and Charlie rode through Mill Square, passing on their right the hardware stores of J. S. Allen and Anselm Manning and finally they rode by the Scriver Building. Boxes of dry goods and displays of merchandise were crowded around the entrances to the two stores occupying the front of the building: Hiram Scriver's dry-goods business and Lee & Hitchcock's general store.

Turning onto Division Street, the three outlaws continued south to the First National Bank, got off their horses, and tossed their reins over the hitching posts. Two of them walked back to the corner. An exterior stairway led down from the second floor of the Scriver, and the two men lounged around this stairway for a few minutes, leaning against the banister and sitting on a wooden box in front of the general store. They seemed to be casually chatting, but they were carefully taking in their surroundings and waiting for Cole and Clell to appear.

Cole rode across the bridge with Clell and saw the guys sitting on the corner up ahead, but Cole also saw quite a few townspeople milling around, and he became alarmed.

"Surely the boys will not go into the bank with so many people about," he told Clell. "I wonder why they did not ride on through town?"

One of the people in town was J. S. Allen, who had been standing in the doorway of his hardware store when the first three outlaws rode through the square. "Who are those men?" he said. "I don't like the looks of them." Allen left his store and walked toward the Scriver to get a better look. He saw someone he knew and turned to him. "I believe they are here to rob the bank," Allen said.

About this time, the two outlaws at the Scriver corner saw Cole and Clell at the bridge, and they immediately stood up and walked around the corner and out of sight.

"They are going in," Clell said.

"If they do, the alarm will be given as sure as there's a hell," Cole exclaimed, "so you had better take that pipe out of your mouth."

Henry Wheeler watched Frank, Bob, and Charlie enter the bank. He took them to be cattlemen. A farmer passing on the sidewalk asked Wheeler if he knew why so many saddle horses were in town. It was a good question, because most folks in that part of the country traveled about in farm wagons and buggies. And there were those dusters the men were wearing, too.

"It made them look kind of uniform," recalled one Northfield resident.

Inside the Dunn & Riddell hardware store (next door to Henry Wheeler's father's drugstore), Mrs. John Handy stared out the glass storefront at the bank across the street. She had also noticed all the saddle horses in town. And in an odd coincidence, she happened to

be from St. Albans. This reminded her of that terrifying day back in 1864. She became so strangely fixated on the men that Mr. Riddell was having a difficult time waiting on her.

She couldn't even say anything as she

Alonzo Bunker, the bank's teller.   watched the three

men step into the First National. Suddenly, Mrs. Handy took a sharp breath and blurted out, "They are robbing the bank! I saw the revolvers"—the flash of those nickel-plated six-shooters. A stunned Mr. Riddell watched Mrs. Handy bolt for his store's back door.

Alonzo Bunker, the First National Bank's teller, was at work at his desk when he heard the door open and footsteps on the wood floor of the small lobby. The sound was nothing new and only meant a customer had arrived. So Bunker turned from his desk and, like always, moved to the open space at the counter.

But this time three large revolvers pointed at his face.

"Throw up your hands, for we intend to rob this bank," Frank James shouted, "and if you holler we will blow your God damned brains out."

Bunker first thought some friends were playing a joke on him and he merely stood there. That's when Frank demanded to know which one was

Frank Wilcox, assistant bookkeeper.

the cashier. Heywood spoke up from his desk: "He is not in."

The three robbers jumped up and over the counter. Shouting commands, they forced Bunker and Frank Wilcox to their knees. Heywood stood up from his desk but was told to get on the floor with his hands up.

Frank James pointed his revolver at each of them in turn and shouted, "You are the cashier"—while each man denied it. At the same time, Bob Younger and Charlie Pitts searched the men for weapons. Younger started patting Wilcox's clothes, the smell of liquor clearly on the outlaw's breath.

Wilcox always kept a large jackknife in his hip pocket, and when Younger felt the knife, he stopped and said, "What's this?" Wilcox nervously explained that it was only a pocketknife, and Younger let him be and began rummaging around the counter for money.

Bunker realized he was still holding his pen in his hand. As he lowered his hand to place the pen on the counter, Younger saw him and brought his pistol to Bunker's nose.

"Here, put up your hands, and keep 'em up or I'll kill you," Younger said. Bunker's hand shot back up.

Frank James kept shouting for the cashier. He stepped up to Heywood, who had been sitting at the cashier's desk, stuck his revolver in his face, and said, "You are the cashier. Now open the safe you God damned son of a bitch!"

Heywood looked up the gun's barrel at Frank and didn't move an inch.

Outside on the street, Cole and Clell had ridden up in front of the bank just moments after the three robbers stepped inside. Cole got off his horse, threw a stirrup over his saddle, and acted as if he was adjusting the saddle's cinch. But the door of the bank had been left open, and Cole could hear the loud voices of the boys inside; he told Clell to get down and close the door. Clell stepped partway into the bank, grabbed the door, and pulled it shut.

J. S. Allen, who was peering around the stairway from the corner of Lee & Hitchcock's store, had seen the three men in the dusters enter the bank. He couldn't stand it any longer—he was convinced these men were up to no good. He rushed down the sidewalk, and as he got to the front of the bank, he could see the bearded Joseph Lee Heywood through the plate glass. Allen stepped to the door just as Clell was closing it, and in an instant, Clell was in Allen's face, his eyes like those of a wild man. He violently grabbed Allen's collar and pushed a revolver barrel to his nose.

"You son of a bitch," Clell said through clinched teeth, "don't you holler!"

By this time, Henry Wheeler had also caught on to what was happening. He got up from his chair and took a few steps into the street. He saw Clell take hold of Allen, and then he saw Allen jerk free and start running toward Mill Square.

"Robbery!" Wheeler shouted. "They are robbing the bank!"

Clell immediately swung his pistol around and fired at Wheeler, the bullet going over the young man's head.

"Get back, or I'll kill you!" the outlaw yelled.

Wheeler did an about-face and ran into his father's store.

The fifty-year-old Allen raced around the corner of the Scriver, his legs moving as fast as they did when he was a child. "Get your guns, boys," he shouted at the top of his lungs. "They're robbing the bank!"

Cole got back on his horse and began firing his pistol in the general direction of anyone who made the mistake of showing themselves on the street or even poking their head out of a doorway or window.

At the same time, he was shouting, "Get in, you son of a bitch!"

Jesse, Jim Younger, and Chadwell were waiting in Mill Square, and they immediately put spurs to their horses and began yelling like fiends and shooting their revolvers as they galloped to Division Street.

Allen reached his hardware store in seconds and began handing out loaded firearms to anyone around there. It was the townspeople's money in the bank, and as was the case with all banks at that time, those deposits were uninsured. In effect, the outlaws were robbing each citizen individually, at least what savings they had in the bank, which was plenty good reason to put up a fight.

Farmer Elias Stacy grabbed a shotgun from Allen and raced to the corner. As he stuck the barrel out around the stairway, he saw Clell Miller getting up on his horse. Stacy aimed at the outlaw's head and let him have it. The charge was only bird-shot, but the blast knocked Miller to the ground. He picked himself up and got back on his horse, but he could not shake off the stinging from

Anselm Manning.

the pellet-size wounds. Cole glanced over and saw the blood trickling down Miller's face.

Guns were also coming from the hardware store of Anselm Manning. The forty-two-year-old Manning had been standing behind his counter when the gunfire erupted. He looked up just in time to see Jesse, Jim, and Chadwell gallop through the square, streams of white smoke streaking from the barrels of their revolvers as they fired them. This was not an everyday occurrence in Northfield, but Manning wasn't especially concerned—at first. His employee, Ross C. Phillips, rushed to the front of the store and asked Manning what all the racket was.

"I think it's that show that's going to be here tonight"—the Great Professor Lingard. But Phillips went out the front door and turned toward Division Street, when he nearly ran into two people shouting the alarm. From inside the store, Manning heard someone yelling, "robbing the bank." A second later, Phillips ran back into the store and headed straight for the glass display case that held the store's firearms and ammunition.

As gunshots echoed through the square like Fourth of July fireworks, Phillips pulled revolvers and cartridges from the showcase and threw them on the glass top. Manning remembered he had a Remington rolling-block rifle in the store's window, one he had practiced with in the spring. It used a .45-70 metallic cartridge. Manning pulled out the Remington, grabbed a handful of the heavy cartridges, and ran out the door, inserting a cartridge into the gun's chamber as he headed for the sound of the gunfire.

When he reached the corner of the Scriver Building, Manning rashly stepped out from the stairway to get a good view down the street. He was immediately drawn to the riderless horses in front of the bank and two men taking cover behind them.

"I knew they were robbers the minute my eye struck them," Manning recalled. "I drew my gun on them."

But the robbers saw Manning and his raised Remington so they ducked their heads behind the horses. Undeterred, Manning lowered his gun ever so slightly and blasted the nearest horse, killing the one that belonged to Bob Younger. It collapsed in a heap in front of the bank.

"Jump back now or they'll get you," George Bates shouted to Manning from across the street.

Manning darted back from the corner to reload. But when he tried to extract the shell casing, he found it jammed tight in the gun's chamber—his rifle had just become a heavy club. He ran to his store to get the shell out.

The gunfire increased as the seconds ticked by, as did the shouts and cursing of the robbers. Bates, positioned in the front door of a clothing store, had secured a shotgun and aimed it at the bandits.

But try as he might, he could not get the gun to go off. Disgusted, he tossed the shotgun away and grabbed a fine revolver—only to discover that it was unloaded. Still, whenever a rider came close, he pointed the empty revolver at him from the doorway, shouting, "Now I've got you." Each time, the robber spun his horse and fired at the druggist, who ducked inside amid showers of glass and wood splinters.

Cole, Jesse, and the others were constantly driving away people who were drawn to the commotion on the street. Some townspeople were slow to react, not believing they were actually in the middle of a bandit raid on their peaceful town.

Dentist Danforth J. Whiting was at work in his office on the upper floor of the Scriver Building when he heard the gunshots and saw several doves flitter past his window, flushed from the street below. He poked his head out of the door at the top of the stairs on Division Street and saw "several men on horseback riding up and down the street firing revolvers, swearing and yelling in the wildest manner. Some man, apparently a foreigner, was coming up the sidewalk.

They wanted him to run but he only took a natural gait which seemed to enrage one of the horsemen as he rode up near to him firing and ordering him off the street."

When the robbers spotted Whiting, they yelled at him to get back in the building. He did, but a moment later he stepped out again, and one of the robbers cursed him and fired his pistol. Whiting jumped back.

"I was wondering all the time what all this meant," Whiting recalled. "A lady in my office said there was to be an Indian show that evening and the show men were advertising."

Forty-three-year-old undertaker Theodore Miller had a shop immediately next door to the bank and came to the doorway of his shop when the shooting started.

"I thought there was going to be a circus in town, and I stood and watched them," Miller remembered.

The robbers screamed at Miller to get away, but he was nearly deaf and didn't move until one of the outlaws shot at him, sending a bullet crashing into the door.

"At the same time, my wife came running down the stairs and told me something was going on in the bank and as she was shouting one of the robbers came right up to the shop and when I saw the pistol I knew he meant business, and I ran to the back door and jumped from the stair." Miller didn't say what he did with his wife.

While things were going to hell in the street, the boys in the bank were having troubles of their own. When Frank ordered Heywood to open the safe, Heywood calmly replied, "It is a time lock and cannot be opened now."

"That's a damn lie," Frank shouted.

All the robbers knew about the Yale chronometer lock. Clell Miller had found the newspaper story about its installation at least a week before, had torn it from the paper, and carried it around with him in his pocket. But they knew that no bank would have a locked safe

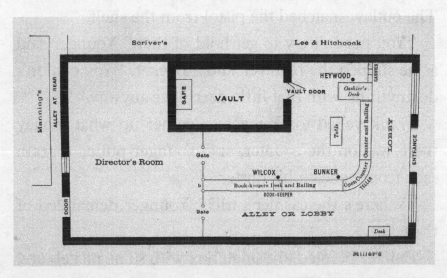

First National Bank floor plan at the time of the raid.

during business hours because the safe's holdings had to be available to the bank's customers. The boys were not new to this game, and they knew the cashiers often lied to protect the monies in their charge. And Frank knew Heywood was lying and he would have none of it.

Frank went over to the open vault and stepped inside to try the safe. Suddenly, Heywood jumped up, sprang over to the vault door, and began to slam it shut. Pitts grabbed Heywood's collar and violently pulled him back.

During the commotion with Heywood, Bunker slowly edged over toward a shelf below the teller's window, his eyes on a loaded .32-caliber Smith & Wesson revolver he could see there. But Younger saw the teller's movement and also spotted the revolver. The outlaw snatched the pistol from the shelf.

"You needn't try to get hold of that," Younger said as he slipped the revolver into a pocket. "You couldn't do anything with that little derringer anyway."

Frank yelled to Younger to gather up what money there was on the counter, and Younger pulled a grain sack from beneath his duster.

"Where's the cashier's till?" Younger demanded of the teller.

Bunker pointed to a small box with some nickels and scrip and said, "There's the money outside."

Younger grabbed a couple of handfuls and hurriedly stuffed them in the grain sack, but then hesitated because he was sure this couldn't be all.

Agitated, Younger pointed his revolver at Bunker: "There's more money than that out here. Where's the cashier's till?"

Younger pulled open a drawer in the counter, saw there was nothing but stationery and slammed it shut. Had he pulled open the drawer next to it, he would have discovered approximately $2,000 in cash.

Now all the robbers were yelling. Frank James kept up his abuse of Heywood, whose resistance both surprised and infuriated him. As treasurer of Carleton College, Heywood knew all the institution's funds were sitting in that safe. If it was stolen, the college would be financially devastated.

"Damn you!" Pitts screamed. "Open that door or we'll cut your throat from ear to ear." He drew a large knife as he said this and took hold of Heywood's hair, jerking his head back. Then Pitts ran the knife's razor edge along Heywood's throat, making a slight cut that oozed a thin red line.

Wilcox and Bunker looked on in horror as Heywood struggled to break free. Finally, Heywood twisted out of Pitts's grasp and started to run away, yelling, "Murder! Murder! Murder!" Frank grabbed Heywood and, in one swift motion, raised his pistol in the air and brought the butt down violently on Heywood's skull, knocking him to the floor. Frank then dragged Heywood back to the vault door.

As Heywood struggled to get up, Frank fired his pistol above the man's head. The sound of the revolver blast in such close quarters caused a ringing pain in everyone's ears. The shot also left a cloud of smoke in the vault.

Frank had purposely missed Heywood, intending to frighten him into cooperating. Bunker, who could not see Heywood well from his kneeling position, thought Frank had just committed murder and that he and Wilcox might be next. With adrenaline coursing through his body, Bunker jumped up and bolted for the rear of the bank. The back door was open, but blinds fastened on the inside blocked half the doorway.

Pitts ran after Bunker, firing his revolver as the man fled. The shot just missed but put a hole in the blinds a split second before Bunker crashed through them and out onto the stairs in the alley. Theodore Miller, the nearly deaf undertaker from next door, was just then at the back of the bank, and Bunker plowed over him.

Suddenly, Pitts was at the door and took careful aim as Bunker ran across an open lot. This time, his shot struck Bunker in the right shoulder.

"The sensation of being shot was as though some one had struck me a sharp blow with a piece of board," Bunker recalled. "There was a jar and a sting as I felt the bullet going through the bones of my shoulder."

Bunker staggered, caught his balance, and kept running.

Henry Wheeler.

After ducking into his father's drugstore, young Henry Wheeler had focused on grabbing the nearest weapon. But when he went for the rifle he kept inside the store, he realized he'd left it at home that day. Then he remembered an old breechloader he had seen at the Dampier House hotel, just two stores to the north. He ran through a back alley and into the hotel and grabbed the gun from the baggage room.

A .50-caliber Smith carbine, it was the type issued to Federal cavalrymen at the beginning of the Civil War. Even years later, Wheeler never saw the irony of using such a weapon against a bunch of ex-bushwhackers who were still living that war, as if time had taken a detour before the Confederate surrender.

But Wheeler wasn't sure the grimy thing would even shoot. It took a paper cartridge that held both the blackpowder charge and a heavy conical bullet. After inserting the cartridge in the chamber, a copper percussion cap had to be placed on the gun's nipple, beneath the cocked hammer. Wheeler got four cartridges and caps from the desk clerk, flew up the stairs to the third floor, and ducked into a room with an open window. Down below and to his left he saw the robbers in the street.

Wheeler, panting hard, his arms shaking, raised the carbine to his shoulder and sighted down its barrel at Jim Younger on his horse. Wheeler was having trouble steadying the carbine's muzzle and keeping its open sights on the moving target, but he pulled the trigger and the old gun answered with a sharp crack. Wheeler immediately lifted his head from the stock and saw a small puff of dust on the street where his bullet had struck the hard-packed dirt. His shot had gone high, just missing Younger. He inserted another cartridge and placed a percussion cap on the nipple. This time he put the gun on the windowsill to steady it.

He aimed at Clell Miller, who was bent over in the saddle, doing something to his left stirrup. Because his shot at Jim Younger had gone high, Wheeler

A fanciful engraving of the Northfield Raid from *The Northfield Tragedy*, 1876.

aimed low on Clell and squeezed the trigger. The gunshot cut through the noise on the street and Clell felt a blow like a hammer as the heavy lead round punched through his shoulder, severing his subclavian artery.

Clell fell off his horse but managed to get up on his knees. He appeared to be yelling orders to the other robbers before his heart finally pumped the last of his blood, and he toppled over onto his face. Henry Wheeler, the medical student, had killed a man.

Meanwhile, the sounds of broken glass and ricocheting bullets mixed with the gun blasts, the urgent shouts, and the clopping of the shod horses as the outlaws raced back and forth in front of the bank. As bushwhackers, Jesse, Cole, and the others had fought as light cavalry, making fast, terrifying charges that struck fear into Missouri militia.

Their surprise attacks and ambushes had usually sent the Federals breaking and running, the bushwhackers riding them down, firing their pistols right and left. If the Federals were ever able to hold fast, the bushwhackers galloped away, disappearing in the Missouri woods and hills to fight again.

But here in Northfield, they were being forced to hold their ground while waiting on the inside men to come out of the bank. And their revolvers were no match for Wheeler's and Manning's shoulder guns, which were far more accurate at greater distances. And while the townspeople were shooting to kill, the outlaws' shots were really meant to frighten, to scare away, to buy time—at least in the beginning.

Division Street, eighty feet wide, had quickly become hell's shooting gallery with the outlaws the targets. With each passing second, the gang's situation became more precarious, and they became increasingly desperate.

Cole jumped down from his horse and ran over to Clell Miller. He kept wondering what the hell was taking the boys in the bank so long. As he rolled Clell over to check his wound, Cole felt a searing pain in his left hip, as if stabbed by a knife. It was a bullet from Anselm Manning's Remington. Manning had popped the jammed shell casing out of his gun with a wooden ramrod from his store and then raced back to the corner. Cole was lucky the shot had not done more damage than it did, as Manning's bullet had first struck one of the stairway's balusters, taking some of the energy off the lead bullet, as well as deflecting its path.

Cole took Miller's pistols and remounted—they needed to get out of this town. Riding up near the bank, he shouted to the boys inside, "Come out of the bank!"

Manning reloaded his Remington, the shell he had used on Cole ejecting perfectly. Adelbert Ames was now at his back, providing calm advice and encouragement. Ames had encountered the gang members as he was crossing the bridge a few minutes earlier while on his way to the mill. He had noticed the strangers in the dusters but thought nothing more of them. But, a few minutes later, he had heard the shout, "They are robbing the bank." He hurried to Mill Square, where he saw the smoke in the air and Manning with his gun at the corner.

Manning again peeked out beyond the stairs to see where the robbers were.

"I saw a man up the street more than half way up the block who was watching the opposite side of the street from me," Manning recalled. "It was evidently this man's business to guard that side of the street."

That man was Bill Chadwell. Manning brought his gun to his shoulder. His hands were trembling, sweat running down his face. From the Dampier House, a traveling salesman watching Manning called out, "Take good aim before you fire."

Manning squeezed the trigger, and the Remington bucked against his shoulder. In the split second before he dodged back around the corner, Manning thought he saw Chadwell wince.

Ermina Kingman, looking out from a store window down the block, saw Manning's shot pierce Chadwell's chest.

"I saw him [Chadwell] reel in the saddle and nearly fall off. He threw his left arm around the horse's neck, and that turned the horse up street again and he came as far as my door, where he fell off and died, after a short period of intense suffering."

One of the outlaws rode up to the dying man, who was stretched out, quivering, holding his upper body off the ground with his arms. The outlaw dismounted and tried to speak to Chadwell, who suddenly rolled over on his back and did not move again. The outlaw hastily grabbed Chadwell's cartridge belt and revolvers and got back on his horse. Chadwell's mount had run off around the block.

Cole Younger, with a grim look on his face, again rode up to the bank door. "For God's sake come out," he yelled. "They are shooting us all to pieces."

Nellie Ames thought she heard gunfire or fireworks. The forty-one-year-old wife of bank director John T. Ames (Adelbert's brother) was driving a small, one-horse carriage up Fifth Street at a little after 2:00 P.M. As she got to the middle of the block between Water and Division Streets, she saw Alonzo Bunker dash out from an open lot, holding his shoulder with his hand.

"What's the matter, Mr. Bunker?" she asked from her carriage.

"I'm shot!" Bunker said without stopping.

Nellie began to pull up on the reins when a man ran up to her, waving his hands excitedly.

"Mrs. Ames, get out of that carriage quick," he said. "You'll be killed."

He helped Nellie down and another man led her horse away.

Nellie hesitated, her curiosity seemingly getting the better of her. The sounds of gunfire became louder as did the yelling and the trampling of horses' hooves. Suddenly, horsemen swept into the intersection in front of her, their revolvers glistening in the sun, firing in different directions. One was Cole Younger, a large, muscular man with sandy whiskers.

Nellie also saw several men clambering up out of a stairwell from the stone building to her left, on the corner. The stairwell led to a basement saloon, and these men had either heard the gunfire or had been alerted to the robbery in progress. The last one to come up was a recent Swedish immigrant named Nicolaus Gustavson. He understood little English and was drunk. He weaved toward the intersection and the robbers on horseback.

Cole Younger wheeled his horse around. Nellie, her eyes now riveted on Cole, was just yards from him.

"Lady," he shouted, "get off the street or you will be killed."

Cole then lowered his revolver and aimed directly at Gustavson. Cole had already seen two of his gang members killed by the people of Northfield, and his wounds, especially the one in the hip, hurt like the devil.

Filled with wrath, he was no longer inclined to use his revolver simply to frighten—and Gustavson was too easy a target.

Nellie saw Cole fire—the crack of the shot thundering off the buildings—and Gustavson toppled over backward. Cole's bullet had struck the right side of Gustavson's head at his ear, fracturing the skull and tearing a path just underneath his scalp before exiting at the top of his head. Still alive, Gustavson lay there bleeding in the street, the entire left side of his body paralyzed.

The two men who had forced Nellie out of her carriage now took hold of her arms. She could hardly walk, but they got her off the street and into a nearby blacksmith shop. But as Nellie came to her senses, she promptly went into a panic because she remembered her husband was supposed to be at the bank that afternoon.

View of the Scriver Block from Division Street showing the exterior stairway going to the second floor. The First National Bank is just to the right of the storefront with the awning (Theodore Miller's undertaking and furniture shop).

Nellie burst out of the shop doors and ran across the lots behind the bank to Mill Square. When she turned toward Division Street, she saw several men gathered at the Scriver corner, including Manning, with his rifle, and her brother-in-law, Adelbert.

Nellie rushed to the corner and

then headed around it to the bank. The men hunkered there grabbed her and pulled her back. Whether or not her husband was in the First National, the battle was still raging.

The robbers inside the bank may or may not have heard Cole Younger's first call to come out, but they definitely heard the second. And there was no mistaking the desperation in his voice. Bob Younger did not have to look at Frank to see what he wanted to do, and neither did Charlie, who had reappeared after chasing Bunker. They both jumped over the counter and hurried to the door and were outside before Frank, who hated to accept defeat, began his exit.

The chaos in the bank was nothing compared to the pandemonium they encountered on the street. Immediately in front of them lay Clell Miller's body and Bob's dead horse. Bullets whistled up and down. Jesse, Jim, and Cole dashed back and forth through a haze of gun smoke. The nostrils of their horses flared, sucking in oxygen, and the animals' eyes bulged from their heads as they sensed the death around them.

In addition to the gunfire, large rocks arced through the air. Elias Hobbs, unable to find a gun, had begun shouting, "Stone 'em! Stone 'em!" Fifty-nine-year-old lawyer Truman Streeter and a twenty-six-year-old black man named Ben Richardson also began scavenging for rocks and hurling them at the robbers.

At the same time, Bob ran down the sidewalk along the side of the Scriver toward the stairway and Manning, who was using the stairs as cover.

"Kill the white-livered son of a bitch on the corner," one of the outlaws shouted.

As Bob swung his revolver up to shoot Manning, the hardware dealer leveled his rifle at outlaw, who promptly darted behind a box beneath the stairs. Bob kept his revolver up, its hammer at full cock, waiting for a chance to fire. For a few seconds the two weaved back and forth in a deadly game of peek-aboo, until Cole yelled at Bob to shoot through the stairs. Manning retreated behind the stone corner as Bob's bullets popped jagged wood splinters off the staircase.

Henry Wheeler, looking down from the third floor of the Dampier, had inserted the third of his four paper cartridges into the old Smith carbine and placed a percussion cap on its nipple. Seeing the duel between Bob and Manning, he pulled the gun's large hammer back and looked down the barrel, centering the weapon's sights on Bob. The carbine cracked and the outlaw jumped, the lead slug slamming through his right elbow. Bob's gun arm fell limp to his side, but in an incredible display of grit, he switched his pistol to his left hand and blasted again at the staircase.

Wheeler reached for his last cartridge, but it had fallen off the bed. The paper of the cartridge had ruptured with the fall, spilling the powder all over the floor. Wheeler could not fire another shot.

With Bob so close, Manning could not risk moving out beyond the corner and needed a different strategy. At the rear of the Lee & Hitchcock store, a side door opened onto Division Street. If Manning went through the store and out that door, he might be able to pick off Bob from behind—that is, if Bob stayed put under the stairs. Manning thought it was worth a try and he left his position at the corner.

Moments after Bob and Charlie exited the bank, Frank James let go of Heywood and ran over to the counter, pulling himself up by the railing. Heywood, his head and neck bloody, staggered over to the cashier's desk.

Poised at the top of the counter, Frank turned and pointed his pistol at Heywood. He blamed the failure of the robbery on this damned fool bank employee. He fired at Heywood but somehow missed. Heywood sank into the chair at the desk, or maybe he was dodging behind the desk. Wilcox simply stood there petrified.

But Frank was far from done. He again pulled back the hammer of his revolver, its shiny cylinder rotating to bring another loaded chamber before the barrel. And with "the expression of a very devil in his face," Wilcox recalled, Frank "put his pistol almost at Heywood's head and fired the fatal shot."

The bullet entered Heywood's left temple, spraying blood and brain matter all over the desk. He tumbled forward and fell behind the counter. Facedown, his body heaved slightly as his lungs continued to breathe for some minutes, blood running out of the hole in his skull. Heywood had prevented another St. Albans, just like he said he would, but his heroics had cost him his life.

Frank leaped over the counter and ran for the front door just as Cole was yelling, again, for him to come out. Wilcox flew out the back of the bank and across the alley to Manning's store.

Frank, shocked to find two men killed, was relieved to see that his brother Jesse was not one of the casualties. He grabbed the reins to his horse and climbed into the saddle. Charlie Pitts had already mounted his steed. The outlaws shouted to one another and began to move south down the street. Bob turned and stumbled after them.

"My God, boys," he cried, "you are not going to leave—I am shot!"

Cole spurred his horse and galloped back to his brother, who grasped Cole's outstretched arm with his left hand and swung up behind Cole, cursing in pain as he righted himself.

Anselm Manning, now in the Lee & Hitchcock store, warily approached the side entrance. It had been open earlier, but once the shooting started, a brave clerk had crawled to the door and closed it, having the presence of mind to spin the combination on the store's safe. The robbers had been near this door many times because it was right next to the bank entrance, and Manning knew he would be exposing himself to those on the street if he opened it, but as he crept close to the door, he noticed the gunfire had stopped.

As he slowly pulled open the door, he looked out and the street appeared to be deserted. He peeked his head out and looked to the left at the staircase—no Bob Younger. Manning stood up and cautiously walked out onto the sidewalk, his rifle at the ready. He looked down Division Street to the south, over a block distant, and saw the robbers riding away. He was tempted to try one last shot with his Remington, but townspeople were already spilling onto the street and gathering in clusters, trying to see the robbers before they disappeared. Manning lowered his rifle and began to take in the carnage around him.

The Northfield Raid had lasted no more than ten minutes, perhaps as few as seven. Albert H. Taisey, who walked out of the bank only a few moments before the robbery, missed the whole thing. Hearing the gunfire as he turned a corner, he thought it was nothing more than a few boys having some fun, so he continued on toward Carleton College. Returning to Division Street immediately after the bandits had left, he was shocked to learn that "the gentleman whom he had so recently pleasantly parted from was a corpse."

News of the robbery rapidly spread through the small town. The fire and church bells were rung loudly. Margaret Evans, Dean of Women at Carleton, had been sitting in her room in the women's dormitory just two blocks from Mill Square when the shooting erupted. She heard the loud popping but did not know quite what to make of it.

When the sounds did not let up, she decided to find out what they might be. She went to the main door, and as she opened it, the matron and a wife of a college trustee rushed in. Both women could hardly speak, having run from Division Street with news of the raid. Finally, the matron got out the words "Keep the girls off the street," and then she collapsed in a faint.

All kinds of wild thoughts went through Evans's mind when she learned exactly what had happened. Evans thought the robbers might attack the college next. She organized her girls to defend themselves. They gathered the fire axes they had in the building and scrambled to the third floor, where they huddled together. Evans shortly learned that the outlaws had fled Northfield, but she still kept her girls inside and did so for several nights following. She and the matron slept alone on the lower floor as guards.

Nine-year-old Dwight Lockerby was sitting uncomfortably at his desk in a warm classroom in the public school, also just two blocks away, when a classmate came into the room looking scared and upset. The boy had come from outdoors and had apparently seen something disturbing, but neither his teacher nor his classmates could get the boy to talk.

At about that same time, the teacher and the students began to hear the town's bells. An elderly woman came in, rushed to the front of the classroom, and leaned close to the teacher's ear. She sobbed as she whispered something, the students straining their hardest to hear her words.

Suddenly, the teacher cried, "My husband!" and fell back into her chair. Dwight's teacher was twenty-five-year-old Nettie Bunker, the wife of the bank's teller.

issed
rtery.
stiff
, but
izzie
rob-
odied
bank,
nger
home
work-
The
tuffy
after-
ed to
step
treet,
it the
ered.
grass
xious
n.
me a
ident
iend.

ier, the couple had celebrated their
ary.

uch for Dwight and his classmates,
the school to see what was going on

Dwight got to Division Street, he
amiliar people carrying all sorts of
hotguns, revolvers, even knives. He
one of the bigger throngs to see what
ng about and abruptly came upon the
n lying in a pool of blood.

grisly sight, Dwight backed away,
d to the other side of the street. Just
nt of the bank, he saw two men car-
ier with another dead body. Dwight

got a fellow teacher to watch the few
g in her classroom and set off to find
anxiously asked each person she
e Mr. Bunker might be. Some told
ed, others said he'd been shot dead.
friend with a carriage who took her
f Dr. Hyram Coon on Water Street,
l was being treated.

bullet had entered Bunker's shoul-
ame spot as the slug that killed Clell
for Nettie and her husband, Pitts's

Sarah Elizabeth "Lizzie" Heywood.

bullet had just n
the subclavian a
Bunker would be
and sore for a tim
he would be fine.

Not so fine was I
Heywood. As the
bers cursed and blo
her husband in the
she and another, yo
woman sat in her
on West Third
ing on a new dress
house had grown
from the warm
noon so they decic
take a break and

outside to get some fresh air. From across the s
they could hear a neighbor shouting to another abo
bank having been raided and Mr. Heywood murc
Lizzie sank to her knees and toppled over onto the
lawn. It was some time before Lizzie's friend and ar
neighbors were able to revive the distraught woma

Joseph Heywood's body was brought to his h
short time later, transported in a carriage, by Pre
Strong of Carleton, who was cradling his dead f

When Lizzie learned the full details of Heywood's death, how he had repeatedly defied the robbers and saved the bank's money, she reportedly said, "I would not have had him do otherwise."

Lizzie Heywood was Joseph's second wife. His first wife, Martha, had died a year after the birth of their little girl in 1871. Lizzie was Martha's old schoolmate and good friend—Martha had named her child for Lizzie—and she was Martha's choice to raise her daughter and be the next Mrs. Heywood.

"This 'friend' was made a widow . . . by an assassin's bullet," Adelbert Ames wrote to his wife after the raid. "The first wife now has her husband, and her friend, her child."

The other victim of the raid, Nicolaus Gustavson, also appeared to cheat death much like Alonzo Bunker had. After a few minutes of lying motionless on the street, the Swede was able to stand up on his own power, seemingly more sober than before he took Cole's bullet.

Gustavson was even able to run to the Cannon River and wash the ugly wound in his scalp. A friend took him to a doctor who treated the injury. Gustavson talked and seemed fine, but as his brain swelled from the trauma, his condition worsened. The next day, he could not rise from his bed, and the day after that he drifted into a coma. The Swede died on September 11.

On Division Street, the crowds of gawkers continued to grow throughout the afternoon.

"The two dead robbers were left lying in the street
in pools of their own blood, to be looked at by the
world," reported Adelbert Ames. "Men, women and
children had their fill. Country folks came in or were
in town and sat in their wagons by the dead bodies and
chatted for hours. . . . All the women and children in
town nearby went to see them."

A traveling salesman from Pittsburgh, who happened to be lodging at the Dampier House at the time
of the raid, wrote that the corpses "presented a terrible
look—a determined, savage, disappointed look was
depicted upon their ghastly countenances. Certainly,
thought I, looking upon their bloody bodies and awful
faces, the way of the transgressor is hard."

Alonzo Bunker, his wound cleaned and bandaged,
carefully stepped into his doctor's carriage to be driven
home. But Bunker asked the doctor to take him home
by way of Division Street so he could look at the dead
gunmen.

"I witnessed women calmly surveying the carcasses
of the robbers," Bunker recalled, "expressing contempt
rather than pity."

Division Street had quickly come to resemble a car-
nival. And the dead robbers were not the only things to

see. There were broken windows, glass shards on the sidewalks, and bullet scars in the bricks and masonry of several buildings—dramatic evidence of how intense the skirmish between the townspeople and the outlaws had been. The bullet holes in the wooden staircase on the Scriver Building were especially impressive. At least one pistol belonging to the robbers had been picked up off the ground after the gang retreated, a .45-caliber nickel-plated Single Action Army revolver with ivory grips.

Druggist George Bates retained a couple of mementos from his encounter with the robbers. One was a slight scratch on his cheek and the bridge of his nose he received from a glancing bullet fired by one of the bandits. There's a good chance the wound was from flying glass, but he liked to say it was a bullet, which made for a more exciting tale. He said he found the bullet lodged at the back of a collar box in the clothing store where he'd been when he challenged the outlaws with his empty revolver.

The druggist told a reporter he would keep the bullet "as a souvenir of the hottest day Northfield ever saw."

At 3:00 P.M., John T. Ames hovered over the telegraph operator at the depot, rapidly dictating the news of the raid. Neither he nor anyone else could have imagined such a calamity. One Northfield man, a good man, was dead, and Ames's own wife had blundered upon the robbers as the bullets were flying.

But the worst came later, when a horrifying rumor reached Ames that the robbers were on their way to his home. He certainly couldn't dismiss the idea of the bank robbers striking his residence as ludicrous, especially after what had just happened on Division Street. His daughters were home, unprotected. He decided he had to go to them.

Adelbert tried to reason with his brother and urged him not to leave. As one of Northfield's most prominent citizens, the people looked to John T. for leadership, to organize a pursuit of the killers. Even if the robbers did go to his home, Adelbert said, they would not harm his daughters. But John T. couldn't be stopped and headed off for his home, with Adelbert following. Fortunately, before the Ames brothers had gotten very far, they met up with a man who told them the robbers had ridden out of Northfield without stopping. Adelbert told his greatly relieved brother to get back to Division Street and he would go ahead to look in on the girls.

Some citizens had already begun to chase the robbers, but John T. realized it would take a much larger effort to apprehend the criminals. These bandits were ruthless, armed to the teeth, and willing to fight to the death. The small town of Northfield had done exceptionally well in defending itself and driving off the robbers, but now it sorely needed help.

Minnesota, like Missouri and most other states, had no state police force. The larger municipalities, with their professional police departments, filled that role in certain situations. So John T. reached out to Minneapolis and St. Paul for help and sent a telegram to the chief of police of each city:

```
EIGHT ARMED MEN ATTACKED BANK AT 2 O'CLOCK.
FIGHT ON STREET BETWEEN ROBBERS AND CITIZENS.
CASHIER KILLED. TELLER WOUNDED. TWO ROBBERS
KILLED. OTHERS WOUNDED. SEND US SOME MEN
AND ARMS TO CHASE ROBBERS.
                              JOHN T. AMES
```

The telegraph operators in the Twin Cities transcribed the messages, becoming increasingly excited as they put each letter, each word, each sentence together. The Minneapolis chief of police quickly read his telegram and frantically went to find the mayor and located him around 3:40 P.M.

When the 4:00 P.M. train pulled out of Minneapolis, the chief of police rode in one of the cars, along with four of his men armed with lever-action rifles and three hundred rounds of ammunition. The St. Paul chief and several of his men also made the 4:00 P.M. train in their city, the two forces joining up at Mendota Junction, just south of the Twin Cities, for the remainder of the journey.

John T. Ames left the telegraph office to look for horses for the manhunters. The telegraph operator continued tapping out warnings to all of southern Minnesota with descriptions of the robbers.

At some point that afternoon, one of the First National Bank's directors came to the telegraph office with an urgent message he needed sent to Philadelphia. The message was for George M. Phillips, the bank's cashier, who had just begun his visit to the World's Fair.

In eight words, the telegram informed Phillips of the tragedy in Northfield. The cashier would return immediately to Minnesota and to the desk he always occupied. But by the time Phillips arrived, the blood and brains of the man who had worked in his place had been cleaned away.

Many Northfield citizens, adults and children, had difficulty sleeping on the night of September 7. If any of them got up and looked out their windows, they would have seen the stars disappear as clouds began to roll in. Civil War veterans eerily recalled how heavy rains invariably followed catastrophic battles. Northfield's fight never reached the level of a battle's slaughter, but a big rainstorm was still coming.

Five
And Then There Were Six

*Long experience in their mode of life has
made them not only desperate men but
detectives equal to the most noted, and to
capture them is no easy matter.*

—*LIBERTY TRIBUNE*

Six men on five horses headed straight for the
Big Woods. All they'd gotten from the bank was
$26.60 in coin and scrip. As the robbers cantered out
of town, they ejected the spent shell casings from their
revolvers' cylinders and replaced them with fresh
rounds. They also took stock of their wounds. All three
Younger brothers had bloodstains on their clothes and
saddles. Cole had the hole from Anselm Manning's rifle
bullet in his left hip, but the wound was not dangerous.
Jim Younger had taken a ball somewhere to the shoulder, though it apparently punched through clean, and

Bob's elbow was busted. The brothers likely had other wounds as well, but Bob's elbow would end up being the most troublesome. Frank's right leg was bleeding where he'd been hit by a pistol ball or buckshot sometime after he exited the bank. Whether or not the people of Northfield nicked Jesse or Charlie Pitts, no one knows for sure. They may have escaped unscathed.

If the robbery had gone according to plan, the gang was going to cross the Cannon River on the iron bridge at Mill Square, pausing briefly at the depot to smash the telegraph equipment at the office there before riding west. But Manning and the other Northfield defenders had undone that plan. Now the robbers would have to cross the river at Dundas, a village of eight hundred people three miles to the south.

Riding five abreast, the gang was in no mood to share the road. Just outside of Northfield, they ran into an elderly farmer driving a wagon loaded down with vegetables. One of the outlaws pulled his revolver, aimed it at the farmer, and shouted, "Take the ditch, God damn you!" The frightened old man jerked on the reins of his big draft horses and forced them down the steep bank, wrecking the wagon and spilling his load all over the ground.

Reaching Dundas, the outlaws paused briefly at the bridge to wash their wounds in the Cannon's cool waters. Someone fashioned a crude sling for Bob's arm. Then they rode cautiously through the tiny business district, their eyes trained on every man in view, wondering if the town had been alerted to the robbery. It had not, but not for lack of trying. The Northfield telegraph operator had sent message after message to the little town, but its operator had been gone from the office for at least an hour. So the people of Dundas didn't think anything more about the passersby than what an odd-looking bunch they were. The owner of the hardware store thought they were "a lot of drunken loafers."

Some of the outlaws cursed at one another, sharply laying the blame for the disaster on what someone did or should have done. The hardware store owner, in a jocular mood, asked the boys if they were a cavalry regiment. A traveling salesman from St. Paul guessed that if Sitting Bull was after them, they would be riding a little faster. In a blur of movement, one of the robbers unholstered his pistol and pointed its big bore at the salesman, snarling, "Get in [the store], you son of a bitch."

On the other side of Dundas, the gang encountered a man driving a wagon of hoop poles, which would be used to make the hoops that hold together wooden barrels and kegs. Bob Younger, in increasing pain, needed a mount, and one of the man's horses looked like it might do. So the gang told the wagon driver an incredible tale: a band of ruffians had robbed the bank at Northfield and murdered the sheriff. They were hot on the trail of the bad men but would need to commandeer one of his horses. When the wagon driver made the mistake of arguing, one of the outlaws jerked out his revolver and cracked its butt on the man's head, sending him tumbling into the ditch.

The outlaws were taking the better of the two horses, and they had begun to help Bob mount it when they spotted two horsemen coming up fast from behind. This could mean trouble, and sure enough the two men rapidly approaching were the first of the pursuers to set out on the trail of the bandits. They were well armed and riding the fastest horses in Northfield—the mounts of the fallen Clell Miller and Bill Chadwell.

One of the outlaws took several steps toward the oncoming riders, held up his hand, and yelled, "Halt!" Suddenly, the two citizens no longer seemed so hell-bent on catching up to the robbers; they immediately reined in their horses and sat there watching as the outlaws saddled up and galloped away. The two Northfield men wisely followed at a good distance, giving the posses time to catch up with them.

After riding no more than a half mile, the gang stopped once more to tend to Bob's wound, which was bleeding so profusely that blood flowed down his forearm and dripped off his fingertips. They got a pail of water from a farmer and poured it over Bob's arm. The farmer, who had followed the gang members out to the road, asked how Bob had been hurt. One of the outlaws explained that "they had got into a row with a blackleg at Northfield, who had shot him, and the blackleg [a card cheat or swindler] had been killed."

The gang galloped west toward Millersburg, three abreast in two ranks. Bob rode in the middle of the first rank so his companions could lead his horse while keeping him propped up. But he desperately needed a saddle. After spotting a house in the distance, two of the boys turned off the rode and talked the farmer there into "loaning" them a saddle, this time claiming they were law officers chasing horse thieves. At approximately 4:30 P.M., the gang reached Millersburg, six miles from Dundas. The hotel owner there got a quick look at the men as they rode by and recognized some of them as his guests from the previous night. Millersburg, hardly more than a spot in the road, was off the route of the telegraph, so no one there could possibly know about the Northfield Raid. Even so, the robbers did not stop to get reacquainted.

But the Northfield telegraph operator had done his job well, and with each passing hour, dozens more men turned out to join the hunt for the bandits. Shopkeepers, craftsmen, farmers, and day laborers dropped everything at the cry of the news and dug out their old muskets, pistols, and knives, loaded themselves into buggies and wagons or saddled their nags, and headed west to cut off the robbers' retreat. Five such manhunters arrived at Shieldsville, deep in the Big Woods southwest of Millersburg, at approximately 6:00 P.M. They had come in a wagon direct from Faribault and, as it had been a long ride and the town appeared quiet, the manhunters decided a glass of beer would taste pretty good. They parked their wagon in front of Joseph Hagerty's general store and saloon and went in, leaving their guns in the wagon—guns that they had neglected to load.

As the Faribault party sipped on their drafts, six men on horseback slowly rode into Shieldsville. Eyewitnesses said the riders looked tired, and one awful-looking man was covered with blood. These men, the James-Younger gang, could not help but notice the wagon with its shotguns and pistols sitting in plain view. One of the outlaws asked a bystander how long the wagon had been there, and the man replied that it had rolled into town only about five minutes earlier.

The riders pulled up to a water pump in front of Hagerty's establishment and calmly watered their horses at the trough. A few of the outlaws dismounted. An old man came out of the saloon and asked the boys where they were going. Jesse James, who had not yet lost his sense of humor, pointed to Bob Younger and said they "were going to hang that damned cuss."

Just then, one of the young manhunters appeared in the saloon's doorway, shouted, "Those are the fellows," and rushed toward the wagon to get his weapon. But he froze in his tracks when the robbers, in a blur of movement, cocked and aimed their revolvers at him. The rest of the Faribault party stumbled outside a second later, all wearing the same shocked look on their faces.

"Let's break their guns," said one of the outlaws.

"You won't break my gun," yelled one of the Faribault men, as he lunged forward. The robbers pointed their revolvers at him and told him to get back. "They are not loaded," he pleaded as one of the outlaws made a move toward the guns. Plainly seeing what a bunch of bumpkins they were up against, the bandit turned away from the wagon and got back on his horse. They left the firearms alone.

After all the horses had gotten a good drink from the trough, the outlaws decided to give the Faribault men a good scare and began firing their revolvers at the water pump. Wood splinters flew every which way as the bystanders dove for cover. A little girl happened to step into the doorway of the saloon as an outlaw fired, and his bullet just grazed her.

As the robbers galloped down the road and disappeared into the forest, the Faribault men scrambled for their guns. They rustled through their supplies in the back of the wagon, searching for their boxes of cartridges. Once they found the ammunition, they hurriedly loaded their firearms, but the men were not crazy about immediately going after the outlaws. The gang's demonstration of firepower had made a big impression. But within five minutes, another squad of manhunters arrived in town, boosting the courage of the Faribault men. The entire party, fourteen in number, set off after the bandits.

Bob's injury, as well as his mount, which was not nearly the same quality of horseflesh as that of his companions, prevented the gang from moving with the speed they were known for. The Faribault posse, despite the wagons they traveled with, steadily gained on the outlaws. Four miles from Shieldsville, the posse caught sight of the bandits in a ravine. The outlaws were out of killing range—the posse had no rifles, which could have done the job at this distance—but the excited possemen opened fire anyway. The outlaws heard the bullets slicing through the air near them, followed by the pops of the guns, and they wheeled around, drawing their revolvers as they did so. The bandits fired at the posse in the distance, their shots so close together it sounded like a single volley.

One of the posse's bullets hit Cole Younger's "crazy bone" on his elbow. The lead bullet had lost nearly all its momentum, but it still hurt like hell, causing Cole, who had hold of Bob's mount, to jerk both his and Bob's horse about. Suddenly, Bob's horse slipped and fell to the ground, throwing him off. He screamed in pain as he tumbled, his companions all cursing in confusion. As he scrambled and struggled to pull himself back up on his horse, the saddle girth broke and his horse ran away.

Cole shouted at his brother to get up behind him, which Bob did, though with difficulty. The outlaws then spurred their horses and raced into the nearby woods. The posse cautiously moved to the spot where the outlaws had fired at them, rounded up Bob's horse and the stolen saddle, but they soon lost all track of the outlaws.

As the sun sank toward the horizon, the gang had the advantage of darkness, but the fading daylight also brought confusion. Most of the boys had purchased Minnesota maps, though they were not especially accurate or detailed, and the bandits would have little time to study them now. "We were in a strange country," Cole wrote later. "On the prairie our maps were all right, but when we got into the big woods and among the lakes we were practically lost."

At dusk, the gang confronted a farmer on horseback named Levi Sager. They told him they were after the robbers and asked if he had seen any posses. Sager knew all about the raid, and said he had seen a squad of man-hunters pass down the road just a few minutes earlier. One of the gang remarked that the posse was heading the wrong way. The robbers had gone to Shieldsville, he told Sager. The boys continued to pump the farmer for information, finally telling him he would have to guide them to the road to Waterville and lend them his horse.

On what authority? Sager retorted.

The boys just laughed and told him he could go to hell. One of the outlaws got up on Sager's horse, but the animal immediately began to prance about. Sager's horse had never been ridden by a man wearing spurs and it didn't take too kindly to the outlaw's long, pointed rowels. The rider tried his best to get the horse to cooperate, but after a quarter mile of fighting the animal, he gave up and let Sager have his cussed mount back. But the gang was not finished with Sager.

They forced him to stay with them for much longer than he cared to, only freeing him when they reached a farm field south of Kilkenny, in southeastern Le Sueur County. As Sager hightailed it back home, the gang melted into the darkness.

The robbers found shelter that night in the farmhouse of Lord Brown, who lived on the Waterville road. Whether or not Brown knew who his guests were has never been clear. The shot-up and bloodied outlaws were not your typical houseguests.

Well hidden at Brown's place, the outlaws dressed their wounds and talked over their plans for the next morning. Even as exhausted as they were, they had difficulty sleeping that night. The James-Younger gang had lost two good men on the streets of Northfield, and they had killed a man—perhaps even two. They had not gotten nearly as far as they needed to, and the Big Woods had left them confused and disoriented. But Jesse, Frank, Cole, and Jim had ridden with the bushwhackers Quantrill and Bloody Bill Anderson. They had been in tight spots before.

And yet, Minnesota was feeling tighter by the hour. All through the night, the manhunters increased in number, reaching at least two hundred men. Parties of horsemen moved in silence over dirt roads and paths. Guards stood watch at bridges, fords, and crossroads.

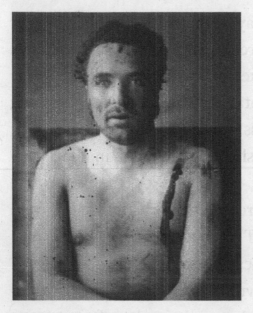

Clell Miller in death.

Using this spotty, makeshift picket line, Sheriff Ara Barton of Rice County aimed to stop the robbers' flight and contain them in the Big Woods, where the posses could eventually flush them out and capture or kill them. Barton and his fellow lawmen felt confident that the next day would bring a new sighting and a fresh trail to follow. Now, as a chill rain began to fall upon southern Minnesota, the manhunters waited anxiously for the morning—as did Jesse James and the gang.

Clell Miller's dead eyes were frozen in a look of surprise. His shirtless body had been carefully propped up in a sitting position for Ira Sumner, a Northfield photographer. A dark ribbon of dried blood flowed down from a jagged hole in Miller's upper chest, and he had large welts on his forehead where Elias Stacy had peppered him with a shotgun. Next to Miller's corpse was the body of Bill Chadwell, also shirtless. Unlike Miller,

Chadwell seemed to glare, his narrow eyes fixed in a look of defiance. He had a small hole above his heart, the fatal wound delivered by Anselm Manning's rifle, and the dried blood ran in a straight line to his waistband.

Bill Chadwell in death.

Sumner bent over behind his large camera, a black cape draped over his head, and carefully focused the ground glass lens on his subjects. Once it was focused, he quickly slid a wooden plate holder into the back of the camera. The holder contained a single glass plate, freshly coated on one side with silver-sensitized collodion. Sumner then pulled up the thin slide covering the plate, the last step before making an exposure. He next reached around with his right hand to the front of the camera and carefully removed the lens cap, holding it to the side as he counted six seconds in his head. He then replaced the cap and reinserted the slide, after which he removed the plate holder from the camera. Sumner repeated this process for each image made—at least five—after which he went to his darkroom to develop the plates before the collodion had a chance to dry.

The bodies were then carried down the stairs from Sumner's second-floor studio on Division Street and returned to the vacant store on Mill Square where they had spent the night. A coroner's inquest was scheduled for 11:00 A.M., and the bodies would need to be stripped and washed clean before then. According to one account, so many people wanted to see the dead robbers that their bodies were displayed for a short time in Mill Square, which became packed with gawkers, sheriffs and police officers from nearby towns, newspaper reporters, posse volunteers, and Northfield's own citizens, both children and adults. The square quickly filled with the excited chattering of the crowd.

"Every man encountered had his story to tell," wrote the *Minneapolis Tribune*'s correspondent, "and the reporter had but to make known his mission and forthwith were opened upon him the floodgates of information."

Everyone wanted to know who the dead men were. Where did they come from? Why Northfield? People tried to find clues in the robbers' clothing and personal items. The shorter one, Clell Miller, wore new-looking clothes under his ulster duster. His shirt, topped with a white linen collar, looked like he had unwrapped it the morning of the robbery. A white linen handkerchief was tied around his neck, and his fur felt hat, "John Hancock make," was also new and of fine quality, although now it had a few small holes in it. Clell also wore a plain gold ring, gold sleeve buttons, and a gold Howard pocket watch worth $175. For socks, he wore "striped half hose," and his boots, although of good quality, did not match, one being finer and lighter than the other.

Clell had a leather money belt hidden in his clothing, although it contained no money. A search of his pockets uncovered a Minnesota map, a pocket compass, the *Rice County Journal* news item describing the improvements at the First National Bank, $5.75 in currency, and a short piece from an unknown Minnesota newspaper listing the "Arab Horse Maxims." "Whoso raiseth and traineth a horse for the Lord," read the first maxim, "is counted in the number of those who give alms day and night. . . . He will find his reward. All his sins will be forgiven him; never will any fear come over him and dishonor his heart."

Bill Chadwell wore a new suit of black clothes worth some $30 and a new colored shirt. His pockets bulged with ammunition, and a cartridge belt circled his waist beneath his suit. He had a fine gold Waltham watch and ten cents in currency. A business card for the livery stable of St. Peter's Nicollet House was found in one pocket, its reverse side featuring a table of distances for the principal towns of southern Minnesota. Chadwell also had an advertisement for Hall's Safe & Lock Co., which he had torn out of the *Rice County Journal.* The advertisement featured a crude engraving of two bearded robbers using various tools to break into a Hall's safe.

"It's no go, Jim," says one of the safecrackers, "it's a Hall."

A *Saint Paul Dispatch* reporter took a tape measure to "the ghastly forms of the two bandits" and carefully examined their wounds. Chadwell's skin, he noted, was "as fair and soft as a lady's." He said nothing about Miller's skin, but he discovered that Miller had several pellet wounds on his back, indicating the outlaw had been hit by at least two shotgun blasts.

Neither of the dead men carried any personal letters or photographs of loved ones. The *Pioneer Press & Tribune* said that the "fact that nothing was found on the dead robbers to indicate who they were or where they came from clearly shows that they were professional brigands, probably from Missouri or Kansas, as it is a rule with such, when on marauding expeditions attended with danger of capture or death, to have nothing about their persons by which their names could be ascertained."

Sometime on Friday, Caleb Peterman of Cannon Falls, fifteen miles away, came to Northfield to view the bodies. The thirty-one-year-old Peterman suspected his ne'er-do-well brother-in-law, Bill Stiles, might have been involved in the raid. Stiles had supposedly written from Texas two months earlier, claiming to have "made a good haul." "If you want $100 or $200," he wrote Peterman, "say so." Stiles had also said he was planning to be in Minnesota in a few weeks and knew where he could make another "good haul."

Peterman did not hide the reason he was visiting Northfield, and a crowd of townspeople and reporters gathered around him, eager to see if he could identify one of the robbers. Peterman looked closely at Chadwell's body and told the several onlookers that if the man was Stiles, there would be a scar under his left arm. Someone lifted the arm and, indeed, the scar was there. Peterman didn't move and refused to say if the outlaw was his brother-in-law. The crowd began urging him to respond, and finally Peterman admitted that the dead man was Bill Stiles.

Peterman said he knew little about Stiles's background: he had been twenty-three years old and had grown up at Monticello, Minnesota, in Wright County, though his father now lived at Grand Forks, Dakota Territory. The Northfield authorities immediately contacted the father, who did not seem surprised that his son had taken part in the holdup. "I thought he was in Texas," Mr. Stiles remarked. "I suppose he got in with a lot of them damned pirates." Mr. Stiles then explained that his son "had always been a wild boy and he could do nothing with him, but he did not think him vicious."

Peterman's identification made a lot of sense. Stiles was the perfect local guide for the Missouri bandits. When others later identified the dead outlaw as Bill Chadwell, people reasoned that "Chadwell" was simply one of Stiles's aliases. According to some newspapers, the bandits had even used the name "Stiles" before. When talking to the Millersburg farmer, the gang had supposedly told him that the "blackleg" they had killed was named Stiles.

But, even though this all made sense at the time, Bill Chadwell was not Bill Stiles. For whatever reason, Caleb Peterman had perpetrated one of the biggest cases of false identification in Minnesota history. And that soon became clear. Several citizens of Monticello, who knew Stiles "almost as well as they know members of their own family," examined Sumner's photograph of Chadwell and said they were "perfectly confident that he is not the man," that the dead outlaw bore no resemblance to Stiles whatsoever. One acquaintance pointed out a problem that should have been obvious to the brother-in-law: Stiles was only five feet, eight inches tall, whereas Chadwell was six feet, four inches. Another associate, who claimed to have been with Stiles in the pinery over the winter, had seen him there as late as May or June. "At that time," said the informant, "Stiles was trapping and hunting with the Chippewas and did not dare to come out of the woods for fear of being arrested for selling whiskey to the Indians."

Even Stiles's father added to the chorus, angrily writing the press that he had never recognized his son in the photographs of the dead robbers, as some papers reported. He asserted having been recently contacted by Peterman, who was also denying much of what was attributed to him in the newspapers. The intriguing letter from Stiles to Peterman quoted by the press did not contain an offer of money, Peterman said. Instead, Stiles was writing from Texas *asking* for money.

Bob Younger had the last word on this when he later stated that no man from Minnesota was part of the gang. "The name of Bill Stiles," he insisted, "is simply a reporter's imagination."

But over the years, writers and historians would perpetuate the myth of the outlaw band's Minnesota guide, and more than a few would embellish it, claiming

that Bill Stiles was the one who convinced Jesse James
that the banks of Minnesota were easy pickings. No
writers questioned why the outlaws found it necessary
to buy several maps, nor did anyone bother to explore
the wealth of evidence, including federal, state, and
territorial census records showing that Bill Stiles and
Bill Chadwell were two very different young men. The
only things Stiles and Chadwell shared in common
were their given names, the year of their birth, and
their willingness to live outside the law.

As the coroner's jury convened in Northfield for
its inquest on the bodies of what one newspaper described as "the two scoundrels who met with such a
richly deserved fate," Minnesota governor John S.
Pillsbury drafted a reward proclamation. He dipped
his steel-tipped pen into a bottle of ink on his desk
and, with a quick flourish, signed his name to the official document, declaring a $1,500 reward for the
capture of the bank robbers. The First National
Bank offered a reward of $500, a sum put up by John
T. Ames and his brother, Adelbert, on behalf of the
bank, which they did because the bank's president and
cashier were out of town and its treasurer lay dead.
Any amount larger would have to wait until the officers and directors could convene.

The news of the bank's seemingly trivial reward caused considerable indignation. The *Saint Paul Dispatch* commented, "If the brave and heroic Heywood could know that after sacrificing his life in the path of duty and preserving the entire contents of the bank, the owners of that institution offer the paltry sum of $700 [$500] for the capture of his brutal murderers, he would rest uneasy in his coffin and feel that his sacrifice had been in vain."

Within a week, the First National raised its reward from $500 to $3,000. Governor Pillsbury also raised the state's reward offer to $1,000 per man, making for a potential payout of $9,000 if all six robbers were caught. The *Saint Paul Dispatch* also noted that the governor's proclamation labeled the robbers "outlaws, which gives every man a right to shoot them down."

There had been plenty of shooting already, and it was fast becoming apparent that this reward was not for just any outlaws, but rather for the most notorious and feared bandits in the nation. Detective Larry Hazen of Cincinnati, still diligently at work on the Rocky Cut case for the Adams Express Company, could not get to Minnesota fast enough. Eight heavily armed men on horseback robbing a bank in broad daylight, committing bloody murder, and standing their ground in a deadly shoot-out with townspeople? Such ruthless swagger could only come from the James-Younger gang.

Hazen stepped off a train in St. Paul on the evening of September 8. The scrappy, forty-six-year-old Irishman, a bushy black mustache under his nose, stood only five feet, five inches tall. But the little man knew his business, having served as Cincinnati's chief of police during the Civil War, and he had been working as a detective for the Adams Express Company since 1872.

A newspaper reporter caught up to Hazen, who did not hesitate to blame the Rocky Cut robbers for the Northfield debacle, accurately naming all eight members of the gang who had traveled to Minnesota. The detective made the short journey to Northfield the following day, where he got his first look at Sumner's photographs of the dead bandits. Hazen, in another testament to the difficulty of identifying the men without accurate portraits or descriptions, misidentified both of them. He said the tall man, Bill Chadwell, was Charlie Pitts, and the shorter bandit, Clell Miller, he named as Chadwell. Not until copies of the photographs had been received by Kansas City chief of police Thomas M. Speers would the dead robbers be accurately identified as Bill Chadwell and Clell Miller.

Based on descriptions he gathered from Northfield eyewitnesses, Detective Hazen said who he thought the robbers in the bank and the man who murdered Heywood were. But he got that wrong, too, although his reasoning was not completely unsound: "Jesse James is always ready for murder," Hazen said, "and he is undoubtedly the one who fired the fatal shot at Heywood, the cashier."

There would be plenty of mistakes and bad hunches to go around in the days and weeks to come—there always were when it came to the James-Younger gang. St. Louis chief of police James McDonough still had men pursuing the outlaws in Texas when news of the raid reached him. "I am of the opinion," he wrote Missouri's governor, Charles Hardin, on September 12, five days after the raid, "that it is quite a different gang who made the late assault on the bank at Northfield, Minn."

Henry Wheeler could not stop thinking about the bodies. As a medical student, he knew firsthand the demand for good cadavers at his university's medical school. Clell Miller and Bill Chadwell were not only outstanding physical specimens, but Wheeler felt a proprietary interest when it came to Miller. It would be a true waste if the bodies were to rot out in the

cemetery when they could be put to good use else-
where. Besides, these wicked men who had terrorized
Northfield were thoroughly despised; no one visiting a
Minnesota cemetery would miss them.

Wheeler and a classmate, Charles Dampier,
approached Mayor Solomon Stewart and told him
they would like to claim the outlaws' bodies for the
University of Michigan's medical department at Ann
Arbor. Stewart initially told the boys yes and good
riddance. But once the mayor gave the matter more
thought, he decided he did not have the right to give
the bodies away, worthy cause or not. He met the boys
again and gave them the bad news: the robbers would
have to be interred in the cemetery. But, and he leaned
in close and spoke in a whisper, the bodies would "not
be covered with any more earth than was necessary."

During the afternoon following the inquest, the outlaws were buried in unmarked graves in the paupers'
section of the Northfield Cemetery. Late that night,
a wagon with four men and two large wooden barrels
quietly rolled through the cemetery gate. A black man
drove while Wheeler, Dampier, and another University
of Michigan classmate, Clarence Persons, steadied
the barrels. The wagon stopped next to the fresh-dug
graves in the southwest corner of the cemetery, and by
the light of a lantern, the medical students went to work

with their shovels. They quickly struck the corpses, just as Mayor Stewart had promised. The bodies were stiff, and it was no easy task stuffing them in the barrels—especially the tall Chadwell. The popping of bones and joints mixed with the grunts of the young men.

Carrying its macabre cargo, the wagon next arrived at a discreet location where the barrels were filled with alcohol or brine and lids carefully sealed. On the outside of the containers, the word *PAINT* was written on each. The barrels were then driven to the depot and unloaded. In order not to excite suspicion, Clarence Persons arranged for the shipment of the "paint" to leave for Ann Arbor the next day.

On the afternoon of September 9, as the corpses sloshed in their barrels aboard a train bound for Michigan, the first engraving based on Sumner's photograph of Miller appeared in the *Saint Paul Dispatch*. Soon after, Chadwell's image would be selling newspapers, too. By any measure, the two Missouri bandits could not have come to a more ignominious end. Such was the fate of outlaws who got caught, and the men fleeing through the Big Woods knew this all too well.

Six
The Great Manhunt

It seems hardly possible that they can escape,
so swarmed with enemies are the woods.

—*THE MINNEAPOLIS TRIBUNE*

Twelve noon, Friday, September 8, 1876
Cannon River, thirty miles southwest of Northfield

George James cradled his single-shot shotgun and
looked across the river to the east bank. A group
of men he didn't know had come to James's house while
he was away that morning and had asked his wife a lot
of questions about the river, marshes, and area roads.
He knew they had to be the robbers, so he grabbed his
shotgun and went off to alert the authorities. Farmer
James found several guards at one of the bridges over
the river, but right around the time he got there, word
came that some suspicious men claiming to be posse

members had questioned a nearby road crew about the closest fords.

The commander of the small force at the bridge immediately sent James and two other men downstream along the west bank to block the lower ford while he and another man started for the upper ford. James and the two men had just reached the lower ford when he saw something move in the woods on the east bank, and then six men leading horses slowly emerged from the brush and started down the bank. Just as their leader and his horse entered the water, James raised his shotgun and yanked the trigger. The boom of the shotgun echoed down the river as bird shot peppered the brush around the leader.

The outlaw cussed and unholstered his revolver. "We must take to the woods," he shouted to the men behind him.

James hurriedly reloaded his shotgun as the robbers scampered back into the forest. "Come on, boys, we have got them!" he yelled. But when he looked back, he saw that both of the men had dropped their weapons and run like hell at the sound of the gunshot. One of the men, a doctor, somehow lost his false teeth while he was getting away. The *Saint Paul Dispatch* even wrote that the doctor "lives to tell the tale how he escaped by the skin of his teeth."

James could see how outnumbered he was and retreated as well. The outlaws, hidden just inside the trees, apparently heard the guards fleeing upstream. The bandits mounted up, wheeled their horses, and trotted out to the bank and splashed into the swollen river. They crossed to the west bank in silence and disappeared into the woods. The manhunters quickly regrouped, and while some attempted to trail the robbers from the ford, word was sent out to the posse leaders that the irregular containment line would need to be shifted west—and fast.

But the outlaws were entering a particularly wild section of the Big Woods, what one correspondent called the "bad country back of Elysian." Roads were scarce—if what they were riding on could be called roads—and there were the marshes to cross, with their soft, muddy bottoms that sapped precious strength from the horses. Farmsteads were scattered, and quite a few people living there still did not know about the raid, which was helpful to the gang.

A half hour after crossing the river, the outlaw band, six men and five horses, reached the secluded farm of fifty-one-year-old Ludwig Rosnau, a native of Germany. Ludwig and his sixteen-year-old son, Wilhelm, saw four of the men at the barn and went up to see what they wanted. The strangers wore India rubber coats, which were unbuttoned, giving the farmer an easy view of their wide cartridge belts. One was a large man, as large as the boy had ever seen— Cole Younger. The "leader" was smaller, a "middle-sized man," and he did all of the talking. This was Jesse James, whom the rest of the gang now followed as they desperately tried to elude the manhunters on their trail. There was no time for arguing over leadership if they were to escape from Minnesota.

Jesse told the Rosnaus that he was the sheriff of Rice County and he was on the trail of horse thieves. He asked the directions and distances to St. Peter, Le Sueur, German Lake, and other places. Jesse then wanted to know if there were any horses in the barn. Wilhelm, speaking for his father, answered yes. Waving a large document in the farmer's face, Jesse said he needed two horses and a guide. The boy recognized the document as a map of Minnesota, but that didn't matter because there was no way his father was letting anyone take a single horse. That is, until the "sheriff" and his "deputies" pulled their revolvers.

The outlaws helped themselves to two horses and saddles and made Wilhelm mount one while one of the robbers got up on the other. Jesse told Wilhelm to take them to the road that ran from Waterville to Cleveland. Farmer Rosnau wasn't happy about this, but he wasn't really worried because he still didn't know about the raid. Wilhelm was a little frightened, but he was a good guide, leading the gang through the woods and around a deep swamp. They traveled slowly because one of the horses had an ugly sore caused by a saddle cinch and could hardly walk. The outlaws talked low among themselves, and several times Wilhelm tried to talk with the men, but they did not answer, and finally Jesse told him not to talk so loud as he might alert the robbers.

At one point, they encountered another boy who knew Wilhelm. The group halted, and Wilhelm and the boy began speaking in German. Jesse did not like that one bit, and he told the boy to hush up. But the young man kept speaking to Wilhelm in German. Suddenly, Jesse cursed and ordered someone to knock down the kid. One of the outlaws pulled his revolver and raised the butt in the air to strike the boy, when the boy jumped back, crying, "Don't! Don't!" He also said his English was poor. Jesse then told the boy he'd better hightail it out of there, and if he turned around, he would be shot. The boy hightailed it.

The gang and Wilhelm reached the Cleveland road after about a mile and a half, where they halted to trade horses with the boy, giving him the lame animal. They told him to stay there for half an hour while they went into the woods and scouted for tracks. Wilhelm watched as the outlaws crossed a cornfield and got onto the road where it led into some trees. Suddenly, the outlaws put their horses into a gallop, the tramping of their hooves gradually growing fainter until all Wilhelm heard were the sounds of the forest. He stayed like he was told until another young man came up the road and asked if he'd heard about the Northfield robbery. Everything instantly came together in Wilhelm's mind, and he started immediately for home.

That evening Wilhelm told a group of lawmen about his experiences with the robbers and that one man carried his arm in a sling and it looked like there was blood on the man's sleeve. Wilhelm thought this man's leg also might be hurt because he kept one foot out of the stirrup.

"They were mild-mannered men and behaved all right," said Wilhelm, "except when they drew revolvers."

The last time the gang was seen was on Friday just before dark. A posse spotted the men riding across a cornfield, heading for cover in some thick trees. The posse had been close enough to see the bloodstains on Bob Younger's sling and also saw where blood had dripped down onto his leg. The men had gone by so quickly, like ghosts, that the possemen hadn't even had time to raise their weapons.

At least five hundred men pounded the roads through the Big Woods on Saturday and Sunday. A special train ran the seventeen miles between Mankato and Janesville, patrolling the tracks and transporting men and supplies. Telegraph operators manned their stations around the clock, transmitting every scrap of news, every rumor, as well as a flood of dispatches coming from the Minneapolis and St. Paul newspaper correspondents who now rode with the manhunters.

But the robbers seemed to have vanished. This area was home to thousands of feral hogs that tore up the earth searching for grubs and roots—one man described it as "the hog pen of the state"—and this made following any trail tedious. And when fresh tracks were discovered, they turned out to be made by other posses. The rain, which only seemed to get heavier and colder, turned the roads into muck and soaked the possemen, causing some guards to abandon their posts.

Fear of the robbers rattled quite a few of the men and boys who made up the posses. "Many, of course, were there who started in the chase as they would go upon a chicken hunt," commented one reporter, "made brave by the excitement of the moment, but worse than useless in case of actual service." Some, he said, were "scared at the sight of a stump." Of course, part of their fear was from them being poorly armed "with weapons little better than garden syringes"—or no arms at all.

The locals were also easily terrified and often mistook the manhunters for the bandits. Instead of waiting and asking questions, they simply ran for their lives, spreading false reports of robber sightings that only caused more confusion. Some others took advantage of having all these warm, hungry bodies and dramatically raised their prices on provisions and meals. The price gouging was so bad that a special shipment of bread, sausage, and cheese was delivered by rail to one group of manhunters.

But the biggest problems for the men from St. Paul, Minneapolis, and other parts of the state were a lack of familiarity with the area and a lack of coordination, which caused them to be as lost in the Big Woods as the outlaws. The best maps of the region were the county maps found in the large (14½×18 inches) Minnesota atlas published in Chicago by A. T. Andreas in 1874. A number of possemen actually toted along the unwieldy 394-page book. Others tore out the maps they needed and tried to piece together the different roads. Unfortunately, even these maps were not detailed enough and contained many errors.

The manhunters had plenty of leaders in their ranks, county sheriffs and prominent citizens, but they still didn't have strict charge of their volunteers, frequently making suggestions on what needed to be done as opposed to issuing direct orders. And no one man oversaw the entire operation or had authority over all the various parties in the field. So a number of escape points were left unguarded because everyone assumed someone else was doing it. Probably the most inexcusable behavior came from the police departments of Minneapolis and St. Paul. The two cities were jealous and bitter rivals in everything: business, transportation, politics, sports, and more. And so, too, with the robber hunt.

Detective Mike Hoy led the Minneapolis squad. A native of King's County, Ireland, the thirty-nine-year-old Hoy had fought with the Tenth Minnesota in the Civil War and had served as chief of police of St. Anthony, Minnesota, before it merged with Minneapolis. Hoy was a large and powerful man with a full beard and bushy eyebrows, and he could also be a bully with an evil temper. His counterpart with the St. Paul contingent, thirty-eight-year-old Detective John B. Bresette, had been with the police force since 1857, except for Civil War duty with the Eighth Minnesota. A native of New York, Bresette was also a good-size man with a florid complexion and a drooping mustache. He was said to be "known for his brusque, quick, off-hand way," which was not necessarily a compliment.

Hoy and Bresette were alike enough to hate each other, and they bickered and quarreled like children, refusing to cooperate, each striving to secure any glory for themselves. "The defeat of the object sought to be obtained," wrote one reporter, "is the inevitable result."

On Sunday afternoon, convinced that the outlaws were being harbored by local criminal types, Detective Hoy led his party to the home of a man named Conway, who had a notorious reputation as the leader of a gang of horse thieves. According to the people at the house, Conway had not been seen for the last three weeks. Not only did Hoy not believe them, he was convinced they were hiding something.

Hoy singled out a young man named Dolan, a former inmate of Stillwater Penitentiary, and forced him to accompany his men to an island in nearby Lake Elysian. Dolan trembled as he watched Hoy uncoil a long rope and then step around behind him. The detective tied one end of the rope around Dolan's neck and threw the other over the limb of a large oak. Hoy then asked Dolan if he had anything he wanted to tell him. When Dolan shook his head no, Hoy signaled his men to hang the poor man. The rope instantly snapped taut and Dolan's feet left the ground, kicking and twisting.

After a few seconds of this torture, Hoy told his men to let Dolan down so he could interrogate the man again. Gasping for air, Dolan still refused to talk, and the torture was repeated. The "hanging bee" went on for some time until Hoy finally threw up his hands and released Dolan, flabbergasted that the ex-con refused to squeal. It never seemed to occur to Hoy that Dolan might have nothing to squeal about.

That same afternoon, as the fears grew that the outlaws had completely escaped, a rider galloped into Janesville, a thick lather dripping off his heaving horse. He pulled up at the railroad depot, jumped off his mount, and rushed inside to the telegraph office. He handed a message to the first man he saw, a reporter for the *Saint Paul Dispatch*. Three robbers had been driven out of the woods, the message said, and were fleeing toward Waterville. The reporter anxiously asked if there was any other information, and the man told him the outlaws had dashed across a bridge over the Cannon River yelling and firing their guns in the air. The guards dove for cover, but they described one of the horses as a buckskin, which matched one ridden by a robber in Northfield.

The reporter turned to the telegraph operator and dictated several messages to points all over southern Minnesota, including his newspaper in St. Paul. The correspondent for the *Minneapolis Tribune* took his turn with the wire next. "The announcement creates a sensation among the few men remaining in town," he reported. "It settles the question that the robbers are still in the country, and we wait now breathlessly for news from the front. It looks as though the end would come today. Every one is excited. Every one talks rapidly and excitedly."

These telegrams did raise excitement across the state and even more men volunteered for the robber hunt. A special train carrying more than one hundred men from Northfield, Winona, Rochester, Owatonna, and Medford soon steamed toward Janesville. Another train departed from St. Paul at 6:00 P.M., carrying Chief of Police James King, private detective Larry Hazen, and twenty armed men. Several hundred people gathered at the St. Paul depot to see the chief off.

The St. Paul train arrived in St. Peter, seventy-five miles down the track, at 9:15 P.M., and Chief King stepped off in a drizzling rain, anxious to get any updates. An official at the station handed the chief an urgent dispatch, and what he read disgusted him. The report of the robbers was false. Yes, some men had terrorized the bridge guards, but they were a bunch of drunken yahoos from Waseca having fun scaring the hell out of people and not the Missouri outlaws.

Topping off the day's bizarre reports, though, was a dispatch received later that afternoon from Waseca. Two manhunters sent word that they had come across a fresh grave in the woods where they believed the out-laws had taken refuge. They immediately assumed it contained the body of the wounded and bloody robber so many people had seen. The men had hurriedly clawed back three feet of soft, black earth and found it . . . empty.

At 3:00 P.M. on a wet and muddy Sunday, as the tele-graph wires sizzled with the false report of the robbers near Waterville, the funeral of Joseph Lee Heywood took place at the family residence in Northfield. A memorial service that morning had drawn a crowd of between eight hundred and a thousand people, and several hundred converged on the modest home on West Third. "The house was literally packed," re-ported the *Rice County Journal,* "the piazza also; the front, quite spacious yard was full, and the street on which the house fronts was full of carriages gener-ally filled with occupants who could not get into the house."

After the funeral, a long procession followed the horse-drawn hearse to the Northfield Cemetery. Among the pallbearers were two men who had played a dramatic role in defeating the outlaws: Anselm Manning and J. S. Allen.

But the true hero of Northfield was the dead man in the coffin. In florid commentaries, newspapers across the country lauded the assistant cashier's bravery and "rare fidelity" in resisting the ruffians in the bank. His "instincts and self-culture led him to prefer death even, to the surrender of truth, duty, trust," wrote the editor of the *Journal.* "It is a glorious finale of a beautiful career."

A dissenting voice, however, came out of Spring Valley, Minnesota. The editor of the town's newspaper, the *Western Progress,* found it difficult to swallow the idea that it had been the assistant cashier's "duty" to give his life for the First National Bank:

> *Do the demands of the employer of the employee extend so far? Is not an employee's life of greater value than a few thousand dollars of the employer's gold? We would not detract one iota from the dead man's laurels, but we fear he gave his life from a mistaken motive or demand of duty. He was a husband and father, with a wife and children looking*

to him for care and protection, whose demands cannot be measured by gold and silver; and was not his duty to them more sacred and of far greater importance than the treasure for which he sacrificed his life? . . . The coldhearted, selfish employers will look with secret satisfaction upon his sacrifice, and the thoughtless world will plaud it as heroic; but a more thoughtful tribunal will judge that in dying for others' gold he transgressed a higher and holier law, and cruelly wronged his wife and children.

Describing the men who ran the First National Bank as coldhearted may have seemed mean and unfair, but it would be hard to prove otherwise when it came to one of the bank's investors: Adelbert Ames. Outwardly, Ames and the other shareholders acted appropriately in offering a respectable reward for the capture of the robbers. But in a letter to his wife, Ames lamented the $400 he stood to lose as his share of the monies set aside for the robber reward and the compensation for Heywood's widow: "This would buy the much-coveted stem-winding watch—and—well, I have forgotten what the other thing is I stand so much in need of."

Nevertheless, numerous banks made certain that Heywood's sacrifice did not go unrewarded. Several St. Paul bankers established the Heywood Fund to benefit the widow and little girl, and soon thousands of dollars poured in from banks in Canada, New York, Boston, San Francisco, and all over Minnesota.

Heywood's murder was a tragedy, but there were other, unforeseen casualties in the days following the raid. Two boys of Henderson, Minnesota, inspired by the exciting events in Northfield, were playing a game of "robbers" armed with a pitchfork and a shotgun when the shotgun went off. The boy with the pitchfork went down clutching an "ugly wound" in his side.

Near Owatonna, a seven-year-old child came up with an antiquated pistol and somehow convinced his mother that he should load it to be ready in case the robbers appeared. The mother consented and watched intently as her son charged the weapon with bird shot. The next thing she knew, the pistol exploded, sending the full charge of lead into her face and neck. The woman lost one eye outright with the other seriously injured. And the attending doctor believed one small shot had penetrated her brain.

Cold and hungry, the James boys, the Youngers, and Charlie Pitts draped their rubber-coated blankets over a framework of branches to shelter themselves as the rain splattered down around them. It was late in the evening of Friday, September 8, and the men were thoroughly soaked, not only from the steady rain but from brushing against the forest's wet undergrowth and slogging through countless bogs. Even if they could have found dry tinder for a fire, it was far too risky to build one.

As one of the outlaws removed the blood-soaked bandages from Bob Younger's swollen and disfigured elbow, the men talked in low tones. They were again down to five horses, and they were thoroughly played out at this point. If the gang wanted to keep moving,

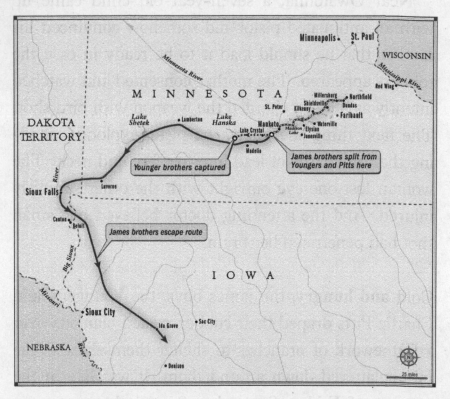

After Northfield: The James-Younger gang escape route.

they would have to abandon their mounts. This might be an advantage, though, because the posses were looking for men on horseback. They had often been dismounted, leading the horses through the timber, so they would likely travel just as fast, at least while they were in the Big Woods. Still, the outlaws would need all their cunning and stealth to avoid being caught.

The men were too miserable and cramped to get any sleep, so they just waited for the gray murkiness of dawn, which came at about a quarter till six. The men took all the bridles and the better saddle blankets from the horses and used the bridles to tie the rolled-up saddle blankets and rubber blankets around their bodies. They left all the horses picketed in the woods with long straps, hopeful that it would be some time before the posses discovered the animals.

The gang moved slowly through the trees and swamps in a westerly direction. Sometime before noon, they reached a secluded island or finger of land, heavily forested. The rain had let up, and they were sure they were far from any homesteads or roads so they started a fire and crowded around it. These men were used to doing nearly everything in the saddle; their tall boots were *riding* boots. All this walking had begun to take its toll on their feet. They had worn out their socks, and blisters had formed on their soles and where the wet leather rubbed against their skin. As they warmed themselves near the fire, they cut up their underclothing and used the cloth to wrap around their feet.

For food, the gang had subsisted on green corn, wild plums, and whatever else they could scavenge or steal (one farmer's wife complained that the gang had run off with her day's baking). But this camp gave them a chance for meat. A stray calf appeared and one of the boys quickly pulled his revolver and shot it, but he stared in disbelief as the wounded animal ran off. The same thing happened when a hog was spotted nearby. The outlaws were afraid to fire follow-up shots, though, because they did not want to draw the attention of any posses that might be close on their trail.

The gang rested until nearly dark before starting out again, marching all night but taking frequent breaks. As the morning glowed in the east, they stopped near the edge of a clearing and started another fire. They placed corn in the husk and potatoes upon the coals and tended to their feet and wounds as they waited for the vegetables to cook. Later, as they devoured their simple breakfast, the men suddenly pricked up their heads at a distinct sound in the distance. It was a bell. They were camped about a half mile north of the tiny hamlet of Marysburg, and the bell of the Catholic church was pealing for early mass.

After breakfast, the outlaws decided to move their camp, most likely because earlier they had been spotted. Two boys, not more than twelve years old, reported having seen the suspicious men near the edge of the woods, not far from the Marysburg church—and they said the men were wearing linen dusters. Detective Mike Hoy listened to the youngsters' story later that same day and scoffed at it. The strangers they saw were "as likely to be pursuers as pursued," he declared. And he did not bother to go to the place where the men had been seen. The Minneapolis detective's mistakes were beginning to pile up.

The gang walked at least three miles to the south and set up temporary camp on the banks of Madison Lake, in Blue Earth County. That night, they tramped nine hard miles west, skirting the north edge of Eagle Lake and arriving within three miles of Mankato, where they discovered an abandoned house in the woods. Finally, they could get out of the rain. They holed up there all day Monday, Tuesday, and Tuesday night, nursing their bodies and letting time and the elements wear on the posses.

On Tuesday morning, the manhunters discovered the robbers' abandoned horses. Two of the mounts had broken free and were found first. About an hour later, the camp was located with the three remaining horses, including the noted buckskin. The tied horses had eaten every bit of foliage within reach, which was not much to begin with, and then had begun eating the bark off the elm trees they were tied to. In addition to being visibly thin, the horses had saddle sores on their backs and cuts on their sides where the outlaws had furiously raked their spurs time and again. On the ground behind a log lay the McClellan saddles the outlaws had purchased in Minnesota. Two bullet holes were discovered in one of the saddles, and a posse member got a prized souvenir when he dug a pistol bullet out of one of the holes.

By that afternoon, the telegraph flashed the news that the robbers were on foot, advising that "every stranger should be carefully scrutinized and detained if any way suspicious." But while the discovery of the robbers' horses made big news, it also delivered a blow to the posse leaders because it was now clear that the outlaws' horses had been abandoned days ago. There had been no positive sightings of the robbers in the last seventy-two hours, which caused many to conclude that the outlaws had escaped the Big Woods and might even be beyond the Iowa border.

"It is hard to account for their escape," wrote the *Minneapolis Tribune*, "but we are compelled to accept it as fact."

The number of manhunters was getting lower and lower, even though the amount of the reward offer had been increased. The *Pioneer Press and Tribune* claimed that the robbers "have, for the time being at least, completely baffled their pursuers."

But then on the evening of Tuesday, September 12, the sheriff of Faribault County rode into Mankato to report that he had spotted five suspicious men, likely the robbers, near Indian Lake, a few miles to the east. The news brought detectives Hoy and Bresette with their posses to Mankato late that night. The detectives made plans—separately, of course—to look for signs of the outlaws at Indian Lake at first light. But another downpour came during the evening, hard enough to obliterate any trail. The detectives decided there was no point in searching any more. The Faribault sheriff's report made little sense, anyway, because the place where he saw the suspicious men was only eighteen miles from where the horses had been abandoned. Sullen, dirty, and tired, Hoy, Bresette, and their men boarded trains for home first thing in the morning. The Twin Cities' best accepted defeat.

About 6:00 A.M. on Wednesday morning, September 13, thirty-three-year-old Thomas Jefferson Dunning stepped out of his house three miles north of Mankato to bring in the boss's cows. Ambling east, toward the woods, Dunning had hardly passed the back of the barn when he came face-to-face with six stout and grungy strangers. They wore black rubber coats and had rolled-up blankets tied around them. Large spurs were tied to their bridles. The men told the startled hired hand that they were hunting the robbers and that they believed he was one of them. Dunning took a step back in shock, strongly proclaiming his innocence, but the men drew their revolvers and forced Dunning to put his hands behind his back, which they bound tight with one of the bridles.

The man whom Dunning took for the leader carried a nickel-plated revolver with ivory grips, and the other robbers called him "Captain." Jesse, the captain, ordered Dunning to show them the way to Mankato and motioned him to start walking. One of the men followed close behind, holding the reins of the bridle securing Dunning's hands. As the group marched south, Dunning begged to be released, saying he had absolutely nothing to do with Northfield. Instead, the men asked Dunning question after question. Which roads led around Mankato? Were there skiffs on the Minnesota River? Could the river be forded? Could they swim it? What was the country like farther south near the Blue Earth River?

Jesse next told Dunning he would have to guide them through the woods around Mankato, but the hired hand claimed he really didn't know the area that well, and he continued to plead with the men to let him go, saying he had a "delicate wife" and a young child at home. When that failed to get a response, Dunning laid it on thicker, telling the strangers he had heart problems, and if he was out long, his family would come looking for him.

"I suppose you know who we are?" Jesse finally said. Dunning answered that he had a good idea. Jesse then asked Dunning if he knew where they were from.

"From Missouri?" Dunning replied in a shaky voice.

"We're a damned long way from Missouri," one of the outlaws said.

Jesse talked about the raid and said they would not have killed the cashier if he had just opened the safe. The outlaw also said the next son of a bitch that was ordered to open the safe would do it pretty quick.

The men talked low among themselves, and when crossing a road, they walked in Indian file, each man carefully stepping in the tracks made by Dunning. But after tramping three-quarters of a mile, the robbers decided Dunning was more trouble than he was worth. Whether or not he was lying about how well he knew the area, he might lead them in an unsafe direction. But what to do with the man? Dunning promised in the strongest terms he would not tell anyone about them.

The outlaws moved off a short distance to discuss Dunning's fate. Jesse and Frank wanted to shoot the man on the spot, arguing that it was the only way they could be sure of Dunning's silence. Short of that, they should tie the man securely to a tree and leave him, although the poor man might not be discovered for some time, if at all. Cole opposed shooting Dunning, and he also did not like the idea of tying Dunning in the woods. Jesse had expected Cole to be contrary as usual, so he suggested that they let Bob decide.

"If we turn this man loose," Jesse said to Bob, "he will have the whole country after us in twelve hours, and with your broken arm, we cannot possibly get away."

Bob thought for a moment and said, "I would rather be shot dead than to have that man killed, for fear his telling might put a few hundred men after us. There will be time enough for shooting, if he should join in the pursuit."

Dunning overheard the outlaws debating whether he would live or die. His palms became sweaty and cold, and he started to shake. He thought about running, but one of the men spoke up and said Dunning "seemed a good sort of fellow" and "they did not want his family to suffer for them." They made him swear a solemn oath that he would not report them. And they warned that if they learned that he had broken his promise, they would hunt him down and kill him, no matter how many years it took. The outlaws promised to mail him a handsome gift, and they asked for his name and postal address, which they jotted down in a small book.

Cole loosened the leather bridle and freed Dunning's hands. Dunning rubbed his wrists as the outlaws bade him good day and told him they might see him again soon. Several sat on the ground watching as Dunning hurried off. One of the outlaws spoke up in a loud voice, obviously intending for Dunning to hear: "Let's shoot the damned son of a bitch, and then he will be sure not to tell." And then the outlaw laughed. Dunning began to run faster.

When he got home, Dunning tried to figure out what he should do. He believed the outlaws when they said they would come after him if he failed to keep his pledge—they were proven cutthroats. But here was an opportunity to capture the bandits and put them behind bars. Dunning sat down to breakfast and thought about it, eventually deciding that, despite the risk, he had to tell someone. He went to the house of his employer, the farm's owner, Henry Shaubut, and told him the entire story of his terrifying hour with the outlaws. Shaubut immediately saddled a horse and rode for Mankato to alert the authorities.

At 8:45 A.M., the rapid tapping of metal on metal stirred to attention telegraph operators up and down the lines. They quickly wrote down the details of the robber sighting. "This report is reliable," read the telegram. "Get men out immediately to hunt them." The exciting news instantly reinvigorated the manhunt. Mike Hoy's party had nearly reached Minneapolis when they received the report. When they arrived at approximately 10:00 A.M., Hoy, Minneapolis chief of police Albert Munger, and their officers rushed to the nearest gun store, where they bought fine Winchester repeating rifles and "an abundance of ammunition." It's never been clear why Hoy's party needed additional arms, but they may have left their original weapons with the posses remaining in the field. Hoy tried to get a special train to take his squad back to Mankato, but he wasn't successful, which meant he, Munger, and five policemen were forced to wait for the 2:30 train.

A correspondent of the *Pioneer Press and Tribune* interviewed Hoy as he stewed about the delay. "We have had but little sleep since we left home and are pretty well played out," he admitted. As for the robbers, Hoy said "they are, without doubt, the James-Younger gang. They are armed with revolvers good for 100 yards, and each man of the gang carries three or four of them, so that when they meet a determined body of pursuers, bloody work will ensue." He believed the outlaws were headed to Sioux City, Iowa, or St. Joseph, Missouri. Hoy felt the newspapers had reported his movements during the manhunt fairly accurately, but "those relative to Bresette's party have been exaggerated."

Detective Bresette's squad of St. Paul policemen had traveled as far as Blakely, thirty-five miles north of Mankato, when they got word about the Dunning encounter. Bresette's manhunters piled out of the smoking car and waited anxiously at the depot for the next train going south.

In Mankato, twenty men started out after the robbers just minutes after Henry Shaubut brought the news to town. The posse traveled to the last place Dunning had seen the bandits and immediately found their trail. The problem was they were a good two hours behind the gang. As this small party scoured the timber, hundreds of men converged on Mankato in response to the telegram calling for help. In addition to the Minneapolis and St. Paul squads, parties of various sizes were being commanded by the sheriffs of Waseca, Finch, Blue Earth, Winona, Faribault, Rice, and Ramsey Counties, and countless more volunteers were coming from neighboring towns and farms. By the end of the day, more than a thousand men were actively hunting the robbers. The pursuit of the James-Younger band had become the largest manhunt in U.S. history, and everyone involved sensed it was nearing a thrilling conclusion.

Throughout the afternoon, Mankato's streets were filled with "eager, excited, expectant crowds, formed of armed men, hurrying to and fro with stolid, firm resolution depicted on their faces," reported the *Dispatch*'s correspondent. "Wherever two persons were seen conversing in the street, there would be a rush of dozens of excited inquirers, and 'What's the news?' 'Are they caught?' 'Have they shot them?' and a host of similar queries would be repeated at once. Every street corner had its throng of crowding, pushing, attentive listeners, and every group had its orator, who was either detailing in wondrous eloquence some new phase of the situation, some impossible movement of the fugitives, or suggesting some sage course of action."

In order not to repeat past mistakes, Mankato's Civil War hero, Brevet Brigadier General Edmund Mann Pope, was chosen to take charge of the manhunt, which now focused on an area of roughly ten square miles. Pope, a veteran of Antietam, Gettysburg, Cold Harbor, and numerous other battles, stationed guards at bridges, crossroads, and little-used trails—any point that might serve as an escape route—and ordered patrols on area roads and along the railroad lines. The general's militarized zone made it seem that "Mankato expected a siege of the combined forces of all the hostile savages paying allegiance to Sitting Bull," wrote a reporter, "rather than that the men were called out to capture six fugitive robbers."

After the fugitives watched Dunning depart for home, they continued toward Mankato, a cold rain pelting their broad-brimmed hats. Making sure to stay in the woods and out of sight, the men reached the outskirts of town, where they halted and waited for nightfall. They saw their pursuers many times through the undergrowth, waiting with their revolvers drawn and fingers on the triggers. But the manhunters would eventually drift by and out of hearing.

The gang decided not to detour around Mankato. They did not know the woods and the river crossings, and the effort would add miles to their journey. But they knew the tracks of the St. Paul & Sioux City Railroad ran through Mankato. They had come to Minnesota on these very tracks. They didn't need a compass or a map; these steel rails could guide them out of the state.

The trick, though, would be slipping through Mankato (population six thousand) undetected. The whole town had been on high alert for the appearance of the robbers since early that morning. It was audacious and risky for even one man to attempt it, let alone six—but doing something like this was part of the James-Younger gang's fabled escapades.

Shortly before midnight, the outlaws entered Mankato from the east. They reached the railroad tracks near the large brick building of the Mankato Linseed Oil Company, at the head of Elm Street. The bandits looked frantically along the railroad siding for a handcar, which would have taken them rapidly down the line, but suddenly the mill's steam whistle sounded a strong, shrill blast. The men ducked and spun about, looking in all directions. They thought they had been spotted, and the whistle was a warning to the town. The outlaws hurriedly retreated to a point behind the mill. But the whistle had not been an alarm; it had sounded to let the mill workers know the clock had struck 12:00 A.M. The gang soon realized that they were not being pursued, and, slowly and silently, they began once more circling back to the railroad a few blocks to the south. At one point, the outlaws had been no more than four blocks from General Pope's headquarters in the Clifton House hotel.

The night, according to one correspondent, was "of almost Egyptian darkness." As the hunted men neared the railroad bridge over the Blue Earth River, they cautiously studied the approach, fully expecting the bridge to have watchmen, but they were relieved to find it unguarded—or so they thought. At approximately 2:00 A.M., the six men marched across the high trestlework in single file, disappearing on the other side of the river. Incredibly, the James-Younger gang had passed safely through Mankato and crossed the Blue Earth River, despite all of General Pope's preparations and manpower to prevent something like that from happening.

Pope had arranged for a strong force to be stationed at the bridge, but the railroad authorities told him they would have their own people there, so Pope redistributed his men to other points. The railroad's guards consisted of two section hands and a boy, posted out of sight. The boy clearly saw the outlaws step onto the trestle, and he urged his companions to shoot. Instead, the section hands turned and left the poor boy to fend for himself (the men would later defend their actions by saying they were "insufficiently armed"). The boy acted like a true hero and ran to the county wagon bridge a short distance downstream and told Pope's men the outlaws had just crossed the river. A messenger galloped to the Clifton House with the news, which hit the general like a load of Rebel canister shot. But he knew it would do no good to send men out in the soupy darkness. They would take up the hunt at first light and hope to God they could find a trail or other evidence of the fugitives and somehow salvage this fiasco.

Immediately after crossing the river, the outlaws discovered a watermelon patch nearby and helped themselves, pausing briefly next to the tracks to devour their booty. Cole Younger would later declare the melons "splendid." The gang then continued west along the tracks. They scored another small victory when they spotted a chicken coop, which they successfully raided, ringing the necks of three good hens and a small turkey to roast later. After tramping three miles from the Blue Earth River, the outlaws left the railroad siding and walked fifty paces into the woods to the foot of a sharp ridge known locally as Pigeon Hill. They built a good fire, draping their coats and blankets over saplings to keep the bright flames from being spotted from the railroad tracks.

Cole did not like this camping spot; he thought it was a mistake to be so close to the railroad, but the rest of the boys were hungry and cold, and as far as they knew, no one had seen them slip out of Mankato. Bob

Younger removed his sling and bloody shirt and tended to his shattered elbow while some of the men plucked and dressed the birds and placed them on the crackling fire, along with several ears of corn. The woods were perfectly still, and the bluish column of smoke rose through the trees and spread out as a thin haze in the morning sky above the campsite. The man tending to breakfast had just turned the poultry and corn to cook it evenly when the gang suddenly heard the hooting and hollering of excited men that sent each bandit's heart racing. The commotion was coming from the railroad tracks, and the yelling men were rapidly getting closer.

Detective Hoy and his squad, along with a small party led by the Winona County sheriff, had gone to the Blue Earth Bridge first thing that morning and were shown the tracks of the outlaws going to and from the melon patch. Encouraged by these fresh signs, Hoy and his men quickened their pace down the tracks. At 6:30 A.M., an engineer on a passing locomotive waved vigorously at Hoy's party and pointed to Pigeon Hill, just ahead of them. The detective broke into a run, but in his excitement, he rushed past the deep, muddy boot prints where the gang had left the railroad siding. A posseman bringing up the rear saw them and yelled ahead to Hoy. The detective raced back to the spot, breathing hard, and caught a strong whiff of burning feathers. Then he saw the film of smoke above the trees.

"Double quick, charge!" shouted Hoy.

The manhunters jumped the fence and dove into the woods with a loud crash, Hoy in the lead, his Winchester raised in front of him. As they burst upon the campsite, the bushes just beyond were still moving from where the outlaws had run through them. In their panicked flight, the bandits had left behind their breakfast, still cooking on the fire, as well as coats, blankets, and bridles. Hoy waited for more of the men to catch up, and then they set off again after the fugitives, the pursuers chattering nervously and loudly up and down the line. The outlaws clearly heard Hoy's orders, and whenever he shouted, "Keep to the left," the gang moved to the right.

By midmorning, more than two hundred men crisscrossed the woods around Pigeon Hill and beyond; by that afternoon, hundreds more tromped over several square miles of surrounding countryside. Detective Hoy took time to jot a note for the telegraph, stating that they had "captured" the robbers' supplies. "We are in hot pursuit," he wrote. But to those who were part of that pursuit, it was painfully clear that the Minneapolis detective had committed his worst blunder yet. Hoy had been cautioned that morning to "take it cool and lay his plans well before he started." But Hoy, with typical arrogance, brushed off the advice. Had he and his squad remained calm and quiet—and waited for additional men—a plan could have been put in place to surround the robber camp. But the noise of Hoy's party and their pell-mell rush into the woods gave the robbers all the warning they needed, with no one on the other side of the ridge to block their retreat.

"It is safe to say," wrote one angry volunteer, "that Mr. Hoy's running so as to be the first to get the glory and reward, was the cause of the robbers' escape."

The outlaws fled southeast from Pigeon Hill, striking the Blue Earth River after about a mile. To foil the manhunters, they had waded in streams, stepped from rock to rock for great distances, walked in each other's footprints, walked only on their heels, then walked only on their toes. They doubled back on their trail, then doubled again. Upon reaching the Blue Earth, they marched upstream for half an hour until halting in a thicket on the river's bank. Bob, his pain exacerbated when moving, desperately needed rest, so the gang hunkered down here for the rest of the day.

Between 3:00 and 4:00 P.M., as the rain poured down, three possemen came near enough to the thicket to hear the robbers' voices. The manhunters strained their eyes to see the outlaws but failed to detect a human figure—they knew better than to go into the thicket after the fugitives. The three waited for some time but heard nothing more. Growing anxious, they shouted and fired their shotguns into the brush, which brought no response. Finally, with no other manhunters appearing to bolster their numbers, and evening coming on, the three men abandoned their watch and hurried off to report what they had heard.

The possemen were lucky because the fugitives later said they had caught a glimpse of one of their pursuers. It would have been an easy pistol shot, one of the outlaws commented.

Never had the James-Younger gang welcomed darkness like they did that night on the Blue Earth River. But their suffering, fatigue, and stress made for hairtrigger tempers, and they got into a heated argument. Jesse and Frank pointed out that they had been dead right about Dunning. The man should have been killed. Now he had put all Minnesota on their trail, and it was critical the outlaws get as many miles behind them as possible before morning. They could not do that with Bob slowing them down. Despite whatever feelings he had for Bob, Jesse believed they had no choice but to leave him behind. Jesse had a wife and a young boy waiting for him, and Frank had a wife at home as well. And if caught, they would all be facing murder charges. That is, if they were not lynched on the spot.

Cole would never abandon his brother, he angrily told Jesse, nor would Jim. If the James boys wanted to go their own way, they should do it. And so it was decided. Charlie Pitts had a family, too, but his loyalty was to the Youngers, and he chose to link his fate with theirs. Recognizing the hopelessness of their situation, the Youngers and Pitts gave the James brothers their gold watches, rings, and most of their cash to keep for them. The timepieces alone were worth a few hundred dollars, and they thought it was better to part with them now than take a chance of them becoming trophies of the manhunters.

The Youngers and Pitts most likely gave the James boys verbal messages for loved ones and, on the chance they all made it back to Missouri, agreed upon a place to meet. After short, knowing nods—that they might never see one another again—Jesse and Frank disappeared into the bushes and the cold night.

Seven
Last Stand on the Watonwan

*I believe that there were in that country
7,000 lakes, and between every two lakes
there was a marsh. . . . We suffered in those
fourteen days a hundred deaths.*

—COLE YOUNGER

Even with the manhunters' failures, near misses, and infighting, General Pope was still insistent that the Northfield desperadoes were within his reach. Yes, a full week had passed since the raid, but the fugitives had not gotten any more than seventy miles from Northfield. Pope knew some of the robbers were badly wounded—a bloody shirt and handkerchief had been found at the Pigeon Hill camp. These injuries, plus their disadvantage of now being on foot, gave Pope every reason to believe the outlaws weren't going to get too far very fast.

Pope decided to relocate his headquarters to the small town of Lake Crystal, on the railroad fourteen miles southwest of Mankato. By the early evening of Thursday, September 14, he had set up a new picket line with hundreds of men that stretched in a twelve-mile semicircle. If a bandit tried to breach that line, or if any of Pope's men saw one of the outlaws, riders were ready to spread the alarm and direct the posses to the point of the sighting. Now, all Pope could do was wait.

As another wave of rain set in, ten men on the outskirts of Lake Crystal, not far from the general's headquarters, were guarding a bridge over a small creek. They kept their collars pulled tight around their necks, and as the hours wore on and the evening became colder and more miserable, nine of the guards had had enough. They scavenged some dry straw nearby, carried it under the trees and bushes, and promptly bedded down for a nap. The nine tried to persuade the one remaining guard, thirty-two-year-old Richard Roberts, to give up and join them, telling him the robbers had already escaped.

"I was sent out here to guard this section of the road," Roberts said firmly, "and I am going to do it."

One of the men called Roberts a "Sunday school boy" and suggested he say his prayers before going to bed. Roberts told his companion to go to hell.

Shortly after midnight, as the nine guards snored nearby, Roberts thought he heard the sound of a horse's hooves in the sand. Peering into the inky blackness, the sound came closer and closer until Roberts made out a moving form, which his blinking eyes soon recognized as a horse with two riders on its back. The riders were Jesse and Frank James on a recently stolen black horse.

"Halt!" Roberts cried. "Who are you fellows?"

The James boys instantly laid flat on the horse's back, and the lead rider said, "Get up," at the same time raking his spurs against the animal's flanks. As the Jameses flew past, Roberts raised his weapon and fired. The horse jumped, and its riders tumbled to the ground. Both men quickly sprang up and dashed into a cornfield. The riderless horse spun around and galloped back in the direction from which it had come.

The nine sleeping men leaped out of their straw beds, confused and scared. Roberts excitedly told them what had just happened, and one of the guards raced for Lake Crystal to deliver the news to General Pope. In a short time, several men returned with lanterns, holding them low to the ground. They carefully examined the scene and found, lying by the side of the road, a fine felt hat, which Roberts immediately claimed. They also discovered two sets of tracks that resembled the ones they had seen for the last several days. One set had been made by a fine boot with a small, high heel and square toe. There were no signs of blood—at least none were reported at the time. Clearly, though, two of the robbers had broken the line—again.

At daylight, as Detective Hoy's squad and others arrived at Lake Crystal, an anxious Baptist minister named Joseph Rockwood came into headquarters and reported that his team of iron-gray mares had been stolen. The horses were taken from a farm three miles to the south at approximately 3:00 A.M. Rockwood had good reason to be upset because his large mares were considered the best team in Blue Earth County.

Now the Jameses, no longer encumbered by the Youngers, had two strong mounts and could move fast and always be a step ahead of the posses. Over the next two days, several sightings of the pair brought frenzied reactions from the manhunters as they tried to cut off the robbers. But while the reports on the James boys kept the telegraph operators busy, the big mystery was the whereabouts of the other four desperadoes. Had they slipped through Pope's picket line undetected? Were they still hidden in the woods of Blue Earth County? The bandits seemed to have melted away with the rain, but how?

The last horses reported stolen in the area were Rockwood's two mares, which told the pursuers that in all likelihood, the rest of the gang was still on foot. Also, no one who had seen the James brothers described either man as wearing a sling, so the robber with the hurt arm (Bob Younger) must be with the other four. This man was obviously "used up" and was relying on his companions as they attempted to elude the manhunters. Perhaps Jesse and Frank's separation from the others was intended to divert the posse's attention away from the rest of the gang and the crippled bandit.

Then again, some even believed the outlaws had killed the wounded bandit so they could move more quickly. Yet another theory held that the four robbers on foot were being harbored by "lawless scoundrels" in a secluded house somewhere, or that they were being comforted and fed at a secret campsite. "There are those who would not hesitate to do so," commented the reporter for the *Saint Paul Dispatch.*

One of "those" immediately suspected was Irishman Jack O'Neil, who operated the whorehouse in the woods across the Minnesota River from Mankato. Some of the gang had enjoyed O'Neil's ladies prior to the raid, and a rumor was whispered around Mankato that O'Neil had transported the robbers across the river in his skiff. According to the rumor, the man with the hurt arm was then recuperating at the brothel.

Early on Saturday morning, September 16, a large posse boarded the ferry for a surprise visit to the local "den of infamy." Without warning, the manhunters burst through the door and made a thorough search of the premises as the female residents screamed and cursed. But instead of a wounded robber, the possemen found only "five pimps and blacklegs."

"The odds are now considered by all greatly in favor of the fugitive cutthroats," wrote a correspondent from Mankato later that day. Various parties continued to comb the woods south and west of Mankato, and Hoy, Bresette, and others chased the James boys toward Dakota Territory. But with little success, many discouraged manhunters were giving up and heading home. After two more days of playing catch-up, Hoy and Bresette called it quits as well. On Monday morning, September 18, Hoy, Minneapolis chief of police Munger, and their squad of policemen stepped aboard the train at Mankato, bound for the Twin Cities. In one of the car seats, they piled their Winchester repeaters and the bridles, blankets, and coats the robbers had abandoned at Pigeon Hill. These were their only trophies from the hunt.

Judson Jones, a forty-eight-year-old lawyer of Le Sueur County, sat in the seat facing the robber booty, and next to Jones was a Minneapolis policeman. The policeman picked up one of the bridles, this one having a particularly harsh Mexican bit, and handed it to Jones. The lawyer ran his fingers along the bit and said that if Hoy and Bresette had been half as smart as the robbers, they would have more than bridles and horses to show for their efforts. Hoy, whom Jones had never met, happened to be sitting three seats ahead, and he apparently heard his name in the conversation—and he began to listen carefully.

The Minneapolis policeman next asked Jones what he thought of the attempts to capture the robbers. The lawyer, who had spent the past week in the field as a member of one of the posses, quickly answered, "I think Bresette and Mike Hoy have been completely out-generaled." Hoy clearly heard this last remark and jumped up out of his seat to face Jones.

"I am Mike Hoy. *Now* what have you got to say of him?"

"Nothing but what I have said, that Bresette and Hoy have been out-generaled," replied Jones calmly.

The bully Hoy, whose face had already turned bright red, began to swear. He threatened to throw Jones out the train window.

"You had better not try it," said Jones.

As the detective's tantrum grew worse, Hoy angrily told Jones he would not dare face him with a gun from the opposite end of the car, or even face him in a fistfight.

"I tell you what I dare do," said Jones. "I dare sit here and face you, Mr. Hoy, and I think you had better sit down."

Hoy glared for a moment, after which he plopped down into an empty seat, fuming. At the same moment, a man walked down from the front of the car and addressed Jones.

"You mustn't have any quarrel with this man. I know this man. This is Mike Hoy—he is a dangerous man."

Jones answered that he had no quarrel and was only expressing an opinion. The lawyer turned to talk with the man sitting next to Hoy and suddenly Hoy threw a swift punch with his left fist, hitting Jones on the right cheek with the force of a sledgehammer.

The lawyer, a slender man, spun around and tumbled forward, somehow grasping a seat so as not to fall completely to the floor. Several shocked passengers rushed forward to prevent the larger Hoy from killing Jones, saying, "That's enough, Hoy—hold on—don't strike him again."

Jones shortly came to his senses and returned to his seat, saying loudly to Hoy, "That blow won't pay you in the long run." When the train arrived at St. Peter, Jones carefully stepped off and walked straight to a doctor's office. The detective's blow had been so violent it had fractured Jones's cheekbone, pushing it in and permanently disfiguring his face. Had Hoy hit him an inch or two higher, the doctor said, Jones would likely be dead.

Hoy's attack made all the newspapers and just fed to the belief that much of the blame for the fugitives' escape lay at Hoy's feet. The *Saint Peter Tribune* pointed out that if such mild criticism could trigger such a violent response, then Hoy "had better commence fighting the whole Minnesota Valley, for there is scarce a man who is familiar with the facts but has indulged in much harsher criticism than that for which Mr. Jones now lies in bed."

Hoy and Bresette did not have to look far for reminders of their failures. Even the Minnesota press could not stop themselves from writing about how the outlaws had vanquished the manhunters:

Here were six men hunted by a thousand in a land comparatively strange to them. Every device was resorted to. Every rod of a vast extent of country was searched. The best detective talent was employed. The best woodsmen were engaged in the hunt. Citizens of every class deserted all else, and took up their arms. Yet almost in the face and eyes of eager pursuers, they have passed through the most carefully arranged traps. . . . Such determination, daring and perseverance was worthy of a better cause, and cannot but evoke the admiration even of those who most desire their extermination. Probably no men were ever more desperately set upon, nor more intrepid daring ever displayed by mortals. Houseless, footsore, hungry and poorly clad, they have passed on, and their miraculous escape excites more wonder than did their daring attempt at robbery.

But the Younger brothers and Charlie Pitts had not escaped. After Jesse and Frank left them, they trudged north until they found a road leading from Mankato. The fugitives followed this road due west. Cole would later say they were out to get some good horses at a farm he remembered that was near Madelia, a village of eight hundred people twenty-five miles southwest of Mankato. But the ragtag band, their various wounds seeping blood and pus, made little progress, camping in one patch of timber for two nights and another near Lake Linden for three.

Minnesota had become their living hell. The rain and cold continued to sap their strength, making their situation nearly unbearable. "The oldest inhabitant has no recollection of such persistent rain-storms as we have had during September thus far," reported the *Rice County Journal* on September 21. The outlaws were living that outside and were drenched by nearly every storm. Plus, they were always famished, surviving primarily on corn from the fields and one night a few chickens they were able to steal.

By now, they had left the Big Woods and were in the prairie country, which meant places to hide were farther apart. When they did travel, they did so under the cover of darkness. Cole walked with a cane he had carved from a stick. Bob's shattered elbow had begun to heal but not in a good way. He could not straighten his arm, nor could he control his fingers on his right hand. When they tried to sleep, Cole lay flat on his back so Bob could rest his arm across Cole's body. Cole had given up trying to remove his wet leather boots. He did not know it at the time, but his feet had been wet and swollen for so long his toenails were separating from his toes.

As the Youngers and Pitts pushed slowly west, one Madelia resident actually expected them. When Cole and Charlie scouted Madelia prior to the raid, they had lodged at a small hotel called the Flanders House, operated by forty-three-year-old Civil War veteran Thomas L. Vought. Colonel Vought, as he was known to the locals, had been intrigued by his guests with their broad-brimmed hats and dusters, their fine horses and saddles and their southern phrases. Cole and Charlie had identified themselves as railroad surveyors and had peppered Vought with questions about the area. Cole, who had registered as J. C. King, seemed to have already gained a familiarity with the locale, mentioning that he and his companion had been to a particular bridge that crossed an outlet between Armstrong and Strom Lakes, a few miles northeast of Madelia.

After Cole and Charlie left, Vought didn't really give them much thought—that is, until news of the Northfield Raid reached Madelia. He instantly thought of his two lodgers, and when the papers said one of the robbers had checked into another hotel as J. C. King, he had no doubts that his visitors were members of the outlaw gang. Suspecting that they might try to escape by crossing at Armstrong Lake, Vought gathered two volunteers and spent two nights guarding the bridge.

Seventeen-year-old Oscar Sorbel happened by while Vought and the Madelia men stood watch and asked what they were doing. They told him they were looking for the Northfield fugitives, and the young man instantly became their boon companion. The raid had been the most exciting thing to happen in Sorbel's short life, and now he was face-to-face with the actual manhunters. Vought knew the lad lived with his parents and six siblings on a small farm about five miles to the west, near the north shore of Lake Linden. And as they were about to return to Madelia, he gave Sorbel a thrill by asking him to keep a lookout for anyone matching the robbers' descriptions. If he saw any of them, he was to bring the news to Vought at the Flanders House as fast as he could.

"Gee!" Sorbel said wistfully, "I'd like to take a shot at those fellows with dad's old gun."

At 7:00 A.M. on Thursday, September 21, Oscar's father, Ole Sorbel, sat on a stool milking one of his cows out on the road in front of the family home. He looked up and saw two strangers walking by. One had reddish whiskers and the other a black mustache—Jim Younger and Charlie Pitts. The men passed on each side of Sorbel, running their hands gently along the back of the milk cow.

"Good morning," they said cheerfully.

Ole nodded a greeting as the strangers continued down the road.

Oscar was carrying empty milk pails up from the barn when the two men passed by. But he was able to catch a good glimpse of them and hurried up to the gate, where he waited until the strangers were out of hearing.

"There goes the robbers," Oscar whispered to his father. Ole looked up, thought carefully, and shook his head. They looked like "nice men," he said.

Oscar stepped through the gate and out into the road and studied the strangers' tracks. After a moment, he called to his father. "Look here," Oscar said, "I will show you how 'nice' they are." The tracks clearly showed impressions of the men's toes in the mud from holes in the soles of their boots.

"Well, never mind," Ole said. They had a lot of work to do that day, and he wanted to get the hay in as well. "Tend to your business," he told his son, pointing to one of the pails.

Oscar grabbed a pail and began milking, but he could not get the strangers out of his mind. They had to be the fugitives; he was sure of it. After milking one cow, he set the pail inside the fence and started walking briskly down the road in the direction the men had gone. He did not ask his father's permission. Ole yelled after the boy, warning him that if they were indeed the robbers, he might get shot, so he best take care.

Young Sorbel trailed the strangers until he saw where their tracks entered some woods. He did not follow them into the woods but proceeded cautiously to alert the nearest neighbors. At a house about one mile to the west, he got up on the roof to see if the robbers had left the woods. They had not. He then hurried to the top of a big hill nearby where he could see the different roads to New Ulm and Madelia and looked all about. But he saw no one.

He returned home to another surprise. While Oscar had been absent, two more strangers had come calling and asked for breakfast. His mother, Guri Sorbel, politely informed them it was not yet ready but would be soon. The men could not wait and instead asked for some bread and butter. They said they had been out hunting and fishing and asked where the best fishing was. Guri told her son that one of the men appeared to have an arm in a sling underneath his coat. This last bit of information excited the teenager even more. He wanted to return to one of the neighbors to warn them that there were four robbers on the loose, but Ole Sorbel, fearing his boy would be picked off by the outlaws, would not allow it. So Oscar found his twelve-year-old sister, Maria, and sent her to get the message out for him. Whether or not Oscar's parents knew about the errand he had given to his little sister is not known.

Oscar begged his father for a horse he could ride to Madelia, eight miles away, to alert the manhunters, but Ole said no—this robber business was a dangerous thing. Oscar was small for his age, but he could be as

Oscar Sorbel.

strong-minded as his father, and Oscar was not about to take no for an answer. Finally, his father gave in, but only on the condition that Oscar take the east road so as to keep out of sight of the fugitives. The horses were hitched to the farm wagon, but Oscar quickly removed one from the harness and jumped on its back. The nag was so fat that Oscar could hardly feel the animal's ribs. Nevertheless, he dug his heels into the horse's sides, urging it into a halfhearted gallop.

The muddy road made for tough going and quickly tired the poor animal. A mile and a half from Madelia, the horse tripped and tumbled to the ground, throwing Oscar from its back. Undaunted, Oscar jumped up, mud dripping from his face and arms, and got the horse back on its feet. He arrived in Madelia an hour after leaving his home, his exhausted mount covered with sweaty foam. Oscar rode straight for the Flanders House, all the while grandly shouting, "Robbers are around—if you want to make money, got to hurry up."

The first people Oscar encountered did not believe a word he said. Plastered head to toe with mud, the boy looked and acted half crazed, and everyone understood the robbers to be out of Minnesota, anyway. Fortunately, Oscar found Colonel Vought on the porch of the Flanders House—and nearby was James Glispin, a slight, undersized, twenty-eight-year-old sheriff of Watonwan County. Oscar jumped down from his horse and breathlessly told his story to Vought. Glispin stepped up and asked Oscar to describe the men. When Oscar mentioned that one of the strangers had a wounded arm, that settled it. Within five minutes, Glispin, Vought, and two other citizens were armed and mounted. As they rode out of town, Glispin left orders for as many volunteers as possible to get their guns and come on.

The incredible news that the robbers had been spotted just a few miles away raced through the village. Shops were suddenly closed as the men of the town scurried around for saddle horses and buggies. Those who could not find a mount started on foot. Oscar Sorbel, the proudest teenager in Minnesota, loaned his tired horse to a citizen and jumped into the back of a wagon for the ride home—and hopefully to the scene of the coming action.

We were very imprudent . . . in going to the house for food," Bob Younger would say later, "but we were so hungry."

And tired. After leaving the Sorbel place, they walked around the north end of Lake Linden and headed southwest, but Bob lagged behind. At one point that morning, he insisted on stopping in a field to rest. His companions urged him to keep moving; even if the Sorbel family believed their story about being sportsmen, a family member might tell someone else who would figure out that they were the robbers. Bob said the others could leave him if they wanted to, but they refused to abandon him. Finally, Bob got up and started walking again.

At approximately 11:00 A.M., as the outlaws approached the marshy outlet to Lake Hanska, they saw four men on horseback, one after the other, coming up fast on their trail. The rider in the lead, Sheriff Glispin, ordered the fugitives to halt. The outlaws broke into a run, splashed across the wide slough, and continued running due south toward the brushy thickets of the Watonwan River's north fork, a little under three miles away.

Glispin's party galloped up to the edge of the slough, which was too deep to cross with horses, and fired several shots at the fleeing outlaws, the balls whistling past their heads. But the fugitives were soon out of range.

It took precious time for Glispin to find a crossing for his horses, and that gave the robbers a good two miles between them and their pursuers. But the delay also brought Glispin more recruits, all now converging on the Watonwan. After navigating the slough and again reaching solid ground, the sheriff and his men spurred their horses and quickly closed the distance with the outlaws. As Glispin and a posse member galloped within shouting distance, the fugitives spun around and raised their revolvers.

"What do you want?" they called out.

Glispin pulled sharply on the reins of his horse and came to a halt. "Throw up your hands and surrender," he shouted.

"Come up closer," the robbers yelled, pointing to their pistols and explaining that they only had revolvers to fight with. If the posse would come closer, they would "give them a clatter."

The fugitives began walking briskly again toward the river. Glispin and his companion opened fire, white smoke streaming from their pistols. The Youngers and

Pitts fired behind them as they continued their retreat, forcing Glispin and the others to jump off their horses as bullets flew dangerously close, one shot drawing blood on the sheriff's mount. The gunfire popped back and forth until the outlaws ducked out of sight in the river's plum thickets.

The Youngers and Pitts reloaded their pistols and pushed through the brush to the river's bank. The Watonwan was less than thirty yards wide, but it had swollen from the rains and was running rapidly. The outlaws had no choice but to plunge in, holding their pistols above their heads. The cold, rushing water pulled against their coats and blankets, nearly sweeping the men off their feet, but they soon drew themselves up on the steep south bank. When they stepped out of the willows growing along the bank, they were in sight of the farm of Andrew Anderson, and they looked about quickly to see if there were any horses. Anderson's wife had heard the gunfire and saw the four men come out of the river. She ran screaming from the yard.

At that time, a small party from St. Paul was out hunting prairie chickens, and they saw the men fleeing across the prairie, followed by their pursuers, and quickly guessed that they had stumbled on the hunt for the Northfield bandits. The party consisted of Horace Thompson, president of the First National

Bank of St. Paul, his son, four ladies, and two children. Thompson had rented two light spring wagons in Madelia, each pulled by a pair of fine horses. After Thompson's party spotted the fugitives, they followed the hunt from the high ground on the south side of the river, stopping about five hundred yards short of the Anderson place.

Mrs. Anderson ran toward the Thompsons, shrieking that the robbers were coming. Thompson tried to calm the woman, who said her husband was working a field about a mile away. Thompson instructed her to go to her husband and tell him what was happening. He then told his son to fetch the shotgun shells with the heavy goose loads. They quickly switched out their shotgun shells, stepped in front of their wagons, and began walking slowly toward the robbers, who were clearly coming in their direction. Horace Thompson recalled that he "never saw four more robust and powerful looking men." The women of the party stood upon the wagon seats waving their scarves wildly, trying to attract the attention of the possemen.

Cole and the others were surprised to see the Thompson party. Hell, they thought, everybody, even the ladies, was after them. But the desperate men recognized the two teams and buggies as a godsend—they must have them. However, as the outlaws closed the distance, it became evident that the Thompsons were moving toward them as well, with weapons at their shoulders. Both parties halted just out of pistol range. The forty-nine-year-old Thompson watched as the Youngers and Pitts huddled together in conversation.

Believing that Thompson and his son might be armed with rifles, the outlaws turned to their left and stepped into some tall weeds. The fugitives crouched down and slowly followed a ravine back toward the riverbank. Thompson and his son advanced to the edge of a bluff, where they looked down and saw the robbers enter a copse of willows in an elbow of the river.

Sheriff Glispin had been forced to ride east for a mile before finding a place to cross the river, but Thompson now saw the sheriff and several horsemen approaching at a gallop and waved them in. Within thirty minutes, more than forty men were on the scene. Guards were hurriedly placed all around the five-acre patch that contained the fugitives, with some men on the north side of the Watonwan to block the gang if they attempted to recross it. The Youngers and Pitts, hunkered in the thickets, could hear the excited shouts and whoops of the manhunters closing in, like the high-pitched howls of hounds nearing the end of the chase. The outlaws were simply too exhausted to run again.

"Cole, we are entirely surrounded; there is no hope of escape," Pitts said. "We had better surrender."

Cole looked at his old friend Pitts and called him by his real name: "Sam," Cole said grimly, "if you want to go out and surrender, go on. This is where Cole Younger dies."

"All right, Captain," Pitts said, "I can die just as game as you can. Let's get it done."

To flush the fugitives, Sheriff Glispin turned to thirty-nine-year-old Captain William W. Murphy, who had arrived with several men from his farm four miles away. Murphy, a veteran of the Fourteenth Pennsylvania Cavalry, had been wounded three times in battle and had also spent time in a Confederate prison camp. His Civil War heroics were well known, and Murphy fully lived up to his reputation, immediately calling for volunteers to accompany him into the brush to root out the robbers.

The outlaws froze in place as they listened to Captain Murphy's call for men. They instantly looked at one another and then hurriedly pulled out all their revolvers, spinning the cylinders of each one to make sure every chamber contained a live round.

Cole spoke in a whisper: "Make for the horses. Every man for himself. There is no use stopping to pick up a comrade here, for we can't get him through the line. Just charge them and make it if we can."

Six men volunteered to join Captain Murphy, including Sheriff Glispin and Colonel Vought. Others were called to join the seven, but not a sound came from the remaining possemen, so Captain Murphy organized his brave handful in a skirmish line, each man five feet from the next. Do not shoot first, he instructed his men, as he intended to call out to the fugitives to surrender once he knew their location. But he told his men, if they did get into a shoot-out, they were to shoot low. The battle veteran had given this same advice countless times to the soldiers in his regiment, as it was well known that most soldiers in battle shot high, missing the enemy entirely.

Captain Murphy now gave the command to march, and the line slowly advanced north through the brushy bottom toward the riverbank. All eyes focused on the ground in front of the skirmishers, the agonizing tension rising with each step, but this sweep failed to disclose the fugitives, so Murphy turned his skirmishers on a sharp left wheel, Sheriff Glispin anchoring the end of the line on the riverbank. Once the men came even with Glispin, they marched west, pushing through thick willows, about five feet high.

Charlie Pitts, crouching in the willows with his comrades, spotted Sheriff Glispin coming toward him, and when the sheriff approached to about fifteen feet, Pitts jumped up and aimed his revolver at the sheriff.

Glispin, who held a single-shot rifle at the ready, saw the huge outlaw rise from the willows and quickly drew a bead on him. Both men fired almost simultaneously. Pitts fell forward like a brick and rolled over upon his back, dead. Glispin, unharmed, dropped to one knee to reload as the Younger brothers stood up and furiously fired their pistols, flame and smoke belching from the barrels.

The manhunters instantly returned fire on the outlaws, a spray of lead flying all through the brush. Across the river, several trigger-happy possemen blazed away into the willows, their bullets snipping twigs perilously close to Murphy's men. Captain Murphy fired all six chambers of his revolver and yelled over to Glispin that he needed to reload. The sheriff yanked his own loaded pistol from its holster and tossed it to Murphy. The captain began to move even closer forward, but then he suddenly jumped back when one of the outlaws' balls slammed into the right side of his stomach. He immediately reached down, expecting to feel blood soaking his clothing but instead felt his large briarwood pipe, now splintered, in his vest pocket. Later, when he pulled back his vest and shirt, all he could find was a slight bruise.

The Youngers were getting the worst of it, taking hits from all directions. Jim winced in pain as a ball pierced his right thigh. Then his head snapped back as one of Colonel Vought's bullets tore into the left side of his upper jaw and lodged in the roof of his mouth near the back of the throat. He fell to the ground unconscious, blood gushing from his face. Buckshot peppered Cole's head and back, causing him to grunt and suck in air. Next a ball penetrated his head behind his right eye. He collapsed near his brother, bleeding from his nose and mouth. Bob took a bullet in the right lung but remained standing, an empty revolver in his left hand. His elbow injury rendered him helpless to reload his pistol.

With the outlaws' guns silent, Captain Murphy shouted for a cease-fire and demanded that the fugitives surrender.

"Do not shoot any more," Bob Younger answered, "as the boys are riddled."

"Throw up your hands," ordered Sheriff Glispin.

Bob held up his left hand.

"Throw up the other!"

Bob explained that his other arm was broken, and Glispin told him to move to Captain Murphy and turn over his weapon.

As Bob stepped forward, he came onto higher ground and was suddenly visible to the possemen across the river. One fired at Younger, striking him under his arm and causing a flesh wound. Bob halted, angrily shouting, "Some damned son of a bitch shot me after I surrendered!"

Murphy yelled again for all the men to cease fire.

"Don't shoot him or I'll shoot you," Sheriff Glispin added for good measure. Bob then advanced to Murphy and handed him his pistol.

The other skirmishers converged on Murphy and Glispin, and all the men farther out began pouring into the willows to get a look at the defeated Northfield robbers. They heard the moans of Cole and Jim before they saw them on the ground. Jim sputtered and hacked, strangling on clots of his own blood. He pointed to his mouth as the possemen crowded around him.

Thirty-three-year-old John M. Robb of Madelia kneeled down and ran his finger between Jim's lips and cleared his mouth, causing the panic in Jim's face to fade away. Robb then told Jim to get up.

"They will shoot me," Jim slurred.

"No," said Robb. "You have surrendered, and I will stand between you and harm."

Jim stood up, unbuckled his ammunition belt, and handed it and his loaded Smith & Wesson to Robb. He had tossed aside his other revolver after emptying it in the fight, although it was quickly recovered—the souvenir-seeking started almost immediately.

Sheriff Glispin called for a wagon to transport his prisoners and Pitts's corpse to Madelia. Cole, eight fresh wounds in his body (not counting those from Northfield), slowly stood, and, along with Jim and Bob, was marched out of the willows to a place where the wagon could pull up. Several men dragged Pitts's body out of the brush by its feet. Colonel Vought walked up to Cole and instantly recognized him as the pleasant southern man who had lodged at his hotel under the name J. C. King.

"He recognized me," Vought remembered, "and held out his blood covered hand and shook my hand and called me landlord."

Captain Murphy could not help but feel compassion for the pathetic-looking fugitives, with their soiled and torn clothing, worn-out boots, and multiple bloody wounds. They were suffering incredible pain. After a moment of silence, Murphy spoke up: "Boys, this is horrible, but you see what lawlessness has brought to you."

There were those who felt no sympathy at all. Some, including several possemen who had remained silent when the call went out for volunteers to go in after the outlaws, clamored for killing the Youngers. With a disgusted look on his face, Sheriff Glispin put a quick stop to such talk.

Oscar Sorbel, who had been relegated to holding some of the possemen's horses during the capture, came up as the wagon arrived and helped load Pitts's body. Once the Youngers were aboard, Bob asked if he could have a chew of tobacco. Several men said he did not deserve any. But Oscar found a man who was willing to give up a ten-cent plug, and he handed it to the outlaw. Bob broke off half with his teeth and began to return the other half to Oscar, but the young man told him to keep it.

The wagon lumbered out of the Watonwan bottom and halted briefly on the bluff to the south. Glispin needed to rearrange his prisoners to make them more comfortable for the ride of several miles into town. Cole and Jim were in such bad shape, they looked like they might die before getting to Madelia.

The Horace Thompson party came up as the possemen tended to the outlaws. The ladies could see that the Youngers desperately needed bandages, and they untied the colorful scarves from around their necks and handed them over to the prisoners. These scarves were the same ones they had frantically waved earlier to get the attention of the manhunters.

At approximately 5:00 P.M., Sheriff Glispin's posse with its grizzled trophies pulled up at the end of

Madelia's Main Street. A large crowd—made even bigger by a special train from Mankato—had arrived at the site of the cavalcade. Many stood in buggies and wagons to get a better view. As the prisoners' wagon passed down the street, huzzahs went up as each throng got its first good look at the outlaw brothers.

Despite their exhaustion and aching injuries, the Youngers suddenly became alert, marveling at the crowd and reveling in the attention. Jim, blood dripping from his face in "clotted masses," waved his hat back and forth and even managed to let out a cheer or two. Cole, his right eye now swollen shut, waved his hand and took a gentlemanly bow.

Twenty-three-year-old Luther Pomeroy never forgot the sight. Cole "may have been an outlaw," he said years later, "but many of us that day admired his nerve, for he was a man who could take it on the chin and still smile."

The prisoners were delivered to the Flanders House and placed in rooms on the second floor, Cole and Jim sharing one with a single bed, while Bob was in another room about ten yards away. They were given clean clothes and told to take off their tattered and dirty garments. The town's doctors immediately set to work patching up the outlaws the best they could. Cole told the physicians his swollen and bruised feet hurt more than all his wounds. When his boots and makeshift socks were removed, his toenails came off with them.

Cole's and Jim's injuries appeared to be fatal. The doctors worried that the ball behind Cole's eye would cause inflammation of the brain, and it could not be removed safely. The doctors stepped away from the bed and discussed this wound and others, speaking in whispers so as not to upset their patients.

"Speak up, Doctor," Cole said. "You needn't mind me. It makes no difference to me. If I die within five minutes, it will be all right."

Jim's ghastly mouth wound presented the greatest challenge. The bullet had shattered his upper jaw so a large piece of the bone needed to come out. The doctors gave Jim morphine to reduce his suffering; afterward they performed the delicate surgery while Cole, lying at his brother's side, watched. When one of the doctors finally succeeded in cutting all the surrounding tissue and removed the section of bone, four teeth were still attached. But try as they might, the doctors could not find the bullet lodged behind the muscles near his throat.

Crowds remained around the Flanders House until late that evening, and a steady stream of men, women, and children were allowed to march up the stairs and peek into the rooms of the prisoners. Still, the guards forbade anyone but reporters from speaking to them. At one point, a man in the crowd shouted excitedly to "hang the skunks," offering to "knock their skulls in with the butt end of his rifle."

Sheriff Glispin immediately stepped before the throng and announced that he would shoot down the first man who attempted to touch the robbers. A lynching was actually the boys' greatest fear. They were almost sure they would be lynched the moment they were captured.

"I don't want any man to risk his life for us," Cole said to the sheriff, "but if they do come for us, give us our pistols so we can make a fight for it."

"If they do come, and I weaken," Glispin replied, "you can have your pistols."

The next morning's train brought more hordes anxious to view the outlaws. They were joined by an enterprising Mankato photographer named Elias F. Everitt, who had gotten permission to capture the outlaws' images on his glass plates. A chair was placed on the porch of the Flanders, and each brother was brought down, one at a time, for his "sitting." The whole affair made a fascinating show for the crowd on the street. After Everitt had exposed plates for all three robbers, one of the guards plopped down in the empty chair. The guard, a rough-looking character

Cole Younger, age
thirty-two, Madelia,
September 22, 1876.

Jim Younger, age
twenty-eight, Madelia,
September 22, 1876.

Bob Younger, age
twenty-two, Madelia,
September 22, 1876.

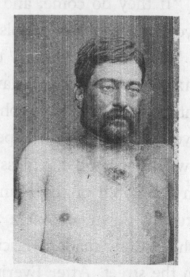

Charlie Pitts in death,
September 22, 1876.

with only one hand, wore a dirty shirt stained on the front with tobacco juice. As he settled into his seat, a young woman standing on her toes in the back of a farm wagon exclaimed, "Look, look, there is the worst looking one of them all."

Before leaving the Flanders House, Everitt made two more exposures. One was of Oscar Sorbel, the young Paul Revere of the Watonwan. Then the photographer lined up all seven manhunters who had bravely gone into the willows after the gang. These men would forever after be known as the Madelia Seven.

It was warm that morning, and Everitt had taken off his coat and draped it over a nearby clothesline that also held the tattered garments of the robbers. When he went to retrieve his coat, he discovered that the buttons were missing. The souvenir hunters had cut them off, just as they had all the buttons on the robbers' clothes.

Everitt also photographed Charlie Pitts, whose body had been lain out on ice in Madelia's tiny jail. But Charlie apparently did not keep well because his nose and mouth had become terribly swollen. The *Saint Peter Tribune* complained later that Everitt's photograph of the stiff corpse, a bullet hole plainly visible in the center of the chest, looked nothing like the outlaw who had visited St. Peter before the Northfield Raid: "[T]he man himself was a fine, genteel-looking person, instead of the gross, brutal rough indicated by the photograph."

The crowd was standing room only in the Flanders House as hundreds of people—eight at a time—filed past the robbers. Bob, his ruggedly handsome face without the slightest scratch, received several bouquets of flowers from admiring ladies. For most of the day, though, the scene was one big crying jag.

"The women were melted to sobs and strong men gave way to sympathetic tears," reported the *Saint Paul Dispatch*. "Prayers, ardent and fervent, were uttered,

The Madelia Seven. From left to right: Sheriff James Glispin, Captain William W. Murphy, G. A. Bradford, B. M. Rice, Colonel Thomas L. Vought, C. A. Pomeroy, and S. J. Severson.

and the two brothers [Cole and Jim] clasped each other's hands and gave way to apparent grief, their features quivering in every muscle, and the scalding tears rolling down their cheeks. Many believe in their contrition. Both brothers speak in feeling tones of their dead mother and living sister, and this touches the women wonderfully."

One sobbing woman stepped into Bob's room and asked the outlaw if he knew her.

"No, madam, I have not that pleasure," he said.

"Don't you know me?" she asked again.

"Indeed, I cannot recollect you, madam," Bob answered.

"Don't you remember the woman who gave you bread and butter?"

"Oh, yes, certainly, and most thankful were we for it."

"Oh forgive me, sir," she blurted out, "indeed, I did not intend to do it."

"I have nothing to forgive," Bob gently assured her. "You were very kind to us, and we shall not forget it."

"But forgive me, sir," she pleaded, "I did not mean to betray you."

"Why, really, madam, we never supposed you did. We do not blame you at all. We are only very grateful for what you did for us."

"But, sir, it was because you were at our house you were caught; but it was not my fault, indeed it was not."

Finally, to pacify the distraught woman, Bob forgave her, and she immediately brightened. Drying her tears, she said good-bye and left the room. But as soon as she stepped out of hearing, Bob turned to a reporter and asked the woman's name.

"Mrs. Sorbel," the reporter answered, "the mother of the lad who informed the people of your whereabouts."

"I shall never forget that name," Bob said.

A flood of telegrams came over the wires with reports of the capture and descriptions of the robbers. One telegram received by the *Saint Paul Dispatch* read:

ST. PETER, MINN., SEPT. 22.—WE HAVE SURREN-
DERED. MIKE HOY CAN NOW COME ON WITH SAFETY.
COLE YOUNGER

Written by some wag, the "Cole Younger" telegram subsequently appeared in newspapers across the state.

Several newspaper correspondents kept the outlaws occupied during their confinement at the Flanders. The boys admitted that they were the Younger brothers, but they refused to identify those killed or the two who broke the line at Lake Crystal. They made it a point, they said, not to speak of each other's affairs, only their own. Still, that did not stop others from trying to coax the Youngers into admitting that the two who had escaped—nearly everyone now believed they were Frank and Jesse—were the notorious James brothers. A correspondent for the *Saint Paul Dispatch* told Cole and Jim of a recent report (which would prove to be false) that the two had been captured and that one was dead and the other dying. The journalist referred to the captured bandits as the James brothers, even though this identification had not been part of the report.

This got the outlaws' attention, and they appeared to be genuinely distressed. Cole asked which one was dead, the smaller or the larger of the two. "Mind," Cole quickly added, "I don't say they are the James brothers."

But, the journalist insisted, the two men confessed that they were the James brothers.

"Did they say anything of us?" Cole asked.

"No."

"Good boys to the last," Cole said with a smile.

The other burning questions were who had killed cashier Heywood and why. Bob Younger admitted to the *Minneapolis Tribune* reporter that he was one of the three robbers who had gone into the bank, but he refused to say who committed the murder.

"[I]t was a bad piece of business and very foolish," he said. "It was not our intention to kill him; we have not wanted to kill anyone. It, of course, would do no good to kill the cashier, because then we couldn't get into the vault anyway. Of course, I cannot say what the motives of the man were when he shot, but I suppose he thought the cashier was reaching down under his desk for his revolver."

The correspondent replied: "Heywood was a brave fellow—do you not think so?"

"Well, I don't know," Bob answered. "I think it was more fear than bravery."

While the Youngers sparred with reporters, Sheriff Glispin sparred with pushy state officials. The Minnesota governor was in Philadelphia attending the Centennial Exposition when he heard the news of the capture. He immediately telegraphed his secretary in St. Paul to have the Youngers and the body of Pitts transported to the capital.

Glispin initially agreed but then changed his mind after consulting with several Madelia citizens. It seemed to them that the Twin Cities were trying to steal the show, when the prisoners properly should go to Rice

County, where there were warrants for their arrest, and where they would eventually be tried.

Sheriff Ara Barton of Rice County, along with a posse of twelve men, set out for Madelia on Friday, September 22. Changing trains in Mankato, Barton met a delegation from the governor on its way to Madelia for the same purpose. The two parties began a heated conversation, with Barton finally declaring that the Youngers were his prisoners, and he would be taking them to Faribault, the Rice County seat, by the most direct route. As a consolation of sorts, he agreed that the governor could have Pitts's body. The governor's delegation had no choice but to go along with Barton's decision. The prisoners were legally his.

Sheriff Barton and his deputies arrived at the Flanders House late that evening. Shortly after 6:00 A.M. the next morning, the Youngers were loaded in a wagon and driven to the Madelia depot. A mattress had been placed in the train's smoking car for Cole and Jim. The two were rapidly improving, but their doctors were still concerned about their condition, particularly the wound behind Cole's eye. Bob rode in a seat behind his brothers. Sheriff Glispin and the other members of the Madelia Seven, along with two doctors, accompanied Barton and his men.

It was not yet 7:00 A.M. when the train pulled into Mankato, where the sheriff's party were going to transfer the prisoners to the Winona & St. Peter line a few blocks away. Huge crowds had already gathered at both depots. The Mankato mayor had made arrangements to put the outlaws on display in the railroad agent's office, which had a large window that fronted the station platform. Approximately a thousand people filed past the open window as the brothers ate their breakfast. When it was time to go to the Winona depot, throngs surrounded the wagon with the prisoners and ran after it.

"A few foolish men and women shook hands with them and begged tokens of remembrances," reported the *Mankato Union.*

The outlaws found similar receptions at each stop as their train chugged eastward, the curious plastering their faces against the windows of the cars, some of the bolder ones even attempting to get inside. Bob "sat complaisantly twirling his moustache during most of the stops at the stations and chatted affably with the officers and others who occupied seats adjacent," observed a *Minneapolis Tribune* reporter. Cole passed the time reading a detailed account of the capture in a copy of the *Mankato Review.*

The last transfer occurred at Owatonna, where the officers forced the crowd back with shouts and orders, quickly ushering their prisoners into the caboose of a freight train that pulled out immediately for Faribault, sixteen miles north.

The use of a freight train for the final leg of the journey had been intentional, Sheriff Barton correctly predicting that Faribault's citizens would be expecting the robbers on a passenger train. But although there were relatively few people at the depot when the prisoners were led from the caboose, word of their arrival raced through the town's streets like a raging flood, and the sheriff hardly had the Youngers in the open wagon before the excited crowds began to form. By the time he had his prisoners locked up in their cells, most of downtown Faribault seemed to be heading up to the jail. But Barton wouldn't allow anyone to see the prisoners until the afternoon, by which time the doctors had removed several bullets from the men and again dressed their wounds.

The number of visitors was respectable, yet it hardly prepared the sheriff and his officers for the next day's circus, when nearly four thousand people passed through the jail to see the Younger brothers.

When the news of the capture of the Youngers reached St. Louis, Chief of Police James McDonough suddenly changed his mind about the identities of the Minnesota raiders. "I am now convinced that the 'old mob' were at Northfield, Minn.," he wrote Missouri governor Charles Hardin on September 22. He assured the governor that should "any of the uncaptured ones find their way into Jackson or Clay Counties, I will be prepared to receive them."

In the meantime, McDonough would leave that night for St. Paul with one of his men, Russell Palmer, "who can fully identify all the captured robbers, dead or alive" (Palmer, thirty-six years old, had lived for a short time with the Youngers' uncle). McDonough had already wired St. Paul's chief not to bury any dead outlaws until he had a chance to view their bodies.

McDonough and Officer Palmer, along with Calvin B. Hunn, superintendent of the United States Express Company, reached St. Paul Sunday morning, September 24. Along with St. Paul chief of police James King, they went directly to the capitol to examine Pitts's corpse, where they found the state's surgeon general in the process of embalming the decomposing outlaw. McDonough immediately confirmed the identification of the dead man as Charlie Pitts, real name Wells, based on a photograph he brought and Hobbs Kerry's detailed description. Every physical detail Kerry provided the chief matched up, McDonough explained, even down to the black hair on the back of Pitts's hands. McDonough's party also carefully examined the Ira Sumner photographs of the two bandits killed in Northfield and agreed they were Miller and Chadwell, the names provided by the Kansas City chief of police.

Making quick work of their visit to the capital, the next order of business was to see the prisoners in Faribault. At 1:30 P.M., they boarded a special train consisting of an engine and "an elegant passenger coach." Several local dignitaries, state officials, and journalists traveled with the St. Louis party, including St. Paul's mayor, chief of police, the governor's secretary, and John T. Ames of Northfield. At Mendota Junction, six miles down the line, the train took on two cars containing a large party of Minneapolis dignitaries: the city's mayor and chief of police, as well as a large number of women. More than seventy people stepped off the special train in Faribault at about 4:00 P.M.

The St. Louis officers found Cole reclining on a couch outside the cells reading a newspaper, a cigar stuck in his mouth. A boy fanned the outlaw to keep him cool.

"Hello, Cole," Officer Palmer greeted the bandit, "how are you?"

Palmer sat down on the couch next to the outlaw, and the two talked a long time, Cole giving Palmer verbal messages for his friends in Missouri. The

St. Louis policeman also recognized Bob, who matched the descriptions assembled by Chief McDonough. But McDonough and Palmer were not at all sure about Jim.

According to McDonough's information, Jim Younger had never fully recovered from a wound in the thigh he supposedly received in the Roscoe gun battle with the Pinkerton men. McDonough had Jim stripped, and after failing to find a wound or scar in the outlaw's thigh, he told Sheriff Barton that the prisoner could not be Jim Younger. Jim did not have the stamina to journey to Minnesota, he declared. No, this man was a Texas desperado named Calvin "Cal" Carter, formerly of Missouri.

McDonough's investigation had convinced him that Cal Carter was "the eighth man of the gang," having filled the place of Kerry. Strangely enough, Officer Palmer, who claimed to be well acquainted with Carter from his time in Jackson County, insisted that Jim was none other than the Texas outlaw. Palmer had never met Jim Younger, only the brothers Bob and Cole.

Sheriff Barton later told Cole about the identification of Jim as Carter, causing Cole to nearly swallow his cigar.

"He's a Younger, and our brother as we have told you," Cole said, somewhat indignant. "If you want to test it, bet them $1,000 that he is our brother, and we will back you and prove it if we have to bring his mother!"

A *Saint Paul Dispatch* reporter summed up the confusion best, writing that McDonough's doubt "seems to arise from the fact that the presence of Jim Younger in Minnesota is not consistent with the detectives' theory of his movements, but then, according to the same theory, none of the Younger-James gang of desperadoes could have had a hand in the Northfield tragedy."

That evening, as the special train rolled north from Faribault on its return journey, the passengers took a vote on what should become of the Youngers. Seventy-one votes were for hanging the boys. Six voted not to hang them, and three were undecided. All the ladies were in favor of hanging, with one young woman adding the following qualification to her vote: "Hang all except Bob."

Eight
The Pursuit of the James Boys

The detectives . . . think the capture of the James boys only a matter of time. Parties have been sent out from St. Louis and other points, but Cole knowingly remarked that they are where they won't get them now.

—THE MINNEAPOLIS TRIBUNE, SEPTEMBER 25, 1876

O ver the past two weeks, there had been so many false reports about the outlaws that the first telegrams with the news that four of the Northfield robbers had been surrounded near Madelia were received with biting cynicism. By nightfall of the twenty-first, it was confirmed that three robbers had been captured and one killed, creating a great euphoria across the state. But nothing compared to the jubilation in Northfield.

"The people were wild," Carleton student Thomas Hughes wrote to his parents and siblings. "Last evening was like a regular Fourth of July night. A huge bonfire was made in the square in the middle of town. Cannon, torpedoes, firecrackers, and guns were fired 'till near midnight. The band was also out."

Adelbert Ames saw the great bonfire and flash of guns that night, too, writing his wife that "Everybody talks and laughs with everybody else, and all is happiness."

But even in that happiness, talk turned to the James brothers, the last of the robbers still on the run. People hoped there would soon be news that these two evildoers had been overtaken or shot dead in the Dakotas or Iowa. With six of the eight gang members now dead or jailed, the citizens of Northfield had to believe the chances of this happening were good.

They did not know brothers Jesse and Frank James.

Three and a half hours after stealing Elder Rockwood's fine iron-gray mares on the early morning of September 15, the James brothers appeared at a farm about two miles northwest of Madelia. The outlaws dismounted and asked the woman of the house for something to eat. She told them breakfast was not ready but soon would be. The brothers said they did not want breakfast but would appreciate a loaf of bread. She encouraged the pair to wait, but when they declined, she gave them the bread, and they paid her ten cents.

Jesse was bareheaded, having accidentally lost his hat when he and Frank were shot at by the Lake Crystal guard. He asked the woman if there might be an old hat about the place, explaining that he had lost his. There was no old hat, she replied, but they had just bought a new one for their boy. Jesse talked her into selling the boy's hat for $1.50.

The brothers also purchased two cloth sacks that they filled with straw or hay and tied to their horses' backs—the brothers had been riding the mares bareback. When one of the outlaws pulled out a large roll of bills to pay the woman's husband for the sacks, the farmer's eyes nearly popped out of his head. The roll was "as large as his arm," and the farmer saw lots of fifty- and one-hundred-dollar bills as the outlaw flipped through it.

Before leaving, Frank dressed the wound in his right leg. The farmer studied Frank curiously as he did this, noting that the wound looked like an old sore. When the outlaws were ready to leave, the farmer helped both men into the saddle. They appeared to be "badly used up," he would later tell the authorities.

Jesse and Frank rode the grays hard all day, covering a good forty miles (and showing just how much Bob Younger had been slowing them down). At sundown, they pulled up to the home of a German farmer five miles south of the town of Lamberton. The farmer gave the boys a puzzled look. Their makeshift saddles were one thing, but their horses were larger than ones used for riding and were obviously a team intended for pulling. The brothers said they had had an accident with their wagon, forcing them to abandon it, and the man appeared satisfied.

They asked the farmer if they could stay there for the night, and he immediately told them to get down off their horses and come in. He noticed that both Frank and Jesse were extremely stiff and favored their right legs. They continued to lie to their host, telling him their injuries had been a result of the wagon mishap. But the German's later statement that both men had wounds in the right leg was the first evidence that the Lake Crystal guard's snap shot had struck at least one of them, that outlaw being Jesse.

The German dressed Frank's wound, but Jesse didn't show his injury. The German thought it was strange that both men slept in their clothes, but the outlaws were not about to let him see the impressive arsenal beneath their rubber coats. At about 7:00 A.M.

the next day, they thanked the German and told him they were going to head into Lamberton. He watched as they rode away, but after riding north for a quarter mile, the brothers suddenly turned at the corner of a cornfield, dug their spurs into the sides of the grays, and galloped south across the prairie.

As the authorities began to hear about these encounters and other sightings, the posses raced to get ahead of the fugitives so they could intersect their route. The brothers were most likely fleeing southwest, but the chances of blocking their retreat, with so much territory to cover and the pair moving so rapidly, were slim. On the same night that the brothers lodged with the German farmer, Mike Hoy's squad had been camped just eight miles to the south. It might as well have been a hundred.

About noon on Saturday, September 16, Sheriff William H. Dill of Winona County, Detective Bresette, and more than twenty men guarded three likely routes south of Lake Shetek, in the direct path of the outlaws. There was no sign of the brothers until dark, when two of Dill's scouts came galloping up and said two men on the gray mares had visited a house on the Des Moines River not five miles away at 2:00 P.M. The outlaws told the woman at the house they were after horse thieves and she gave them her bread, milk, and meat—which they devoured while sitting astride their steeds and then rode to the southwest.

Sheriff Dill located their trail the next morning and sent this message to General Pope: "We struck the trail of the two fugitives, still on the gray horses, five miles south of here. We have started after them, and are in hot pursuit."

Dill neglected to say that the outlaws had avoided his checkpoints the day before and were now seventeen-plus hours ahead of him—too far to have much hope of catching the James brothers. Dill and Bresette would never even lay their eyes on the boys.

Frank and Jesse rode all through the night Saturday, and on Sunday morning, September 17, arrived at the farm of Charles and Sarah Rolph on the west bank of Rock Creek, about nine miles northeast of the town of Luverne. Charles was away from the house so Sarah greeted them. They asked for breakfast, and, without the slightest hesitation, she invited them into her home. Ten days after the raid, there were still people like Mrs. Rolph who had not heard of the robbery or the great manhunt.

The brothers had trouble getting off their horses because of their injuries and how many hours they'd spent in the saddle. They shuffled along, hardly able to lift their legs. Over breakfast, Jesse said something had startled their team, causing a runaway, which wrecked their wagon before they could get the animals under control. He said Frank had received two broken ribs in the accident. Sarah noticed that Frank was suffering so much he could hardly sit up to eat his breakfast. Jesse's stiffness, he told her, came from a recent bout of rheumatism.

Frank and Jesse kept their rubber coats on at the table, even though Sarah offered to hang them up. And when they paid her for breakfast, they reached up under their coats instead of unbuttoning them. Mounting the grays to leave was even more interesting to watch. The men finally led the horses next to a fence, stepped up on the fence rails, and then, their faces contorted in pain, slid onto the horses' backs. Before riding away, they asked Sarah if there was a telegraph office in Luverne. She thought they wanted to send a message about their broken wagon, but Frank and Jesse were trying to figure out how much time they might have before their visit was telegraphed to the posses.

Telegraph or not, word got out quickly about the boys being at the Rolph farm. Charles's brother-in-law visited later that morning and told Sarah and Charles about the Northfield robbery. They looked at each other, stunned. Charles left immediately to go to

Luverne to give the alarm. On his way to town, he saw the outlaws in the distance, moving slowly southwest, their horses nearly played out.

When Charles reached Luverne about noon, he told Sheriff Ezra Rice of Rock County everything Sarah had told him about her visitors. They "looked enough alike to be brothers," he said. One was taller than the other, the taller man having sandy whiskers. The shorter man had a sandy mustache. And one of them wore a fine pair of boots with small heels and square toes.

Within minutes, several parties set off on the bandits' trail, including Sheriff Rice with three men. Rice caught up to the outlaws, at which time the sheriff suddenly became timid. He pulled out a rifle, and the bandits were within easy rifle range, but the sheriff chose not to get into a gun battle with the Missouri desperadoes, even though he had the advantage in weapons and men. In a move that would be roundly criticized, Rice chose to follow the two fugitives at a distance, eventually abandoning the chase that night.

About dusk, Frank and Jesse reached the farm of Andrew Nelson on Split Rock Creek, in Dakota Territory. The Nelsons' sod home was located a few miles downstream from the jagged quartzite cliffs of today's Palisades State Park and about twenty miles southwest of Luverne. They found Nelson, a native of

Sweden, sitting on a fence. Nelson lit his pipe as they talked, and the brothers asked him several questions about the fords and roads. Finally, Frank, who had been eyeing the farmer's stable, asked the man if he intended to sit there all night. The boys had left their coats open, and Nelson could see their revolvers. He took Frank's question as a strong hint, answered no, and went into his house.

Frank and Jesse led the grays to the stable, brought out two black horses, and transferred their straw-filled saddles. The mares had been as good as their reputation, having carried the brothers for at least 150 miles. But now the animals had raw backs and cruel gashes in their sides due to the brothers' unrelenting pace. As Jesse and Frank were about to leave, Nelson's teenage son ran out of the house and asked them not to take the blacks. The outlaws quickly told the young man there were at least four men on their trail, and they had no choice.

As they rode off, one of the brothers gave the lad a message for their pursuers. The newspapers later described the message as "a vulgar invitation."

Young Nelson may have told the Jameses about a defect with the blacks. If not, they soon discovered it: one of the horses was completely blind and the other was blind in one eye. After about twelve miles, the brothers stole a pair of gray geldings to replace the blacks. The fugitives boldly passed through the town of Sioux Falls in the middle of the night and, two miles south of town, stopped the stage en route to Yankton. They asked the driver where he was going and asked about a certain road.

When the driver asked them where they were going, the outlaws rode off without answering. The time was 3:30 A.M.

Frank and Jesse were smart to keep out of sight during daylight hours because there were posses scouring the countryside along the Big Sioux River, and telegraphs were alerting the communities south of Sioux Falls that they were likely in the path of the Missouri-bound outlaws. About dusk, the fugitives found a place to stay with an unsuspecting Norwegian immigrant named Ole Rongstad (or Rogustad), seven miles northeast of the town of Canton. They told the sixty-four-year-old Norwegian they were laborers looking for work. Early the next morning, September 19, the bandits continued south, determined to cross the Big Sioux. On the road, they encountered two men, both driving teams. The outlaws unholstered their revolvers, leveled them at the terrified men's heads, and told them a horse trade was about to take place. Jesse and Frank picked out the two best horses from the lot and rode off.

A short time later, a small posse, which included a mixture of locals and a Minnesota squad of eight men from the Worthington area, spotted the Jameses as they splashed across the Big Sioux into Iowa. Three of the pursuers rode a good distance in advance of the main posse. Not keeping together was a big mistake, but an even greater blunder was that the three manhunters in the lead were *unarmed*. As Jesse and Frank galloped up the side of the bluff overlooking the Big Sioux, the three possemen boldly crossed the river right after them.

Reaching the top of the bluff, the outlaws stopped and got down from their horses. Suddenly, bullets began whistling past the surprised pursuers, who, because of the distance, saw the puffs of smoke in front of the outlaws' outstretched arms before hearing, a split second later, the reports of the revolvers. One of the possemen's horses reared when a bullet ripped through its neck. The possemen could instantly see that they might actually get killed, so they turned and raced for cover. Frank and Jesse got back on their horses and galloped away over the hills to the southeast.

The posse decided they needed reinforcements (preferably men with guns), so they abandoned the hot trail of the outlaws and headed for Beloit, just across the Big Sioux from Canton. Within an hour, approximately twenty-five men from Canton and Beloit had answered the call and were headed out to capture Jesse and Frank. But soon after hitting the trail, claps of thunder echoed overhead, followed by sheets of rain. In only a few minutes, the heavy, pelting drops had washed out all trace of the outlaws' horses.

A little past twelve noon on Wednesday, September 20, Sioux City doctor Henry Mosher received an urgent message asking him to come to the home of Rudolph Mann, twenty-five miles northeast of town on the west fork of the Little Sioux River. Mann's wife, Phoebe, was seriously ill. The forty-year-old doctor dropped everything, grabbed his medical case, and walked to Broadbent's livery stable. The roads were in terrible shape from the rain, and the doctor dared not take a buggy through the remote, broken country between Sioux City and the Mann place. Instead, he hired a stout bay horse with a good saddle and bridle.

After about ten miles, Mosher became concerned that he had strayed from his route. He saw a man working in the distance, rode up to him, and said he was headed for the Mann place. The man, a German, sent Mosher to a road about a half mile away that ran parallel to the road he was now on. Mosher tipped his

hat to the German and started across the prairie for
this other road. But he still worried that he might be
going the wrong way, and with the Mann woman desperately needing his attention, he could not afford to
get lost. Soon after he left the German, Mosher spotted two men riding toward Sioux City. Hoping these
men were locals, he changed his course to intercept
them.

The doctor got to within sixty yards of the pair when
he shouted, "Hold on!"

The men stopped and turned their horses to face
Mosher, who rode up to within a few feet of them.
The taller of the two, Frank James, rode a bay. Mosher
saw that Frank's hands were white, long, and slender,
and he had a long, thin face. He wore black pants, a
snuff-colored coat and vest, a fine shirt made of ladies'
cloth, and a felt hat. The blacking on Frank's expen-
sive calf boots had worn off from traveling through the
wet grass and mud, and the boots had several holes.
Frank's expression struck the doctor as "the highest
degree intelligent and dignified, resembling the countenance of a Presbyterian minister."

Jesse rode a gray horse. Mosher thought Jesse
exhibited intelligence also, and noted that he was well
proportioned and muscular, probably weighing 150
pounds, and had a squarely built face with firmly set

lips. He wore a striped cotton or gingham shirt with no collar, and his gray pants and coat were heavily soiled. Both Jesse and Frank had a mustache and whiskers that appeared as if they had been roughly trimmed with shears. Jesse's hair was sandy brown, while Frank's had a reddish cast. Everything about the pair suggested "hard travel."

"Do you live about here?" Mosher asked.

"We do."

"Do you know a family here by the name of R. Mann?"

"We do."

"Where does he live?" the doctor asked, relieved that he had found someone who knew the family. But the outlaws now became vague, never really answering his questions. The doctor was about to ask more questions when one of the outlaws suddenly spoke up: "Who are you?"

"I am Dr. Mosher, of Sioux City, and I am going to visit a patient. Are you hunting the robbers?"

"We are. Can you tell us anything about them?"

Mosher actually knew a good deal about the robbers and the robber hunt, all of which he proceeded to tell the brothers. A large sheriff's posse from Sioux City was on the fugitives' trail at that very moment, he told them, and there was a very good chance the posse would catch the outlaws this time. As Mosher spoke, Jesse and Frank slowly urged their horses forward until the brothers were on either side of the doctor.

When the doctor finished, Jesse said, "We guess you are one of the robbers, and you had better go with us."

This surprised and angered Mosher. "Such smart, intelligent-looking men as you ought to know better," he said. "You know I do not look like a robber."

Mosher had hardly finished uttering the word *robber* before two big revolvers were pointed at his head.

"We are two of the Northfield boys," Jesse said, his blue eyes blazing. "And you are a detective, and, God damn you, we will kill you!"

The blood drained out of Mosher's face. Never in his wildest imagination had he supposed he would encounter the Northfield ruffians. He swiftly raised his open hand in the air.

"Stop! I am Dr. Mosher and nobody else! Give me a chance! If I am not he, shoot me!"

Jesse and Frank looked at each other. They were highly suspicious because this man had come up on their trail as if he'd been following them, and he seemed to know far too much about the robber hunt. Slowly, the brothers lowered their revolvers until the shiny weapons pointed at Mosher's chest.

"We are honorable robbers," Jesse said, "and if you are Dr. Mosher, we won't shoot you. Hand me your pistol and get down from your horse!"

Mosher dismounted, telling the brothers he carried no weapon. Frank took the reins of Mosher's horse in one hand while keeping his pistol trained on the doctor with the other. Jesse holstered his revolver and slid off his horse. He ran his hands inside Mosher's coat and along the man's torso, finding no revolver. Jesse then took Mosher's medicine case and opened it. It contained several vials of medicine and nothing more. Mosher certainly appeared to be what he claimed, but Jesse and Frank were not satisfied quite yet. Jesse next removed Mosher's overcoat and rubber coat from behind his saddle. He unrolled the garments and carefully went through all the pockets.

There was a farmhouse not far from where they were, and soon the entire family stood in the yard taking in the odd scene, talking to one another and gesturing at the men with the guns. Jesse got on the doctor's horse and rode over to the family. He told them he was one of the bandit hunters and asked if there was anyone who lived nearby named Mann and if they knew if anyone in the household was sick. Members of the family said yes to both questions. Jesse then asked if they had heard of a Dr. Mosher of Sioux City. Again, the answer was yes.

Jesse reined his horse around and rode back, chuckling as he neared Mosher and brother Frank. "Doc, I guess you are right, but we'll have to keep you till after dark."

"But I am in a hurry," the doctor protested. "My patient is very sick, and I must go."

"Oh, we'll take you right there," Jesse said. "Get on the gray horse and come with us."

As the three men ambled toward the West Fork, Frank behind Mosher with his gun trained on the doctor and Jesse in the lead, Jesse remained talkative. Suddenly, he blurted out, "Are you Dr. Mosher?"

"Yes."

"Hell! You are not him. I know Dr. Mosher. I have been in his office twice in Chicago, and you are not the man."

Mosher thought either Jesse was trying to get his goat or he was crazy—maybe both. "I am Dr. Mosher and nobody else," he said.

The doctor had not had his lunch when he received the urgent message from Rudolph Mann, so by 4:00 P.M., he was famished, and he told his captors so. They said they were hungry, too. As they neared a small farm, Frank took the doctor to a nearby grove while Jesse rode up to the house. He soon returned loaded down with bread, butter, and cake and gave the doctor first pick, before passing any to Frank or taking anything for himself. Mosher accepted some bread and butter, but he passed on the cake.

"Take some, Doctor," Jesse said, holding the cake out in front of him. "You needn't be afraid; we haven't put anything in it to hurt you." (The ever-suspicious Jesse was always scared that someone was trying to poison him.)

"But I never eat cake," the doctor replied, drawing a strange look from the brothers.

The party shortly came to the house of a farmer named Wright. Frank kept Mosher back as Jesse rode ahead and knocked on the door. Jesse had found some of Mosher's business cards while going through the doctor's clothes, and now he presented a card to Mr. Wright, stating that the doctor was on his way to attend to Mrs. Mann but his buggy had broken down, and they were taking him down by horseback. The doctor wanted to know if Mr. Wright might have a saddle they could borrow for a day or two. The farmer gladly gave Jesse a saddle.

Jesse returned very pleased with himself, taking great delight in telling how he had tricked farmer Wright out of a saddle. Jesse and Mosher now helped Frank, stiff and weak, off his horse. Mosher got a good look at the hole in Frank's bloodstained pants, just above the right knee. Frank said he got the wound at Northfield. Frank then removed the hay sack he had been using for a saddle, pointed to it, and said to Mosher, "You can get that for [a] saddle tomorrow when you come back."

And then, in a boastful tone, Frank added, referring to himself, "The man that shot Heywood has ridden one hundred miles in the last twenty-four hours."

Jesse placed Mr. Wright's saddle on Frank's horse, and Jesse and Mosher helped "the man that shot Heywood" to get back up. The brothers seemed more relaxed now, and the doctor was chatting pleasantly with the two. At some point, Jesse reached into his pocket, pulled out a piece of clean white paper, no rumples or creases whatsoever, and began reading a description of one of the detectives who had traveled to St. Paul and Northfield to help the authorities, possibly Detective Larry Hazen.

The brothers had initially thought the description matched up well with Dr. Mosher, which is why they were suspicious. No one knows where they got the paper.

"Tell the bankers of Sioux City when we come there not to do as Heywood did," Frank said, "but to give up the keys and there will be no trouble." Jesse added that "they were not robbing farmers, or the poor, but were trying to put down monopoly by taking from the men who were robbing the poor, and they were holding a good hand at it, too!"

Near dark, they met a man on the road driving a team of mules and asked for directions to the Mann place. Then they rode on.

"Remember when we let you loose," Frank warned, "to do just as we tell you to. If you do, it will be all right. If you don't, it won't."

About 8:00 P.M., they stopped and ordered the doctor to get off his horse and take off his pants. Frank then got down and removed his own pants, exchanging them with the doctor. "Hadn't you better let the doctor dress your wound now?" Jesse asked his brother. Frank said nothing.

Frank also took the doctor's drawers, socks, and coat. Jesse dismounted and claimed Mosher's rubber overcoat, giving the doctor his old one, which had several bullet holes. Jesse said it had been shot full of holes while he was on horseback.

"Are you ready?" Jesse finally asked Mosher.

"I am."

"Do you see the light yonder?" Jesse said, pointing to a single, flickering orb about a mile distant.

"I do."

"That is Mann's house."

Jesse was lying, of course. It was not Rudolph Mann's house. The brothers had only wanted to get the doctor far enough away from Sioux City that he wouldn't be able to spread the alarm before morning.

Jesse took Mosher by the shoulders and walked him a few feet forward, guiding him. "Go for that light," he said. "Don't you look around or turn to the right hand or the left. Run!"

Mosher now remembered the fear he'd had when he first met up with the outlaws. He was convinced that these murderers intended to shoot him in the back. He ran like hell into the darkness—or tried to; Frank's pants were a good six inches too long. After going some distance, Mosher stumbled into a big slough more than four hundred yards wide with water up to his waist, but he did not stop. When he reached the house, he nearly collapsed from exhaustion. The owner, a German, listened to the doctor's incredible tale and gave him a place to stay the night.

Mosher started for Sioux City the next morning, the twenty-first, arriving about noon. Frank's bloody pants with the bullet hole were enough evidence to convince the authorities that Mosher had really encountered the Northfield robbers. The doctor would later state that Jesse, too, had a wound, just above the heel. Mosher stayed in town only long enough to report his experience with the robbers and get more medicines from his office (the Jameses had taken his medicine case). He then rented a team and buggy from the same livery stable and left again to care for Phoebe Mann.

After hearing Mosher's tale, Woodbury County's sheriff, John M. McDonald, suspected the fugitives would continue to move in a southeasterly direction, possibly to Denison, on the Chicago & North Western Railroad. Warnings flashed ahead over the telegraph, and descriptions of the outlaws were given to railroad conductors in case the outlaws slipped on board a train.

But several exciting reports that came in over the next couple of days placed the robbers all over the map. One had them on the bluffs of Broken Kettle Creek, north of Sioux City. Another claimed the fugitives hired a farmer northwest of Le Mars to take them in his buggy several miles south, telling him they were after the "damned robbers." The farmer and his buggy had not been seen since.

Later reports confirmed Sheriff McDonald's suspicions. A posse "armed to the teeth" under Plymouth County sheriff James Hopkins took up the bandits' trail at the point they parted with Dr. Mosher. This posse traced the brothers to the Little Sioux River, which the outlaws swam with their horses, and then southeast to the Maple River near Ida Grove. The Jameses were on no particular road, often cutting across country. Several farmers spotted them, riding by at a gallop. When the outlaws did stop for food and water, they told the curious they were after horse thieves.

Near Ida Grove, Jesse and Frank stopped for a few minutes to talk to a little girl out in the road. They asked her what she was eating, and she told them a raw potato. This made the brothers laugh. They joked with the girl for a bit, politely declined her offer of some of the raw potato, and, spurring their horses, dashed away. When last seen, Jesse and Frank appeared to be riding for the North Raccoon River, below Sac City.

Sheriff Hopkins's posse and another formed later at Correctionville on the Little Sioux, the last two posses on the outlaws' trail, abandoned the pursuit on the night of September 23. As with previous posses, they had not been able to match the brothers' speed and near superhuman stamina. "The robbers had two days' the start of the sheriff's party, as well as our own, and were making good time," wrote one posse member, "and we concluded to let someone else head them off."

But with no more sightings of the outlaws, there was little interest in manhunting. "It is a pity that more efforts have not been set forth to capture these two villains," lamented an Iowa newspaper. Aside from the two posses that had recently given up, "nothing has been done in this state." And nothing else would be done. Jesse and Frank James had simply disappeared, as they always did.

Chief McDonough hoped and prayed Jesse and Frank would make it home to Missouri so he would have a chance to capture them. He told Governor Hardin he had posted Sergeant Morgan Boland and a squad of officers in the northwest part of the state, "guarding their crossings, and haunts." But Boland's squad consisted of only a handful of men; Jesse and Frank would be able to gallop around them all day, and they would never know it. And the detectives who staked out hot spots like Kearney, Missouri, were embarrassingly easy to pick out, especially by Mrs. Zerelda Samuel. She found that the detectives invariably passed themselves off as either itinerant sewing machine salesmen or lightning rod salesmen. Not long after the Northfield Raid, she called the bluff of the lightning rod men, by telling them she would pay them well to come out to the farm and put up three rods. But the men never showed.

"I was sorry they did not come," she said later. "Lightning would never have troubled them again."

On the other hand, McDonough did have trusted informants in Clay and Jackson Counties who were looking out for the brothers to return. Once McDonough heard from even just one of these spies, he would order his men to swoop in. They would nab the surprised outlaws, just like Hobbs Kerry.

"I feel assured of their capture, should they make for the state," he wrote confidently to the governor. It would be his greatest achievement as a law officer, bringing him lasting fame as the man who brought down the infamous James brothers.

During the first week of October, McDonough got the news he had been waiting for: the James boys were hiding out at two rural homes in Jackson County. Chief McDonough immediately sent thirty-four-year-old Boland, Officer Russell Palmer, and two other policemen to work the case. Two of the officers hired out as woodcutters at Independence, although one man spent most of his time on the town square and at the local livery, listening to the gossip and watching.

Very soon, Boland told the chief the report was true. A man matching the description of Frank James was then staying with Dr. William Noland, who lived about five miles south of Independence. More important, the man had an ugly gunshot wound above his right knee. The wounded man had arrived secretly at the Noland residence by a roundabout and tedious route. The man seemed to move from place to place, sometimes accompanied by another suspicious man. The wounded man had to be Frank.

Boland had learned that armed men guarded the house at night, and, during the day, men watched the road leading to the residence for two miles in each direction. Boland also believed that Jesse was hiding at Dick Talley's home, about a half mile from the doctor's. Boland asked for more men, well armed, to help capture the fugitives, and Chief McDonough happily sent four additional officers to Jackson County on October 12.

Boland, apparently not a superstitious man, planned his raid for the next day, Friday, October 13. He got additional information about the layout of the Noland place the night before by sending an officer, pretending to be a retired Black Hills miner, to the doctor's door. The officer asked if he could sleep in Noland's barn, but the doctor refused, telling him he was welcome in the house. Late that evening, the "miner" slipped away and told Boland what he had gathered. And the most important information was that Frank James was there.

On the afternoon of the thirteenth, Boland and his seven officers silently moved in on the Noland house, coming from the brush so as not to be seen from the roads. At 4:00 P.M., they burst through the front door, guns drawn and cocked. The doctor was away at the time, but the women were home, and they shrieked and cowered as the armed intruders raced from room to room. The officers quickly located their quarry, resting on an elbow on a bed in a corner, his right leg bandaged.

"Hello, Frank," said one of the officers, pointing his revolver at the man's chest.

"My name is not Frank," the wounded man replied in a shocked voice.

The officers were not fooled by this. Any time they made an arrest, the criminal protested that the wrong man was being taken. No, they told him, you are Frank James, and they ordered him to get out of bed. The man said he could not walk, but the officers forced him to stand up.

"Damn you," one of them snarled, "if you could travel here from Minnesota, you can walk across this room."

The man took a step and collapsed in pain. The officers, cursing, placed him back on his bed and picked up the mattress, using it for a litter.

Polly Noland, the doctor's wife, slowly recovering from her fright, begged Sergeant Boland to let the man be. He was not Frank James, she insisted, but John Goodin, a cattle trader from Louisiana. Boland asked about the bullet wound in the right leg, above the knee.

That was an unfortunate accident, she explained. Mr. Goodin shot himself while squirrel hunting, and he had come to Jackson County a few weeks ago for medical treatment. Doctor Noland's son, Columbus, told Boland the same story.

The Nolands seemed sincere, but Boland knew that most of the Jameses' sympathizers—and there were plenty in that part of the state—would lie to protect the outlaws. He directed his officers to take the prisoner to the waiting train and also to detain Columbus Noland. He did not want the doctor's son to send out an alarm before his officers had a chance to visit the Talley place and bag Jesse. But they made a thorough search of the Talley residence and did not find Frank's brother.

Boland's squad moved next to the home of the widow of former bushwhacker Bill Pettis, and they didn't find Jesse there, either. And Frank James was not talking.

With one very important prisoner, then, Boland and his officers boarded their train. But Boland wasn't taking Frank James to the jail in Kansas City, just a few miles away. No, this was entirely a St. Louis operation, and their prize would be going to Chief McDonough.

The train arrived in St. Louis at 7:00 P.M. on October 14. There was no crowd waiting at the station to see the famous prisoner; the arrest had been kept quiet. The officers carried the stretcher with the prisoner three blocks to the Four Courts Building and Chief McDonough's private office on the second floor. McDonough interrogated Frank, who again strongly denied being one of the James boys or having any knowledge of the Northfield Raid. Next a tape measure was used to measure the prisoner's height. At five feet, seven and a half inches, the man was not nearly as tall as Frank James. He also had a jet-black beard and black hair, whereas Frank was known to have light hair and short, sandy whiskers.

These discrepancies should have worried McDonough, but the self-important chief simply refused to believe that this mysterious man with a gunshot wound in the exact same place as Frank's was purely a coincidence. Still, the evidence began to mount that it was. Dr. Noland signed an affidavit stating that his patient was John N. Goodin, and that he had been recuperating at his home on the day of the Northfield Raid. Several others claimed they knew the James brothers, but when they visited the jail, they failed to recognize the prisoner. And Red Wing, Minnesota's mayor, then visiting St. Louis, proclaimed that McDonough's man was not one of the four Northfield robbers who had bought horses in his town.

Frank James's mother—admittedly, not the most trustworthy source—also cast doubt on the identification. When asked by a *Kansas City Times* reporter if the prisoner was her son, she replied, "Do you think I would be here, laughing and talking with you, if my boy was in jail?" The reporter continued to prod, and Zerelda finally commented, "All I have to say is this, when either Frank or Jesse is caught, it will not be here."

As the likelihood that Frank James sat in a St. Louis cell began to diminish, McDonough continued to believe the wounded man was one of the Northfield robbers. By now, McDonough knew he had been mistaken in proclaiming Jim Younger to be Cal Carter, but the chief remained convinced that Carter had gone to Minnesota with the gang. His prisoner had two letters postmarked Henrietta, Texas, the supposed home of Cal Carter, and an old photograph of Carter received from Jackson County bore a remarkable resemblance to the prisoner.

"This is the man who escaped from Minnesota with Jesse James after the Northfield affair, and I know it," the chief said emphatically to a *Globe-Democrat* reporter. "And whether his name is Carter or Goodin, I don't care, so long as I am able to prove his connection with the robbery. In that will be glory enough."

But by the afternoon of October 18, it was clear that McDonough had apprehended neither Frank James nor Cal Carter. A council of three respected physicians visited the prisoner that day to give an opinion about the leg wound and how old it was. One of the doctors, J. C. Nidelet, sat on the board of police commissioners. After carefully examining the wound, the physicians unanimously declared it several months old "at least." This verdict, combined with pressure from prominent St. Louisan Colonel Celsus Price, who remembered Goodin as a member of his father's bodyguard during the war, caused McDonough to capitulate. John N. Goodin was free.

"I now think that an innocent man has been captured," a glory-deprived McDonough admitted to Governor Hardin in a letter of October 19. But the chief defended his actions and those of his men, blaming the fiasco on "one of the most remarkable coincidences on record." And he was dismissive of his critics, writing the governor that "a few of our citizens here, of the old Confederate element, seem to differ with me, and are disposed to characterize the affair as an outrage, &c. &c."

That McDonough's Jackson County raid amounted to nothing short of kidnapping never seemed to enter the chief's mind. It did John Goodin's, though, who promptly sued McDonough for $20,000 in damages.

Sheltered by friends in Missouri, Jesse and Frank James licked their wounds. The route of the final leg of their journey may never be known. An Independence man, one "quite intimate with the James family," informed a *Kansas City Times* reporter that the brothers had arrived in Jackson County direct from Lamar, 120 miles south in Barton County, about October 5.

After escaping Minnesota, he told the reporter, the boys had passed through eastern Dakota Territory, Nebraska, and Kansas and into Indian Territory (present-day Oklahoma) and then turned northeast, crossing into southwest Missouri. Such a route made for an incredibly long, although not impossible, ride for the wounded men, but it had the advantage of having Jesse and Frank arrive at their home base from the south, when they were expected from the north.

Later, gang members Bob and Charley Ford, interviewed after Jesse's death, said the outlaws had made their way through Dakota Territory and Nebraska to Missouri. Another former gang member, Dick Liddil, told of how the James boys got a two-horse wagon, either through purchase or theft, and with the "wounded one" (presumably Frank) in the back, traveled through

Iowa, Nebraska, Missouri, and Kansas before reaching their destination.

Plenty of wild tales eventually surfaced, too. A Sioux City newspaper editor claimed years later that he helped the James brothers escape the Iowa posses in his buggy, transporting them to the banks of the Missouri River at Little Sioux, where the James boys jumped on a skiff and floated to St. Joseph. The editor had gone to such intrepid lengths, he said, all in exchange for what amounted to an exclusive interview with the James boys. He claimed to have obtained their plan for the raid, the details of their flight from Minnesota, and "the biographies of all their associates who had participated in" the raid. Not surprisingly, the editor never seems to have published his "scoop."

Another story came from a man who, although only five at the time of the raid, believed the James brothers had passed very close to his family's farm near Lancaster, Wisconsin, during their escape. He said his father and a companion had actually seen the two outlaws on the side of the road. One sat on a log while the other applied a bandage to the man's leg.

"There has never been any doubt in my mind, or of any other person's in the neighborhood, that these were the James brothers," he wrote.

Perhaps the most fanciful tale came from old Jim Cummins, a former pal of Jesse and Frank. In a 1916 interview, Cummins said he was writing a book that would tell the truth about the James gang. "The truth has never been told," he said. "I am going to tell it and tell it all." According to Cummins, the brothers made it back to Missouri by "a roundabout way that took them out in Arizona and New Mexico. They nearly starved and ate raw rabbit and roots."

But like most everybody else, Cummins didn't really know the truth.

Once they reached Missouri, one of Jesse and Frank's first stops was the family farm near Kearney. This seems unbelievably reckless, but the brothers visited their mother from time to time throughout their outlaw career, a testament to their daring and, more significantly, the debilitating fear the boys struck in many of their fellow Clay Countians.

Jesse seems to have spent most of his time recuperating at the home of the venerable General Jo Shelby near Aullville in Lafayette County. Shelby, then an even greater hero for unreconstructed Southerners than Jesse (rather than surrender at the end of the war, Shelby had led the tattered remnants of his army across the Rio Grande to Mexico), had long been friends with the James boys. The general loved to tell the story of how the brothers, part of a guerrilla unit under his command, had once saved him from certain capture.

"I do not feel it incumbent on me to betray a set or class of men who offered to sacrifice their lives in defense of mine," Shelby once explained to a reporter. Shelby also credited Jesse with single-handedly backing down a mob bent on killing the general's teenage black servant in November 1872.

As the brothers recovered, Jesse remained strangely silent. There were no letters from the outlaw denying that he and Frank had participated in the raid, no naming of alibis from the best citizens of western Missouri, no offer to come in if guaranteed a fair trial. The brothers had had the wind knocked out of them, and in addition to lying low, there was much to ponder. Meanwhile, their law-abiding enemies celebrated the end of the infamous James-Younger band.

"The breaking up of this powerful and dangerous gang of outlaws is the most important event which has happened in the criminal history of the country," proclaimed the *St. Louis Globe-Democrat*.

But Jesse and Frank were not done yet.

Nine
One Last Escape

But they are outlaws, and nothing but the fate
that is certain to overtake them—death—will
relieve them from their ceaseless wanderings.

—*St. Louis Republican*

4:00 A.M., October 3, 1876
Rice County Jail

It was his first night on guard duty, and nineteen-
year-old Frank E. Glazier heard footsteps on the
sidewalk. Glazier was one of four armed guards posted
each night at the jail, two inside and two outside, after
Chief McDonough warned Sheriff Ara Barton that
some friends of the Youngers might attempt a jail-
break. Young Glazier was one of the outside guards,
his post being on the east side of the jail. He and the
other outside man had strict orders to stop anyone who
approached the building.

At the sound of the footsteps, he ducked behind some bushes and watched as a man approached the yard. Once the man walked through the gate, Glazier stepped forward and ordered him to stop. But the man kept coming, heading straight for Glazier.

"Who are you?" Glazier shouted, taking two steps back.

The man did not slow a beat but appeared to be trying to get between Glazier and the jail. The guard raised his rifle.

"Don't you know I'm a policeman?" the man asked, getting closer.

Glazier saw the man's hand move to his pocket and begin to draw something out. Terrified, Glazier imagined the man was reaching for a knife or revolver. He pulled the rifle's trigger, sending a ball crashing through the man's chest and knocking him to the ground with a heavy thud. The man died without making a sound.

The rifle's smoke prevented Glazier from seeing the man fall. But after the smoke cleared, Glazier saw the motionless body, and he yelled to the other guards to come quick; he had killed or wounded a man. Someone bent over the lifeless form and then stepped back in horror. Glazier had killed William Henry Kapernick, city policeman number three.

The Youngers wouldn't be brought before the District Court for Rice County until the fall term started in several weeks, so they passed the time reading the papers, smoking cigars, and eating three square meals a day. As far as Sheriff Barton was concerned, the boys were model prisoners, not causing any trouble with the other inmates or even using any bad language. Under the care of physicians, they continued to recover well, although Bob would never regain the full use of his arm, and the inside of Jim's mouth, with the bullet still lodged in the roof, refused to heal.

Sheriff Barton had ended the mass public viewings after the first few days of their incarceration, but the Youngers were still allowed visitors. *Pioneer Press and Tribune* reporter J. Newton Nind came by every day to be locked up with the brothers. He mostly played cards with them, but Nind was not there to keep the brothers company. Working with the authorities, his primary job was to learn the identities of the two gang members who had escaped. But Nind failed because the Youngers remained tight-lipped about their companions, even in their most unguarded moments.

The brothers' eighteen-year-old sister, Henrietta, and their brother-in-law, Richard S. Hall, arrived in Faribault from Jackson County, Missouri, in early October. Henrietta was attractive, with a slight figure, fair complexion, and light brown hair. She had been so young at the time of her father's death that she had grown up with Cole serving more as a father than a brother. And all three brothers were extremely fond of the "baby" of the family.

Sheriff Barton wanted to put to rest all questions regarding Jim Younger's identity, so he kept Cole and Bob out of sight so only Jim could be seen when Henrietta entered the cell block. The instant she spotted Jim, she ran over to her brother, placed her arms around his neck, and kissed him, tears streaming down her cheeks. She told Jim she knew he was innocent and that "in the sight of God he was not a murderer." Sheriff Barton had the confirmation he needed.

All the brothers became emotional when their sister arrived and during a second visit the next day. Bob, the most cheerful of the three, did most of the talking; Jim's injury made it difficult for him to have a conversation. Sheriff Barton allowed Henrietta inside the cage surrounding the cells, where she trimmed Jim's fingernails and did her best to make her brother more presentable. Cole told Henrietta to let the family know he had no one to blame but himself for their predicament, and that he was resigned to whatever the future held.

Photographer Ira Sumner heard that Henrietta was in Faribault and quickly came over from Northfield to see her. He had made a small fortune selling his photographs of the dead Miller and Chadwell and a composite image picturing all the robbers captured and killed in Minnesota (Sumner had apparently ripped off Mankato photographer E. F. Everitt). He had sold more than fifty thousand copies, and he believed a portrait of the outlaws' angelic teenage sister would be another sure moneymaker. He offered Henrietta $500 if she would sit before his camera (roughly $10,000 in today's dollars), but she quickly turned him down.

On October 19, the last person the brothers expected to see stepped through the heavy door to the cell block: attorney Sam Hardwicke. Clell Miller's family had enlisted Hardwicke to help them recover Clell's body and any remaining personal effects of the bandit. Accompanying Hardwicke was Clell's nineteen-year-old brother, Edward T. "Ed" Miller. Ed had been leery of traveling to Minnesota, fearing that the people of Northfield would try to take their revenge out on him. But Hardwicke had assured him that everything would be okay.

Exactly what was said between Hardwicke, Miller, and the Youngers during their brief meeting (conducted in the presence of the sheriff) is unknown. Perhaps Miller just wanted to know a little more about his brother's last weeks, to have a few memories to comfort his aged mother back in Clay County. But Minnesota's newspapermen, who were constantly at the jail, failed to report any part of the conversation—they didn't even interview Miller.

But a few days later, a *Saint Paul Dispatch* reporter appeared at Sam Hardwicke's St. Paul office. An intriguing story had appeared in the *Chicago Times*, written by an unnamed journalist after a recent visit with Zerelda Samuel. The James boys' mother was her usual cantankerous self, damning the cowardly detectives who had raided her farm and threw the "hand grenade" that killed her boy and shattered her arm. Jesse and Frank were innocent of crime, she said emphatically, but the "murder of that boy, and the loss of my arm will be avenged some of these days, as certain as my boys are living."

It was that bitter threat of vengeance that had brought the reporter to Hardwicke's door. The same article also revealed that the James-Younger gang's real reason for the Minnesota expedition was to kill a Liberty attorney who had assisted the Pinkertons and later fled to St. Paul. Hardwicke was the only St. Paul lawyer from Clay County, Missouri, and the reporter

Samuel Hardwicke, a previously unpublished portrait.

wanted to know if he was the lawyer referred to in the article.

Hardwicke admitted he was indeed the man, but he said that fear of the James boys had nothing to do with him leaving Missouri. He pointed out that he had remained in the state for nearly two years after the Pinkerton raid on the James farm (it was actually a year and four months). But he didn't mention that he'd wasted no time moving from his home in the country into town once the word got out of his involvement with the Pinkertons. Then Hardwicke said something he surely did not believe, as if he was trying to convince himself as well as the reporter.

"Their business is robbery, not murder," he said of the Jameses. "I do not think they came to Minnesota on any other business, and have no apprehension whatever for my personal safety on their account."

Their business is robbery, not murder? Hardwicke knew full well that Jesse had assassinated a neighbor,

Daniel Askew, because he had helped the Pinkertons. He also knew that Jesse had murdered the Gallatin cashier in the mistaken belief that the victim was the Federal commander of the bluecoats who killed Bloody Bill Anderson. Jesse, like his mother and like the bushwhackers he had ridden with in the war, lived for revenge. Everyone in Clay County, including Hardwicke, knew this. The attorney was putting on a bold face, at least publicly.

Privately, the James boys were on Hardwicke's mind enough that he wrote a letter nine weeks later urging a prominent Missouri friend to contact Governor Hardin about the rewards for the outlaws. Hardin had refused to pay the rewards for some of the bandits who had participated in the Northfield and Rocky Cut robberies because the Rocky Cut rewards were for "arrest and conviction"—Chadwell, Miller, and Pitts had been killed. Hardin's legal interpretation prompted the First National Bank of Northfield to consider withdrawing its standing reward of a thousand dollars for the capture of the James boys. The reasoning was that Jesse and Frank had boasted that they would never be taken alive, so Missouri's rewards for their "arrest and conviction" were worthless.

Hardwicke asked his friend to urge the governor to pay the rewards to "insure the continued offer of the liberal reward offered by the bank here." If the governor could not do that, then Hardwicke suggested that he recommend a resolution to the legislature authorizing that the rewards be paid.

"Sometime ago, I adopted it as a rule never to give myself any concern about those outlaws again," Hardwicke wrote. "This occasion has made me break over the rule, in the hope that it might be the means of doing some good to the state." And to Sam Hardwicke.

On the morning of November 15, the grand jury convened in the court of Judge Samuel Lord to consider the four bills of indictment prepared against the Youngers. District Attorney George N. Baxter charged the brothers jointly with the murder of Joseph Lee Heywood; the murder of Nicolaus Gustavson; assault with intent to do bodily harm upon Alonzo Bunker; and robbery of the First National Bank. The grand jury interviewed seventeen witnesses during the course of the day, including Alonzo Bunker, Frank Wilcox, and Northfield postmaster Henry S. French, who swore he'd seen Cole Younger shoot the Swede.

That afternoon, Henrietta Younger and Mrs. "Fanny" Twyman, the Youngers' aunt, arrived by train. They came to Faribault unexpectedly and against Cole's wishes because he was afraid that his relatives being present during the trial would only add to the circus. Sheriff Barton, in an act that reflected his growing fondness for the outlaws, allowed the Younger women to stay in his home during their stay, preventing any unwanted encounters they might face at a hotel. Hordes of curious people were in town to witness the court proceedings and get a look at the outlaws.

The grand jury reported all four indictments at noon the following day, and the judge set the time for the brothers' arraignment for 3:00 P.M. A distance of three hundred yards separated the door of the jail from the door of the courthouse, and an estimated two thousand people waited anxiously to see the prisoners. Finally, at about 3:30 P.M., Sheriff Barton opened the door and walked out of the jail with the Youngers and their sister and aunt, the women wearing veils. Two squads of six armed guards waited at the door, one squad marching before the sheriff's party and the other falling in behind. The handcuffs and shackles clanked as the Youngers, handcuffed together with Cole in the middle, slowly shuffled along.

The brothers, "neatly dressed and cleanly shaved," looked nervous. One newspaper commented that the brothers looked "anything but the desperate men they are claimed to be." Cole remarked that he had never before worn handcuffs. Jim said he had had them on once before when he'd been a prisoner during the war. They marveled at the size of the crowd, and when they entered the courtroom, they found it so packed it was suffocating. Men and women strained and jostled to get a better view of the outlaws, some even climbing up on their seats.

The proceedings were short and somewhat anticlimactic. The brothers remained standing as the district attorney read the indictments. When Judge Lord asked the defendants to enter a plea of guilty or not guilty, their attorney requested more time to plead, which the judge granted. Sheriff Barton then marched the Youngers back through the ogling crowd to the jail.

Most Minnesotans thought they had a good idea how the Youngers would plead. The press had been pointing out for weeks that because of a peculiar Minnesota law, the Youngers could escape capital punishment by simply pleading guilty. Under that law, only a jury could hand down the death sentence, and if a defendant pleaded guilty to a charge, there was no need of a jury. Thus, the harshest punishment that a defendant who pleaded guilty could get was a life sentence, regardless of how heinous the crime.

"Any innocent soul who supposes the robbers can be adequately punished, labors under a grave mistake," wrote the *Pioneer Press and Tribune*. "Their lives are as safe as that of the saintliest person in the state."

The belief that the brothers would take advantage of this law led to enough anger that there was concern that a lynching party of citizens from Northfield, Faribault, and other towns planned to raid the jail. But Sheriff Barton and Faribault's mayor were confident they had plenty of armed men and were adequately prepared to defeat such a mob. The mayor announced in a particularly strident tone that they would "shoot down every man like a dog who tried to violate the law." The rumored mob never surfaced.

But the Younger brothers were actually inclined to take their chances with a jury and plead not guilty to the two murders. Cole strongly denied shooting Gustavson, and Frank Wilcox, the witness in the bank, would testify that Bob had exited before Heywood was shot. If they were lucky, perhaps they could get off with a few years in prison on the robbery charge. But over the next three days, Henrietta and Aunt Fanny begged them to take the safer course and get life in prison. The stakes were far too high for what amounted to a throw of the dice. They urged the brothers to think of their family and loved ones in Missouri.

On Monday morning, November 20, the Youngers stood before Judge Lord and another packed courtroom, with everyone quiet and straining to catch each spoken word. When asked for their plea to the charge of murdering Joseph Heywood, the brothers answered guilty. The district attorney immediately turned to the judge and requested that a jury be impaneled to determine the "degree of guilt." It was a hopeless legal maneuver to get around the law shielding the brothers from capital punishment, and it led to a delay of the sentencing until that afternoon.

At 2:00 P.M., the Youngers again shuffled into the courtroom, their sister and aunt at their sides. The judge announced that he was denying the district attorney's motion for a jury, after which the defense stated that the prisoners were ready to receive their sentence, if the state was prepared. The district attorney said the state was ready. The judge gestured to the Youngers to step to the bench.

"Have you anything to say," the judge asked, "any reason why sentence should not be pronounced?"

"No," the brothers said, shaking their heads.

"Not one of you?" the judge said directly to Cole.

"Nothing."

"It becomes my duty, then, to pass sentence upon you. I have no words of comfort for you or desire to reproach or deride you. While the law leaves you life, all its pleasures, all its hopes, all its joys are gone out from you, and all that is left is the empty shell. I sentence you, Thomas Coleman Younger, to be confined in the State prison at hard labor to the end of your natural life, and you, James Younger, that you be confined in the State prison at hard labor to the end of your natural life, and you, Robert Younger, that you be confined in the State prison to the end of your natural life."

The Youngers displayed not the slightest emotion as the judge spoke, but when he finished, and the brothers returned to their seats, the courtroom spectators saw "an expression of satisfaction and relief" sweep "over their faces." Jim sat down next to Henrietta, who burst into tears and buried her face in his shoulder. He hugged her gently with one arm as the guards placed handcuffs on his other hand. He also leaned over and spoke words of comfort to his aunt, the tears wetting her cheeks as well. But the outlaws didn't shed a tear, nor did their eyes even become watery.

"I have seen a good deal of the world," Cole had told a reporter earlier, "and might as well retire any way."

On Wednesday, November 22, with Cole and Jim shackled together and Bob shackled to a guard, the Youngers were escorted behind the high walls of the state prison at Stillwater, accompanied by Sheriffs Barton and William H. Dill and Henrietta and Aunt

Fanny. The reporters were there, too, peppering the prison's new celebrity inmates with questions.

"This is quite different from a county jail," Bob told them. "There we always had plenty of people to talk to, but here everything appears to go by clockwork." Each brother was asked in turn to name the two robbers who escaped, and each flatly refused. "If this cell door was opened now, and I taken out to be hung," Bob said, "I would not reveal their names—but they are not the James brothers. . . ."

Clay County sheriff John S. Groom did not really care if the James brothers had been involved in the Northfield robbery, but he did care if they were in his county. Years ago, as a Kearney storekeeper, the forty-seven-year-old Groom had been on friendly terms with Zerelda and her boys, and he had known Jesse as a good, honest young man. But on the same day the Youngers became inmates at Stillwater, one of Frank and Jesse's cousins walked into Groom's office and told him the outlaws were visiting their mother. The cousin had had a falling-out with Jesse and was worried the quick-tempered outlaw might kill him. Groom quickly enlisted four men to ride with him to the James farm.

At about 9:00 P.M., as a light rain fell, Groom's posse slowly approached the farmhouse. Frank was walking from the barn to the house, and even though it was good and dark outside, he somehow spotted (or heard) Groom's men. He swiftly unholstered his revolver and fired a shot into the air to alert Jesse inside. The sheriff and one of his men instantly fired at Frank, the flash of flame from the gun barrels giving Frank an excellent idea of where they were. The outlaw calmly leveled his revolver and fired, his bullet splitting the bark on the tree shielding the crouching sheriff.

Groom next heard the stamping of hooves as Jesse and Frank mounted and spurred their horses. "Come on you cowardly sons of bitches," one of the brothers taunted as they galloped away. The sheriff and his men jumped on their horses and chased after the bandits, but they had squandered a rare opportunity to capture the brothers and allowed them—the most elusive outlaws in history—a head start. For a brief moment the next day, the posse saw the bandits, but the James boys' horses were much faster than any horseflesh the sheriff could come up with, and his posse failed to overtake them.

It would be a long time before Jesse and Frank were seen again in Clay County. The boys may have been visiting their mother to say good-bye. They needed to disappear and tend to their families, take them to a place where the law was not hunting the James boys. That place was Tennessee. The Volunteer State was actually a familiar hideout; Jesse's son, Jesse Edwards James, had been born in Nashville in August 1875. And as the Nashville region was then seeing an influx of settlers from Ohio, Indiana, and elsewhere, no one questioned two more nondescript families.

As J. D. Howard and B. J. Woodson, Jesse and Frank settled into a new life that did not include talk of the next haul. They kept their revolvers close, of course, hidden in saddlebags or in shoulder holsters beneath jackets, but they were going straight, or at least making a solemn effort. Frank rented a farm and got a job driving a four-mule team for a lumber company. Jesse took up farming (although not as seriously as Frank) and raised cattle, but he also acquired several fine racehorses and soon devoted most of his time to racing and gambling. Both brothers were seen from time to time in Nashville's faro banks and at the Nashville Blood-Horse Association racetrack. Frank acquired a racehorse or two as well.

Jesse James.

But the new life suited Frank more than it did Jesse. Jesse, not yet thirty-two years old, had spent most of his adult life riding like the devil, terrorizing bluecoats, bank tellers, and Pinkertons. The rush of that wind-in-your-face, gun-in-your-hand lifestyle was like a drug. And Jesse craved attention, the kind he got on a national scale—racehorse owners did not make headlines. At the same time, he continued to spend money fast and easy, just like in the old days, and he accumulated creditors even faster. For Jesse, the answer was obvious—or inevitable. Even though the nightmarish memories of Northfield were still vivid, Jesse began putting together a new gang sometime in the summer of 1879.

The new gang was nothing like the old one though. Its size and makeup varied over time, but the young scamps Jesse scrounged up had not fought with Quantrill or Bloody Bill; there were no bonds forged in fire. And they sure as hell could not be counted on to give their lives in the street while waiting on a man in the bank. But they could point a revolver and hold a horse, and that was about all Jesse needed.

On October 8, 1879, Jesse and five men, including Ed Miller, stopped a Chicago & Alton train at Glendale, just southeast of Independence, Missouri. The boys rode away with $6,000. A reporter commented that the robbery "brought up recollections of the desperate doings of the James boys, the kings of border train robberies." Those were not pleasant memories for the United States Express Company, which promptly offered a reward of $25,000 for the arrest and conviction of the gang. The railroad offered $15,000.

A holdup of two tourist stagecoaches near Mammoth Cave, Kentucky, in September 1880 netted $1,200 in cash, jewelry, and timepieces, and the robbery of a U.S. Army Corps of Engineers paymaster in north Alabama in March 1881 brought the bandits $5,240.18. Nobody was shot during these robberies, but with the holdup of a Chicago, Rock Island & Pacific train near Winston, Missouri, in July 1881, Jesse and the boys returned to murder. Significantly, this job also marked Frank James's return to being an outlaw. (Frank would later claim he was hundreds of miles away in Indian Territory when the robbery took place—he was lying.)

As Jesse and Frank rushed through the cars to take control of the train, they shot and killed two men, conductor William Westfall and a passenger who made the mistake of raising his head for a peek. Jesse would say the conductor was going for a pistol, and even though he warned him not to draw it, the foolish man did anyway—and Jesse had no choice but to kill him. But one of the passengers told a different story. According to the passenger's account, Jesse ran up to Westfall and said, "You're the man I want!"

No sooner had these words left Jesse's lips than the outlaw fired his pistol, striking Westfall in the arm. The conductor turned and ran for his life, and Jesse fired two more quick shots. Finally, as Westfall reached the end of the car, another robber, presumably Frank, fired a bullet that dropped the conductor, killing him instantly. Interestingly enough, William Westfall had served as the conductor on the special train that carried the Pinkertons to Clay County the night of the infamous raid on the James farm.

When Jesse divided the spoils from the Winston robbery, it came to a pathetic $130 each. That would not go very far, and less than two months later, on September 7, the gang hit another Chicago & Alton train at a place deep in the Missouri woods known as Blue Cut, very close to the site of the Glendale robbery. When the express safe proved to be nearly devoid of cash, the six bandits turned to the passengers, relieving the frightened travelers of their money, watches, and jewelry—all that they were unable to hide, that is. A newspaper report placed the loss to the passengers at more than $15,000, although gang members later testified that each man's share amounted to only about $140.

By spring 1882, Jesse was ready for another bank. Trains were too much of a crapshoot; one never knew how much the express safes held. But a prosperous bank was bound to have money in the vault. Jesse had in mind the Platte City bank, about thirty miles from the house he now rented on a bluff top in St. Joseph, Missouri. A murder trial was coming up in Platte City, and Jesse planned to hit the bank during the trial. He figured that many of the town's citizens would be glued to the proceedings at the courthouse. It would be "a fine scheme and would be published all over the United States as a daring robbery," he boasted. And Jesse would shoot any man who interfered, even if he had to "clean the entire town out."

But while Jesse fantasized about his next headline-generating exploit, this gang was really in shambles. Frank had wisely gone back into hiding with his family. Jesse had murdered Ed Miller in October 1881, because Miller had complained about his share of the loot, or because Jesse was afraid of Miller, or because of a quarrel over a woman, or for any number of reasons—no one knows for sure. Some gang members had been caught, and some were lying low, fearing Jesse would do to them what he did to Miller. And unbeknownst to Jesse, the two young men he needed for the Platte City job, who were then living in his home with his family, were conspiring with Missouri's governor to end the outlaw's fabled run.

Governor Thomas T. Crittenden had offered brothers Bob and Charley Ford, aged twenty and twenty-four, respectively, $40,000 for Jesse alive and $10,000 for Jesse dead, the reward money courtesy of the railroads. At least that's what Charley said later. Either sum was a fortune, but the brothers had ruled out taking Jesse alive and waited for an opportunity to assassinate him. It came on Monday, April 3, 1882, the same day Jesse planned to leave to go to Platte City.

It was a warm spring morning, and Jesse had removed his coat and holsters with their two revolvers, a Colt and a Smith & Wesson, and laid them on a bed in the front room—he did not want anyone seeing him armed if he stepped outside. Jesse's wife, Zee, was at work in the kitchen, separated from the front room by the dining room. Their two children were playing in the front yard.

Jesse sat down and pulled off his tall leather boots. He then looked up at the wall in front of him and remarked to Bob and Charley that Miss Mimms's picture needed dusting. He was referring to a framed picture of Zee's niece, Nannie Mimms. Jesse stood up and began to dust the picture but accidentally pushed it out of place.

"With an exclamation of pettishness," Jesse slid a chair under the picture, stepped up on it, and began to reposition the frame.

At that moment, Bob Ford moved between Jesse and his guns, and both brothers drew their revolvers. Bob got his revolver out first, and as he raised and cocked it, Jesse heard the unmistakable metallic hammer clicks and began to turn his head. At that moment, Bob's .44-caliber bullet crashed into Jesse's skull.

Zee heard the loud shot and rushed to the front room. She saw Jesse outstretched on the floor, blood beginning to pool under his head. She next glimpsed Bob and Charley running across the yard, each with a revolver in his hand.

"Robert, you have done this, come back," she shouted.

Jesse in death,
St. Joseph, Missouri.

"I swear to God I didn't," Bob answered.

Zee knelt down next to Jesse and cradled his head in her arms, and she began to cry. He was not dead yet, but his brilliant blue eyes had gone dark. She frantically tried to wipe the blood away, but it kept coming.

The Ford brothers returned to the front room, and Charley

tried to explain to Zee that "a pistol had accidentally gone off."

"Yes," Zee said angrily, "I guess it went off on purpose. You have killed my husband!"

Bob and Charley quickly grabbed their hats and also Jesse's revolvers and gun belt and hurried off for the town's only telegraph office. Once there, Charley paced nervously up and down as Bob tried several times to write out a telegram.

"Shall I write it for you?" the operator asked.

"I can write it myself, all right," Bob snapped.

Finally, Bob handed the operator the piece of paper with his message. He wanted to first send it to Governor Crittenden and then to several law officers. It said: "Meet me in Kansas City tonight or tomorrow. I have my man."

In spring 1882, Frank James, his wife, Annie, and their four-year-old boy, Robert Franklin, were living in a rented house in Lynchburg, Virginia. The modest factory town in the Blue Ridge Mountain foothills was more than a thousand miles from St. Joseph, and only rarely did Frank hear news from his old stomping grounds. But during the first week of April, Frank's wife read a stunning headline in the *New York Herald* that had arrived that morning at the Jameses' door.

Frank had been out walking, and as her husband approached their house, Annie came running toward him with the newspaper in her hands. "Jesse James is killed," she blurted out.

"My God," Frank exclaimed, "where, and how, and who killed him?"

Robert Ford, Jesse's assassin.

Frank quickly scanned the article, looked up at Annie, and said, "This is the end."

If Jesse, who had become obsessively suspicious of nearly everyone he knew and met, could be deceived and shot down like a dog, so, too, could Frank. How could he be certain that a friend, or even a relative, would not find the Missouri governor's reward too enticing? As Annie later put it, Frank "could not even cut a stick of wood without looking around to see whether or not someone was slipping up behind him to kill him." It was time to strike a deal with Governor Crittenden, for several reasons.

There had been a good deal of celebration across Missouri over Jesse's death, but the governor had been criticized for the way it was accomplished, especially from the state's "old Confederate element." Jesse's widow, Zee, and his two young children, Jesse Edwards and Mary Susan, as well as his mother, Zerelda, became objects of sympathy. So, too, to a certain extent, did Frank. He or his supporters masterfully played on this mood by sending Zerelda and Annie James to make a direct appeal to the governor for clemency. The visit even included a brief meeting with the governor's wife, who, according to a reporter, "expressed herself pleased with the modest and lady-like bearing of Mrs. Frank James. Mrs. Samuel, she said, appeared to make an effort at composure, and to keep her countenance from wearing a defiant look. She had evidently been weeping."

The governor refused to make any comment to the press, other than to tersely say a pardon could not be granted before trial and conviction. But negotiations were going on behind the scenes, and in the thick of them was Frank's old friend, the powerful newspaperman John Newman Edwards. The criminal charges against Frank in Missouri were one thing, but an even greater worry was that Minnesota would attempt to extradite him once he surrendered. And Minnesotans, disappointed that they'd been robbed of Jesse, desperately wanted Frank.

Edwards's negotiations with Crittenden went on for several weeks, but they finally reached an agreement by the end of September. Exactly what that agreement was is unknown. Crittenden always denied that he made any promises. But, at the least, the governor must have indicated that he would not honor a Minnesota requisition. He may even have let it be known that he would look favorably on pardoning Frank if he were convicted in the Missouri

John Newman Edwards.

courts. But first, Frank had to turn himself in. The capstone of the governor's campaign to destroy the James gang depended on Frank's surrender. It would vindicate Crittenden's methods, as well as give him the glory, when Frank James surrendered to the governor in Jefferson City.

On Thursday, October 5, Governor Crittenden invited the state's officers, several prominent citizens of Jefferson City, and a number of his close friends to his private office. He did not tell his guests why they'd been summoned, although they expected something involving food and drink. At 5:00 P.M., John Newman Edwards stepped through the office door followed by "a young looking man of slight physique, with pale and extremely intelligent face," recalled the governor. "He walked with a quick, nervous tread and at one glance took in the whole assemblage."

Edwards raised his hat in a grand sweep and announced to the gathering, "Gentlemen, this is Mr. Frank James."

The governor's guests did not really know what was happening, and considering that Edwards had a well-deserved reputation for being fond of the bottle, some no doubt thought he was drunk. Most of the men continued with their conversations. Frank immediately stepped forward, hat in hand, and said: "Governor Crittenden, I am Frank James and will now deliver myself into your hands."

Frank unbuttoned his coat, and with a movement so quick it seemed more a blur, he slid his hands to his waist, a loud click was heard, and he drew forth a heavy cartridge belt and holstered revolver. Everyone in the room froze as their eyes were instantly fixed on the outlaw. Frank swiftly pulled the pistol, a Model 1875 Remington, from its holster, took hold of the barrel, and presented the gun, butt first, to the governor.

"I make you a present of this revolver," Frank said, "and you are the first, except myself, who has laid hold of it since 1864."

Obviously, the Model 1875 did not exist in 1864, but Frank's words, undoubtedly crafted by Edwards, made for a very dramatic presentation, reminiscent of a defeated general presenting his sword to the victor.

Jackson County still held an indictment against Frank for the 1874 murder of a Pinkerton detective, so his first stop was the county jail in Independence. But it would be some weeks before Frank was arraigned, and even longer before any trial would take place. In the meantime, large crowds flocked to the jail, where they greeted him like a visiting dignitary, or, as one Minnesota newspaper put it, the "darling of Missouri society."

He politely shook hands with his visitors and told them he was glad to meet them. Frank's wife and son were often with him at the jail, and the crowds—and reporters—observed Frank lovingly holding his boy, laughing and playing with the youngster.

John Newman Edwards, thrilled with how the press and the public fawned over Frank, wrote his friend on October 26:

> *Your stay in the jail has been worth millions to you as far as public opinion is concerned. In fact, it was the very best thing that could have happened. You can have no idea of the number of friends you*

*have, nor how rapidly public sentiment is
gravitating in your favor. You have borne yourself
admirably, and every man who has seen you has
become your friend. Do not refuse to see any
body, and talk pleasantly to all. . . .*

*Be patient. Make no sharp issue. . . . Lose your
identity as much as possible, and so sure as you
live you will come forth from it all a free man. I do
not believe that the Minnesota authorities will
send a requisition for you. There is not one
scintilla of evidence to base an indictment upon.*

Edwards was overly optimistic regarding the evidence for an indictment. Among the hundreds and hundreds of visitors to the Independence jail were several of Frank's old friends and acquaintances. But there was one whom Frank failed to recognize. Of course, Frank had only seen him for a few moments six years previous—in the First National Bank of Northfield.

At the behest of the Rice County attorney, Frank Wilcox had traveled to Independence in November to see if he recognized Frank James as the man who murdered his friend Heywood. Wilcox not only got a good, close look at Frank, but he also had a short conversation with the outlaw, at the same time being careful not to reveal his own identity. Two months later, Wilcox appeared before a Northfield justice of the peace and swore out a complaint and affidavit naming Frank James as the killer of the bank's acting cashier. The county attorney then forwarded these documents to Governor Lucius F. Hubbard, who signed a requisition for Frank James on January 18, 1883, and forwarded it to Governor Crittenden.

Crittenden received the Minnesota requisition by mail on February 7. His secretary returned it the same day with a short note explaining that the governor would not surrender Frank James to the authorities of any other state as long as there were charges pending in Missouri. Governor Hubbard filed the requisition away in his papers.

After Crittenden made his response public, a reporter visited the Independence jail and asked Frank for his thoughts. "I am not at all afraid to return to Minnesota," Frank calmly replied, "if they will only give me a fair show and an honest trial. I was never in Minnesota in my life, and it is all nonsense about trying to connect me with the Northfield robbery."

That was essentially Frank's answer to every crime charged against him, and prosecutors had an exceedingly difficult time proving otherwise. With the passage of time, some witnesses had died. Others did not have the clearest memories or could not actually identify

Frank James in 1883.

Frank. And some, such as former gang member Dick Liddil, were not good witnesses because they lacked integrity. Sympathy for Frank played a role as well—as did a politically connected defense team. Trials at Gallatin, Missouri (for the murder of the passenger during the Winston robbery), and Huntsville, Alabama (for the Muscle Shoals robbery, of which Frank truly was innocent), ended in acquittals. By March 1885, all other cases, including an indictment for the Rocky Cut robbery, had been dismissed.

But Frank still fretted about Minnesota. John Newman Edwards knew this, and on March 18, 1885, excitedly wrote his friend with good news. Edwards had just left the office of Missouri's new governor, John Sappington Marmaduke, a former Confederate major general and one of the state's war heroes:

> *Now Frank, I think you have perfect confidence in*
> *my judgment and my knowledge of men, and I*
> *here say to you under no circumstances in life will*

*Gov. Marmaduke ever surrender you to the
Minnesota authorities, even should they demand
you, which I am equally well satisfied, will never
be done. . . . You are as absolutely safe as if you
were the Governor himself. Never mind what any
alarmists or busy bodies say to you, trust me. I tell
you that you are a free man, and can never be
touched while Marmaduke is Governor.*

Frank James, after one of the most sensational and
long-lived careers in American outlawry, had pulled
off his greatest escape—this time from justice.

Epilogue

Be true to your friends, if the heavens fall.

—COLE YOUNGER

I n 1897, Stillwater warden Henry Wolfer asked Cole Younger to write down his version of what happened during the Northfield Raid. The newly created pardon board would be considering Cole and Jim's application for a pardon, and Wolfer believed a public statement in Cole's own words, especially one that included any extenuating circumstances, would help their cause. Eight years earlier, Bob Younger had died of tuberculosis at Stillwater, and

The Younger brothers, Bob, Jim, and Cole, with their sister, Henrietta, photographed in Stillwater Penitentiary shortly before Bob's death in 1889.

even after doctors declared that Bob had only weeks to live, the governor refused to issue a pardon. Cole and Jim could use all the help they could get.

In the twenty years since the Northfield Raid, Cole had had a lot of time to craft a version of the debacle that made the Youngers look as good as possible. In his account for Warden Wolfer, he admitted that while the gang had considered other banks besides Northfield's, they felt those banks "had enough to do to care for the farmers who had already suffered too much from grasshoppers to be troubled by us." The gang chose the Northfield bank, he wrote, because they understood it held $75,000 belonging to Adelbert Ames and his father-in-law, General Benjamin Butler. Cole hoped that by presenting these two former Union generals, both Radical Republicans, as their only intended victims, he could paint the raid as Southerners still fighting the war. Although only partially true, it is an interpretation that persists to this day.

Cole wrote that the gang had agreed they would not shoot to kill and would only frighten people off the street. But "all of the trouble" came about because of a quart of whiskey. According to Cole, the three inside men drank most of the quart and were dead drunk by the time of the robbery.

"Had it not been for the whiskey," Cole asserted, "there would not, in all probability, have been a man killed, and I can truthfully say had I known they had whiskey, I never would have gone into town."

Blaming the Northfield disaster on liquor was clever. It suggested that the gang's defeat was more their own making, as opposed to the stubborn resistance put up by Northfield's citizens. But none of the gang was truly drunk. Some of the outlaws did visit the saloons prior to the robbery, and Frank Wilcox recalled smelling liquor on Bob Younger's breath, but no eyewitness accounts, including those of Wilcox and Bunker, describe any of the robbers as acting drunk.

Cole also explained the Heywood murder, writing that the last of the robbers to leave the bank told him he saw Heywood jump up and run for his desk. The robber thought Heywood was going for a pistol and ordered him to stop and sit down. When Heywood failed to stop, the robber shot him. And Cole denied being near that part of Division Street where Gustavson was shot. He believed one of the townspeople shooting at the gang had fired the bullet that hit the Swede.

"I know that neither Jim nor myself fired a shot in that part of the city," he insisted.

These last statements are mostly fiction as well. Though it is possible that Frank James told Cole he believed Heywood was going for a pistol, Wilcox's testimony makes no mention of Heywood's killer shouting at the acting cashier to stop. On the contrary, Wilcox makes it vividly clear that the shooting was nothing less than cold-blooded murder. And despite Cole's repeated denials that he shot at Gustavson, eyewitnesses identified him as the Swede's killer.

The pardon board received an impressive stack of letters and petitions in support of clemency. As was to be expected, many came from Missouri, including a petition signed by members of the state's General Assembly.

"To a certain extent," the petition read, the Youngers were "the last victims of the Civil War, having been so unfortunate as to live upon the border at a time when bad blood was hottest and evil passions most fully aroused." Former governor Crittenden also urged a pardon "on the grounds that they have paid a severe penalty; that they have been exemplary prisoners for twenty years; that they are now old and broken down; the law has been vindicated. . . ."

A surprising number of Minnesotans supported the pardons as well; among the petitions submitted favoring clemency was one signed by eighty-six citizens of Madelia, including three surviving members of the Madelia Seven. Another active supporter was one Horace Greeley Perry, the girl Cole had taken on horseback rides in St. Peter, before the raid. Now grown up, the attractive, twenty-eight-year-old Miss Perry served as the *St. Peter Journal*'s editor. She visited the Younger brothers monthly.

But there were plenty of Minnesotans, especially in Northfield, who opposed the pardons. The townspeople were incredulous over Cole's published account of the raid, and not only did they forward their own petition, but the town sent a delegation to the pardon hearing in St. Paul to demand that the board keep the brothers in prison—for life.

The board listened to testimony on the Youngers' application on Monday and Tuesday, July 12 and 13, and of all those who spoke either for or against clemency, Mayor A. D. Keyes of Faribault made the most penetrating comments:

> These men come here and ask for a pardon on the ground that they have reformed in mind and morals as well as in heart, and they are prepared to become good citizens, if they are released. We claim that it is not too much to ask that they shall remain where they are until they disclose the name of the man who killed Heywood. It is not an element of good citizenship to conceal a murderer. Good faith on their part demands that they disclose

the name of the man who killed Cashier Heywood, that that man may be brought back to Minnesota and punished. If the murderer was Frank James, as we are led to believe, then he has never suffered anything for his crime. He has never even been imprisoned, and it is no more than right that he should suffer the penalty in some measure at least. If the Youngers are now the good citizens they claim to be, they would go on the stand, and, by telling the truth, would assist the authorities of this State in bringing the Northfield murderer to justice.

The board refused to pardon the Youngers. But the brothers did not have much longer to wait. In 1901, the Minnesota legislature passed a bill permitting the parole of life prisoners after serving thirty-five years, minus a deduction for good behavior, which made for a minimum requirement of twenty-four years and seven months. The bill was clearly aimed at the release of the Youngers, who had already served nearly twenty-five years at Stillwater and, as inmates, had not a single mark against them.

Following the legislature's lead, then, the pardon board approved the Youngers' parole on July 10, and in a display of just how much the world had changed since that fateful September day in 1876, the brothers received the news by telephone. There were conditions, however. The Youngers could not leave Minnesota, nor could they exhibit themselves in "any dime museum, circus, theater, opera-house, or any other place of public amusement or assembly where a charge is made for admission."

Not surprisingly, there were few opportunities for former bank and train robbers who had spent a quarter of a century behind bars. Their first jobs were peddling tombstones for a St. Paul granite company. Jim left that position after two months and became a clerk in a St. Paul grocery's cigar department, changing jobs again a short time later for work in a Minneapolis cigar store. In April 1902, he surprised Minnesota's governor with a letter asking if there would be any objection to him marrying. He was in love with a St. Paul socialite and newspaperwoman named Alix J. Muller, twenty-seven years his junior. Miss Muller had met Jim on a research visit to Stillwater, and

Cole Younger on parole in Minnesota, 1902.

she had subsequently worked hard for the Youngers' release.

But according to the attorney general, Jim was still a ward of the state. Only with a full pardon could he legally marry. The pardon board dashed that hope the following July, reasoning that the brothers had not spent enough time on parole.

Becoming increasingly despondent and unstable, Jim quit his cigar store job in the fall of 1902. "I've been down the line and all I can get out of it is what I'm worth as a freak advertisement for some firm or other that believes people will be glad to stare at a reputed murderer and cutthroat," he bitterly complained to an acquaintance.

On the morning of October 18, Jim reached a depressing low from which he could not return. He took a .38-caliber pocket revolver, put it to his head, and pulled the trigger. He left a rambling suicide note folded in an envelope, on the outside of which he had written, "All Relations just stay away from me. No Crocodile tears wanted. Reporters Be my friend. Burn me up. Jim Younger." His words "burn me up" referred to Jim's desire to be cremated, a wish that was not honored.

Brother Cole, sick in bed when he received the news of Jim's death, anxiously asked if his brother had left any letters. What Cole really wanted to know was whether or not Jim had named Heywood's killer? He did not.

By taking his own life, Jim gave Cole the pardon they had both longed for. On February 4, 1903, less than four months after Jim's death, the state pardon board released Cole from parole, with the condition that he never return to Minnesota and that he uphold the previous obligation to never exhibit himself "as an actor or participant" at any place that charged an admission.

Ten days later, at approximately 3:00 P.M., Cole crossed the Missouri state line on a train bound for Kansas City. The fifty-nine-year-old outlaw sat up in his seat, his eyes glowing as he gazed out the window.

"If I could only give a hearty Confederate yell," he exclaimed.

The Northfield Raid had cost the Minnesota treasury $7,000 ($3,000 for reimbursement of "extraordinary expenses" for the manhunt and $4,000 in reward money. In today's dollars, it roughly equals $155,000). The distribution of the reward monies, delayed by lawsuits among the fifty-plus claimants, did not come until January 1878. Of the First National Bank's $2,000 for the four captured robbers ($500 apiece), the claimants received equal shares of $45 to

$48. The State's $4,000 bounty was apportioned by a district court judge based on the merits of each posse member's contribution to the capture. Thus, each of the Madelia Seven received $240. The judge allotted Oscar Sorbel $56.25.

Minnesota's governor Pillsbury wanted to send young Sorbel to the University of Minnesota, all expenses paid, "as the State's acknowledgement of his valuable services." But either nothing ever came of the governor's idea or Sorbel did not want to go. He took up a homestead in Dakota Territory in 1883 and never said much about his role as Minnesota's "Paul Revere" or of his past in general. He did become well known, though, as the best horse doctor around Webster, South Dakota, albeit "a rather rough old codger" in his later years. He died in Webster on July 11, 1930, at the age of seventy-one.

In February 1877, the Minnesota House passed a bill to appropriate money to Anselm Manning and Henry Wheeler "for shooting and killing Bill Chadwell and Clell Miller." But there were apparently second thoughts about the bill, and instead, the Minnesota legislature passed a joint resolution giving special thanks—but no money—to nine heroes of Northfield, including Manning and Wheeler, for their "gallant conduct" in resisting the Northfield robbers.

There were no reward monies or thanks for Detectives Hoy and Bresette, or St. Louis chief of police James McDonough. The goats of the manhunt, they returned to their jobs, never to achieve the national stage again, always jealous that the glory for the one great capture had gone to a bunch of amateurs from Madelia. Bresette retired a senior captain of the St. Paul police force in 1890 and immediately took a job as a detective with the Northern Pacific Railroad. On a spring afternoon in 1892, he collapsed while walking up Minneapolis's Hennepin Avenue, probably from a stroke. He was dead at the age of fifty-four.

Detective Mike Hoy never changed, remaining his belligerent, abrasive self and doing things only his way. In 1887, the politically connected Hoy was appointed to Minneapolis's board of police commissioners, and President Grover Cleveland made him a deputy U.S. marshal. But at the same time, he faced accusations of fixing boxing matches and misusing city travel funds. When a newspaper reporter got the upper hand in a game of pool, Hoy, in a fit of rage, drew his revolver on the terrified young man. He somehow outlived his St. Paul nemesis by three years, dying of a tumor at the age of fifty-eight.

By June 1881, James McDonough had overstayed his welcome. The St. Louis board of police commissioners asked McDonough to resign so that they could appoint "a younger and more active man for Chief of Police," but his forced removal was really about squabbles and infighting in the police department and among the commissioners. He started the St. Louis Detective Agency after resigning and then gave that up two years later to raise hogs and cattle on a ranch near Caldwell, Kansas. He died in St. Louis in 1892, four days after Bresette, aged seventy-six.

The First National Bank gave Joseph Lee Heywood's widow $5,000 outright, and the Heywood Fund presented her with $6,301.03. The fund gave another $6,301.03 to the First National Bank's president in trust for Lizzie May Heywood, the only child of the slain bank employee. The bank's president also became Lizzie's legal guardian. Lizzie left Northfield with her mother only a few months after the raid, but she returned as a young lady to attend and graduate from Carleton College with a degree in music. After marrying in 1897, she settled in Scranton, Pennsylvania, where she taught piano. Lizzie May died in 1947.

Adelbert Ames, who fretted over the monies the raid had cost the bank, later battled with his brother, John T., and father, Jesse Ames, over money troubles with their Northfield mill. Lawsuits, involving tens of thousands of dollars, flew back and forth between the partners for years. One suit in 1888 claimed that Adelbert never gave John T. his share of the proceeds from Northfield flour sales in the East. General Ben Butler, who also had a financial stake in the mill, served as Adelbert's defense attorney, which made for an interesting family rift.

When the Spanish-American War broke out in 1898, Ames rejoined the army, serving in the Santiago Campaign as a brigadier general of volunteers. He died a very wealthy man in 1933 at the age of ninety-seven, the oldest West Point graduate and the last surviving full-rank Civil War general.

In 1890, the Rice County prosecuting attorney presented the Minnesota Historical Society with a fine linen duster and a two-bushel wheat sack that had been left behind in the Northfield bank as the robbers fled. Former St. Paul police chief James King also presented the society that year with a pistol supposedly taken from the body of Clell Miller. The raid relic that received the most attention was the section of bone from Jim Younger's upper jaw, complete with teeth, that had been removed by the Madelia doctors. But the society's staff grew weary of the macabre artifact; accession records show that it was "discarded" in 1919, along with the wheat sack.

Exactly what became of the bones of Charlie Pitts, Clell Miller, and Bill Chadwell remains something of a mystery, or at least a convoluted tale. In December 1878, a family near St. Paul's Como Lake made a gruesome discovery when they pried open a wooden box sticking out of the ice and found a human skeleton. The bones of the feet were small, like a woman's, and a hole from a large bullet was clearly visible in the upper part of the hipbone. The county coroner carefully transported the remains to the morgue, where it was determined that they belonged to a man, and he had obviously met a violent end.

In the midst of the coroner's murder investigation, Dr. John H. Murphy arrived at the morgue to claim the skeleton. Murphy was the surgeon general who embalmed Charlie Pitts. He informed the coroner that after he and his students had dissected the outlaw, he had instructed one of his students to sink the remains in the lake so that the tissue would decompose, after which the skeleton could be easily cleaned and reassembled for display. Case closed.

Murphy took what was left of Pitts and later presented the bones to a young Chicago physician. It is not known where Pitts's skeleton ended up after that. However, at the time the remains rested in the county morgue, a newspaper reporter mentioned to Murphy that there had been no hair or scalp with the skull. "His scalp is in my office," Murphy answered. "I removed his skin." Today, a dried piece of skin containing an ear, labeled as the ear of Charlie Pitts, is in the collections of the Northfield Historical Society.

Clell Miller's family and friends had successfully obtained his body before the University of Michigan medical students could carve it up. A letter published in the *Liberty Tribune* in November 1876 stated that the body had been recently buried in Muddy Fork Cemetery north of Kearney. "There can be no doubt about his identity," the writer stated, "as a number of persons came to see the corpse who had known him from childhood."

Bill Chadwell's body does seem to have been dissected by Henry Wheeler and his fellow students. Afterward, the bones were cleaned and wired, and years later, Wheeler, then a prominent doctor of Grand Forks, North Dakota, proudly displayed the skeleton in his office. According to an old newspaper story, Wheeler received a surprise visit at his Grand Forks office sometime in the 1890s from Elisha Stiles, the father of Bill Stiles, the man who had been confused with Bill Chadwell shortly after the robbery. Stiles reportedly told Wheeler that his son had disappeared at the time of the raid, and he had been trying to trace him ever since. The elderly man stared at the skeleton a long time, suspecting that it might be the remains of his missing son. Of course, they were not the bones of Stiles because he had not been at Northfield. But they apparently were not Chadwell's bones, either.

Years later, Dr. Wheeler admitted that the bones hanging in his office were actually those of Clell Miller. Wheeler had been responsible for Miller's death so it made sense that he would want Miller for his trophy. And not wanting the Miller family to know they had been duped, he was understandably happy to let the curious believe the skeleton was Chadwell/Stiles. Wheeler reportedly donated his trophy to the Odd Fellows sometime before his death, and the skeleton ended up with a private collector in the 1980s. In 2011–12, a forensic team studied this skeleton's skull using "craniofacial superimposition" (Miller's postmortem photo was superimposed over an image of the skull) and found matches to Miller that were "remarkable."

But who, then, is buried in the Miller family plot in Muddy Fork Cemetery? And why did Clell's Missouri associates identify the body as that of their old friend? The forensic team is seeking permission to exhume the remains to do a DNA test.

The First National Bank gave Frank Wilcox a permanent position immediately following the raid. He remained at the bank a number of years, eventually becoming the assistant cashier. He also served several years as the treasurer for the Minnesota State Fair. In 1909, he moved with his wife to Yakima, Washington, where he operated a fruit farm. But every morning, as he sat at his kitchen table, he heard the exact same sounds he had heard the morning of September 7, 1876: the steady, loud ticking of the walnut-framed calendar clock that had hung in the First National Bank. When the bank replaced the clock, Frank had asked for it. And even at Frank's death in 1921, it kept perfect time. Today, that same clock hangs in its old spot in the restored First National Bank, which is now a museum operated by the Northfield Historical Society.

Sam Hardwicke and his family returned to Clay County in the summer of 1877. With the James-Younger gang broken up, and Jesse and Frank in hiding, he did not fear for his safety as he once did. He still had an enemy in Zerelda Samuel, however—until one Sunday in 1894. On that day, Hardwicke gave a funeral oration at the old Shady Grove church; in the audience sat Zerelda. After the benediction, she approached Hardwicke, tears running down her cheeks. "Mr. Hardwicke," she said, "I have long been prejudiced against you, but since hearing your address today, I am willing to let the past be buried, knowing that God is to judge one another."

The two shook hands warmly, and Zerelda invited Hardwicke to have dinner with her, which he accepted. The words spoken and unspoken between the two at that dinner are unknown, but they had lots to talk about. Just a year later, in 1895, Sam Hardwicke died at his home south of Liberty. Zerelda joined her son Jesse in 1911.

After Cole Younger returned to Missouri, he immediately became involved in a Wild West show with his old pal Frank James. The ever-crafty Cole sidestepped the conditions of his pardon by lending his name to the show (for a 25 percent share of the profits) but not participating in any of the performances. He also rushed out his colorful but not-to-be-trusted autobiography, *The Story of Cole Younger by Himself*, to sell at the shows. The Minnesota pardon board was furious, of course, but there was little they could do, and no one was inclined to go down to Missouri and bring the man back.

The Great Cole Younger & Frank James Historical Wild West, which was not nearly as exciting as the illustrated posters and newspaper ads promoting it, ended abruptly in September 1903, with charges and lawsuits flying between the show owners and the former

REAL FACTS
NORTHFIELD
BANK ROBBERY

~BY~
COLE YOUNGER

CONVICT LIFE
MINNESOTA STATE
PRISON

Cole's account of the Northfield Raid was the big selling point of this 1909 book on prison life at Stillwater Penitentiary.

outlaws. This was the last time Cole and Frank would be business "partners," although they remained close for the rest of their lives.

In 1906, Cole caused another uproar in Minnesota with the announcement of his scheduled appearance at a Fourth of July picnic near Kansas City, where he was to give a lecture and show a "moving picture film" depicting a train robbery. There was to be a small admission for the show. Even so, Minnesota's governor John Johnson wanted nothing to do with the old rascal.

"It seems to me Minnesota is well rid of him," said Governor Johnson. "We don't want him back, and I am not in favor of trying to bring him back. Let him stay away."

Cole died at the home of his niece in Lee's Summit on March 21, 1916. On his deathbed, he met privately with Jesse's only son, Jesse Edwards James, and friend Harry Hoffman. As the two leaned attentively toward the prostrate old man, hanging on every word, Cole told them of the fight on the streets of Northfield and the escape through the Minnesota woods. Then, swearing them to secrecy, he spoke of the man who shot Heywood. He spoke to Jesse's son about the gang's split and assured him that the James boys' "acts and treatment of us were honorable and loyal."

Frank James died at the old family farm near Kearney on February 18, 1915. He had made good on the promise he and Jesse had offered time and again. All they wanted was a fair trial, they had said. Frank had gotten his trials and lived the remainder of his life—more than thirty years—a peaceable citizen. He had worked at different times as a shoe store clerk, a starter at horse races, a doorman for a St. Louis theater, and a farmer.

For the last few years of his life, he collected an admission of fifty cents to

Frank James, studio portrait, 1898.

Frank James, circa 1910.

see the old home place—the site of Jesse's birth and the scene of the Pinkertons' biggest failure. Thanks to what John Newman Edwards had started, and the dozens of dime novels that came later, his brother Jesse had become the most famous—and most popular—outlaw on the planet. And, somewhat ironically, a big part of that legendary status had come from the defeat in Northfield. If nothing else, Jesse and Frank's wild ride through a thousand manhunters cemented their reputation as among the most remarkable and notorious outlaws to ever live.

Many journalists paid the price of admission over the years, although it did not always guarantee a visit with Frank. Still, several reporters did manage to get stories from the former bandit, and during one interview, Frank was asked something he had not been asked before. The reporter wanted to know if Frank thought what he had done with his life had been "worthwhile."

Frank paused for a moment, as if his mind was racing over the scenes of his past: foolhardy charges, smoking revolvers, bloody corpses, the faces of Quantrill, Bloody Bill, Cole, Jesse, his mother—and Joseph Lee Heywood, stumbling to his desk.

Finally, Frank answered: "If you're not a quitter, anything you've done has got to be worthwhile. You can make it worthwhile. I guess, if I had it all to do over, and had the choice, and had to make the choice as a young man, I'd rather have all the pain and danger and trouble than to be just a plain farmer. If I had an old man's head, I would choose different. . . ."

Appendix

The following poem was published anonymously in the September 23, 1876, issue of the *Winona Daily Republican*. It was reprinted in several other Minnesota newspapers.

THE ROBBER HUNT
This is the bank at Northfield.

This is the malt, that lay in the vault
That was in the bank at Northfield.

This is the eight, that smelled the bait
That is, the malt, that lay in the vault,
That was in the bank at Northfield.

These are the six, that got in a fix,
That's left of eight, that smelled the bait
That is, the malt, that lay in the vault,
That was in the bank at Northfield.

These are the men, that mounted then
To chase the six, that got in a fix,
That's left of eight, that smelled the bait
That is, the malt, that lay in the vault,
That was in the bank at Northfield.

This is Brissette,[1] the capital pet,
Who swore, you bet, he'd have 'em yet,
That joined the men, that mounted then,
To chase the six, that got in a fix,
That's left of eight, that smelled the bait
That is, the malt, that lay in the vault,
That was in the bank at Northfield.

This is Mike Hoy,[2] that broth of a boy,
Who shouldered his little Winchester toy,
To beat Brissette, the capital pet,
Who swore, you bet, he'd have 'em yet,

---

[1] St. Paul detective John B. Bresette
[2] Minneapolis detective Mike Hoy

That joined the men, that mounted then,
To chase the six, that got in a fix,
That's left of eight, that smelled the bait
That is, the malt, that lay in the vault,
That was in the bank at Northfield.

And this is Dill,[3] who went to fill,
With silvery speech, the deadly breach
Between Mike Hoy, that broth of a boy,
Who shouldered his little Winchester toy,
And Johnny Brissette, the capital pet,
Who swore, you bet, he'd have 'em yet,
That joined the men, that mounted then,
To chase the six, that got in a fix,
That's left of eight, that smelled the bait
That is, the malt, that lay in the vault,
That was in the bank at Northfield.

This is the Governor's right hand bower,[4]
Who waved his hand with majestic power,
And ordered in words that might appall,
The prisoners sent to "ye great St. Paul."
O, where was Dill, who went to fill,

---

[3] Winona County sheriff William H. Dill
[4] Captain Coleman I. Macey, secretary to Governor Pillsbury

With silvery speech, the deadly breach,
And where Mike Hoy, that broth of a boy,
Who shouldered his little Winchester toy,
And where Brissette, the capital pet,
Who swore, you bet, he'd have 'em yet,
That joined the men, that mounted then,
To chase the six, that got in a fix,
That's left of eight, that smelled the bait
That is, the malt, that lay in the vault,
That was in the bank at Northfield.

And this is the surgeon general,[5] too,
Who probed with a telegraph wire, and knew,
Better than Cooley[6] and Overhott,[7]
Whether the men could travel, or not,
Who backed the Governor's right hand bower,
Who waved his hand with majestic power,
And ordered in words that might appall,
The prisoners sent to "ye great St. Paul."
O, where was Dill, who went to fill,
With silvery speech, the deadly breach,
And where Mike Hoy, that broth of a boy,

---

[5] Dr. John H. Murphy of St. Paul
[6] Dr. Charles O. Cooley of Madelia
[7] Dr. George H. Overholt, Watonwan County coroner

Who shoulderd his little Winchester toy,
And where Brissette, the capital pet,
Who swore, you bet, he'd have 'em yet,
That joined the men, that mounted then,
To chase the six, that got in a fix,
That's left of eight, that smelled the bait
That is, the malt, that lay in the vault,
That was in the bank at Northfield.

And this is Glispin,[8] who knew his "biz,"
And sat right down on the St. Paul "phiz,"
And when 'twas squelched, he upward rose,
And put his thumb to the end of his nose,
And this to the surgeon general, too!
Who probed with a telegraph wire, and knew,
Better than Cooley and Overhott,
Whether the men could travel, or not,
Who backed the Governor's right hand bower,
Who waved his hand with majestic power,
And ordered in words that might appall,
The prisoners sent to "ye great St. Paul."
O, where was Dill, who went to fill,
With silvery speech, the deadly breach,
And where Mike Hoy, that broth of a boy,

---

[8] Watonwan County sheriff James Glispin

Who shouldered his little Winchester toy,
And where Brissette, the capital pet,
Who swore, you bet, he'd have 'em yet,
That joined the men, that mounted then,
To chase the six, that got in a fix,
That's left of eight, that smelled the bait
That is, the malt, that lay in the vault,
That was in the bank at Northfield.

Acknowledgments

I saw him occasionally at my daughter's elementary school. Oscar Lindholm was an old horseshoer, and, from time to time, he would demonstrate his craft with a small forge in the school's parking lot. The teachers loved to have him, although they were always a bit nervous about Oscar's salty language in front of the kids.

I'm sorry to say that I never introduced myself to Oscar. I probably nodded hello as I walked by, but, to be honest, Oscar seemed a little intimidating. I only got to know him after his death, through his daughter, Myrna.

Oscar, I learned, had grown up in the teens and twenties on a farm near Webster, South Dakota. As an adult, he served in the army, and it was while stationed in Panama that he picked up a paperback copy of Homer Croy's *Jesse James Was My Neighbor.* While reading this book, Oscar came across a name that was a bit of a shock to him. The name was Oscar Sorbel, the teenager who had spread the alarm about the fugitive Northfield robbers.

Oscar Lindholm instantly recognized Oscar Sorbel as the crusty old horse doctor he had known as a child. Lindholm was amazed that no one around Webster had ever said anything about it or even seemed to know that Sorbel had a famous connection to the James-Younger gang. And, for whatever reason, the horse doctor had never talked about it, either.

Later in his life, Lindholm made Oscar Sorbel a personal research project, writing historical societies and even Sorbel descendants. He gathered his Sorbel materials in a notebook, which his daughter, Myrna Wey of Green Mountain Falls, Colorado, kindly let me borrow. As I thumbed through this notebook, I came to realize—just as Oscar Lindholm had—that the past is not always such a distant place. Sometimes it's as close as a simple hello.

Numerous others have assisted me in my pursuit of the story of the Northfield Raid. Chip DeMann of Dundas, Minnesota, has not only studied the raid for decades, but he has been an integral part of the painstakingly accurate raid reenactments held each September during Northfield's Defeat of Jesse James Days. Chip shared with me his considerable research and thoughts on the raid. But more than that, Chip challenged me to look critically at the available evidence and to question old interpretations. Chip may not agree with all of my conclusions, but there is no question that because of him this is a much better book. For that, and his friendship, I am truly grateful.

Hayes Scriven, director of the Northfield Historical Society, gave me open access to the collections in his care and always had time for my questions and requests. I enjoyed tremendously our many conversations about the several conundrums associated with the raid and manhunt. He has done an exemplary job leading his organization in the care of Northfield's Scriver Block (which contains the restored First National Bank museum) and the society's extensive historical collections. Several illustrations in this book are from the Northfield Historical Society.

My friend and fellow Old West enthusiast Donna Tatting of Forest Lake, Minnesota, made at least two trips to the Minnesota Historical Society on my behalf. On one of those trips, I had given her the task of looking in the papers of Governor Lucius F. Hubbard for the Frank James requisition sent to Missouri's Governor Crittenden in 1883. She found it easily. That requisition, previously unknown to scholars, is the most important new find in this book. Thank you, Donna.

Another friend, Robert G. "Bob" McCubbin of Santa Fe, has carefully assembled the finest private library of Western Americana anywhere, and his collection of historic Old West photographs, a good number of which are outlaw images, is unsurpassed. Visiting with Bob and exploring his library is always a big highlight of my trips to Santa Fe, and he has graciously allowed me to use some of his photographs in this book.

I also want to single out Minnesota historian and author John Koblas. His many books on the Northfield Raid are excellent resources, as are his extensive research papers and notes, now part of the collections of the Northfield Historical Society. I spent several days going through his collection, which took him years to gather. John is also a pleasant and gracious man, and I was fortunate to have the opportunity to visit with him while I was in Northfield.

The staffs of several historical societies, museums, and libraries were most helpful, including Elizabeth Beckett and Liz Murphy at the James Farm; Katherine Keil at the Missouri State Museum; Matthew Anderson at the Minnesota Historical Society; my sister, Terri Gardner, at Watkins Woolen Mill State Historic Site; Susan Garwood at the Rice County Historical Society;

Tim Blevins and Dennis Daily in the Regional History Department of the Pikes Peak Library District; and also the staff of the Interlibrary Loan Department at PPLD.

During breaks in my Missouri research trips, my uncle Curly Gardner of Pattonsburg, Missouri, always made sure I had a good time at the weekly trap shoots near his home. My cousin, David Wayne Gardner of Breckenridge, Missouri, made sure there was a place for my boy and me to hunt wild turkeys, as did my old schoolmate, Dave Greenwood, and Montie Maddux. And friend Charlie Miller of Hamilton, Missouri, kept me supplied with his fine handmade turkey calls. My pursuit of the James-Younger gang is over for now, but I'll still be returning to Missouri every spring to chase gobblers.

My mom and dad, Claude and Venita Gardner, of Breckenridge, Missouri, took me and my sisters to see Jesse James's St. Joseph, Missouri, home when we were children. I still remember the guide pointing to the chips in the front room's floor and explaining that a former owner would sprinkle chicken blood there and allow visitors to chip off a piece of "Jesse's blood." As I researched this book, Mom and Dad gave me a place to stay and sometimes a vehicle for my trips across the state.

While in Northfield, Duane and Joan Olson provided a room and welcome companionship, as well as research leads—Joan was formerly the archivist at the Northfield Historical Society. I also want to acknowledge the Olsons' daughter, Ruth Olson Khan, of Colorado Springs, for first putting me in touch with Chip DeMann, introducing me to her parents, and showing my family a great time during Defeat of Jesse James Days.

For various kind favors, many thanks go to David Dary, Dale Blanshan, Nancy Hitt, Nancy Samuelson, Shirley Wells, Roy Young, the late Mark Dworkin, Jerry and Judy Crandall, Mike Pitel, Judith Sims, Mindy Smith Heine, Dr. James Bailey, Quinn Jacobson, Paul Seydor, Marc Simmons, Ron Kil, Rex Rideout, Andy Morris, and Jack and Mary Ann Davis.

My literary agent and good friend, Jim Donovan of Dallas, Texas, continues to provide excellent advice, whether it be about my writing, books, or a good movie to watch. Thanks also to Jim's assistant, Melissa Shultz.

My editor at William Morrow, Henry Ferris, is, I'm convinced, the best editor in the business. He knows what makes a great book (a lot harder than it seems), and he's a great guy, too. Also at William Morrow, I would like to thank editorial assistant Cole Hager, my publicist Camille Collins, designer Jamie Lynn

Kerner, and production editor Tamara Arellano. My copy editor, Laurie McGee, did another exceptional job. I would also like to acknowledge mapmaker Chris Erichsen.

Lastly, thanks to my family, Katie, Christiana, and Vance, for the love and support they give me—and for being so good about vacations that always seem to be tied to a current writing project.

Mark Lee Gardner
Cascade, Colorado
November 26, 2012

Notes

One: Rocky Cut

5 The Rocky Cut holdup is one of the best-documented
train robberies of the nineteenth century. My narrative is drawn, in part, from the reports in the following
publications: *Boonville Daily Advertiser,* July 8 and
11, 1876; *Boonville Weekly Advertiser,* July 14, 1876;
Sedalia Daily Democrat, July 8 and 9, 1876; *Weekly
Sedalia Times,* July 13, 1876; *St. Louis Republican,*
July 9 and 10, 1876; *St. Louis Globe-Democrat,* July
10 and 11, 1876; *Kansas City Daily Journal of Commerce,* July 9, 1876; and *Kansas City Times,* July 9,
1876. A detailed account, largely lifted from the July 10
Globe-Democrat, appears in the August 1876 issue of
the *Expressman's Monthly.* The eyewitness account of
passenger Christine Peabody is in the *Globe-Democrat*
for July 13, 1876. Baggage master Louis Peter "Pete"
Conklin was interviewed by the *St. Louis Republican*

shortly after the holdup, but he was also interviewed nearly fifty years later by Jesse James biographer Robertus Love. See Love's *The Rise and Fall of Jesse James* (New York: G. P. Putnam's Sons, 1926), 178–185. Conklin believed that Jesse James and Cole Younger were among those robbers inside the cars and Frank James was outside, giving orders to the others.

8 Just east of Otterville, Missouri, on State Highway A, a roadside park on the bluff overlooking Rocky Cut features a granite marker noting the famed robbery.

15 The reader may wonder at the repeated cursing by the robbers. *The Expressman's Monthly* commented that the "whole affair was redolent of profanity." The James-Younger gang was composed of hard men used to course language, but their swearing also served as another way to intimidate their victims.

22 For the Pinkerton attack on the James farm, I have relied upon the *Liberty Tribune*, Jan. 29, 1875; Robert J. Wybrow, *"My Arm was Hanging Loose": The Pinkerton Attack on the James' Family Home* (London: The English Westerners' Society, 2005); and T. J. Stiles, *Jesse James: Last Rebel of the Civil War* (New York: Alfred A. Knopf, 2002), 277–284.

24 For the Roscoe gunfight, see *The History of Henry and St. Clair Counties, Missouri* (St. Joseph, MO: National Historical Company, 1883), 930–934; the *Leavenworth Weekly Times*, Mar. 26, 1874; the *Liberty Tribune*, Mar. 27, 1874; and the *Daily Inter-Ocean*, Chicago, Mar. 23 and Apr. 1, 1874.

26 For the Edmund Graves arrest, see the *St. Louis Missouri Republican,* July 10, 1876; the *St. Louis Globe-Democrat,* July 11, 1876; and the *Kansas City Daily Journal of Commerce,* July 11, 1876.

28 For the accidental killing of Margaret Harris, see the *Kansas City Times,* July 27, 1876; the *St. Louis Globe-Democrat,* July 26, 1876; the *Weekly Sedalia Times,* July 27, 1876; the *Boonville Daily Advertiser,* July 25, 1876; and the *Sedalia Daily Democrat,* Aug. 18, 1876. Albert Harris subsequently filed a lawsuit against the Adams Express Company, the United States Express Company, and the Missouri Pacific Railroad for $5,000 in damages for the death of his wife. Margaret Harris is buried in the La Monte Cemetery.

29 A physical description of Hobbs Kerry is found in the *St. Louis Globe-Democrat,* Aug. 4, 1876; and in Register of Inmates, Missouri State Penitentiary, Vol. F, Missouri State Archives, Jefferson City. Kerry is enumerated as "Burr Carey" in the 1860 U.S. census for Granby township, Newton County, Missouri. My narrative of Kerry's arrest and subsequent confession is drawn from the *St. Louis Globe-Democrat,* Aug. 5, 10, 13, and 28, 1876; the *Daily Inter-Ocean,* Chicago, Aug. 9, 1876; the *Kansas City Times,* Aug. 13 and 15, 1876; and the *St. Louis Missouri Republican,* Aug. 13, 1876. Kerry was released from prison in the spring of 1880 and, two years later, was living somewhere in the East. After that, he disappears from the record. See the *Kansas City Journal,* Oct. 9, 1882.

33 James McDonough's career as St. Louis's chief of police is briefly covered in Allen E. Wagner, *Good Order and Safety: A History of the St. Louis Metropolitan Police Department, 1861–1906* (St. Louis: Missouri History Museum, 2008). Criticism of McDonough's handling of the Kerry arrest and confession is as quoted in the *St. Louis Globe-Democrat*, Aug. 17, 1876. McDonough was also taken to task in the *Sedalia Daily Democrat*, Aug. 27, 1876.

34 The Suppression of Outlawry Act is in *Laws of Missouri: General and Local Laws Passed at the Adjourned Session of the 27th General Assembly, Begun and Held at the City of Jefferson, Wednesday, January 7, 1874* (Jefferson City: Regan & Carter, 1874), 5–6.

Two: Band of Brothers

36 The best source for Henry Washington Younger and his family is Marley Brant, *The Outlaw Youngers: A Confederate Brotherhood* (Lanham, MD: Madison Books, 1992).

Cole Younger's recollections of his father as a Unionist are in his *The Story of Cole Younger by Himself* (Chicago: The Henneberry Co., 1903), 16.

For the jayhawker raids against Henry Younger's property, see Brant, 20; *The History of Jackson County, Missouri* (Kansas City, MO: Union Historical Company, 1881), 272; and Albert Castel, "Kansas Jayhawking Raids into Western Missouri in 1861," *Missouri Historical Review* 54 (Oct. 1959): 2.

37 Cole's run-in with the militia officer, Captain Irvin Walley, is recounted in *The Story of Cole Younger by Himself*, 15–16; and "Cole Younger's Career as Reviewed by Himself," the *Minneapolis Journal*, Mar. 4, 1903.

Cole's story of his father's death is in *The Story of Cole Younger by Himself*, 8–9. Irvin Walley and his men are thought to have been the murderers of Henry Younger. See Brant, 30.

For the burning of the Younger home, see Brant, 42; *The Story of Cole Younger by Himself*, 11; and "Cole Younger's Career as Reviewed by Himself."

38 For the collapse of the women's prison, see Charles F. Harris, "Catalyst for Terror: The Collapse of the Women's Prison in Kansas City," *Missouri Historical Review* 89 (Apr. 1995): 290–306; John McCorkle, *Three Years with Quantrill* (1914; reprint, Norman: University of Oklahoma Press, 1992), 120–123; and *The Story of Cole Younger by Himself*, 9. Cole claimed that his two cousins had been arrested and confined in the prison because they had witnessed the murder of his father the year previous.

39 For the Lawrence Raid/Massacre, see Richard Cordley, *Pioneer Days in Kansas* (Boston: The Pilgrim Press, 1903), 178–220; Edward E. Leslie, *The Devil Knows How to Ride: The True Story of William Clarke Quantrill and His Confederate Raiders* (New York: Random House, 1996), 193–244; and John N. Edwards, *Noted Guerillas, or the Warfare on the*

Border (St. Louis, MO: Bryan, Brand & Co., 1877), 191–199. Quantrill's "kill" order is as quoted in William Elsey Connelley, *Quantrill and the Border Wars* (Cedar Rapids, IA: The Torch Press, 1910), 343.

John Newman Edwards, a James-Younger gang apologist, makes the claim that Cole saved a dozen lives in Lawrence, adding that the bushwhacker "killed none save in open and manly battle." *Noted Guerillas*, 196.

For Cole's "secret mission" and dubious adventures as an Indian fighter, see *The Story of Cole Younger by Himself*, 50–51; and "Cole Younger's Career as Reviewed by Himself." J. W. Buel wrote that Cole's secret mission was to recruit a Confederate regiment in California. Buel's source was almost certainly Cole, and the story is just as bogus as the others Cole spun. See Buel's *The Border Outlaws . . .* (St. Louis, MO: Historical Publishing Co., 1882), 110.

40 Little is known of Jim Younger's service with Quantrill, but see *Noted Guerillas*, 282 and 401; *Three Years with Quantrill*, 195–196; *Quantrill and the Border Wars*, 457; and Paul R. Petersen, *Quantrill of Missouri: The Making of a Guerrilla Warrior, The Man, the Myth, the Soldier* (Nashville: Cumberland House, 2003), 401–402.

An interesting account of Quantrill's foray into Kentucky by Allen Parmer, brother-in-law of the James boys, is found in "Quantrill's Raiders Hold Reunion and Recall Wild Exploits," *New York Tribune*, Sept. 5, 1920. For the surrender of the last of Quantrill's men at Samuels Depot, see *Quantrill and the Border Wars,* 478–479. Frank's parole document from Samuel's Depot, dated July 26, 1865, is reproduced in Gary Hendershott catalog 84 (Oct. 1994), 2.

42 Frank James gave his version of the events at and near Centralia in an interview published in the *St. Louis Republic,* Aug. 5, 1900. It is this same article that contains Frank's explanation as to why the bushwhackers never took prisoners. For more on the Centralia Massacre and the Battle of Centralia, see *Noted Guerillas,* 293–302; and Albert Castel and Thomas Goodrich, *Bloody Bill Anderson: The Short, Savage Life of a Civil War Guerrilla* (Mechanicsburg, PA: Stackpole Books, 1998), 79–95. Frank James always said it was brother Jesse who killed the Federal commander, Major Andrew V. E. Johnston. John Newman Edwards also identified Jesse as Johnston's killer in his *Noted Guerillas,* although Edwards was not present at the engagement.

43 For Robert James, see "A Dead Desperado," *St. Louis Globe-Democrat,* Apr. 4, 1882; "The James Family," *St. Louis Globe-Democrat,* Apr. 6, 1882; the *Kansas City Journal,* Apr. 6, 1882; Jesse James Jr., *Jesse James, My Father* (Cleveland: The Arthur Westbrook Co., 1906), 21–23; and Ted P. Yeatman, *Frank and Jesse James: The Story Behind the Legend* (Nashville, TN: Cumberland House, 2000), 25–26.

Zerelda James, her memorable personality, and her marriages have been chronicled often. Only in recent years has information been published on her prenuptial agreement with Dr. Reuben Samuel. See Yeatman, 27–28.

Frank James's description of the conditions in Clay County at the outbreak of the Civil War is as quoted in Edward H. Smith, "Frank James, Bandit, as He Saw Himself," The Sunday Press Illustrated Magazine Section, the *Pittsburgh Press*, Mar. 21, 1915.

A brief but valuable synopsis of the Civil War careers of both Frank and Jesse James is found in *History of Clay and Platte Counties, Missouri* (St. Louis: National Historical Company, 1885), 266–268.

44 Frank James's statement that the Federals drove Jesse to join the bushwhackers is as quoted in the *Pittsburgh Press*, Mar. 21, 1915.

45 My account of the violent episode at the James farm in May 1863 draws upon the research of Yeatman, 38–40. For the James family version of the incident, which differs considerably from the militia officer account quoted by Yeatman, see the *Pittsburgh Press*, Mar. 21, 1915; *Jesse James, My Father*, 28–30; and the *St. Paul Dispatch*, Oct. 27, 1876.

The Frank James quote on Jesse "out for blood" is from the *Pittsburgh Press*, Mar. 21, 1915.

46 The story of Jesse shooting off the tip of his middle finger and how it led to his nickname is from *History of Clay and Platte Counties, Missouri*, 268.

Jesse's wounding by the German Unionist is from Yeatman, 53; and *History of Clay and Platte Counties, Missouri*, 267.

47 For Jesse's second wounding and his surrender, see Yeatman, 75–77; and Jim Cummins, *Jim Cummins the Guerilla* (Excelsior Springs, MO: The Daily Journal, 1908), 49. The James family always claimed Jesse was on his way to Lexington to surrender when he was attacked and wounded. See *History of Clay and Platte Counties, Missouri*, 268; and *Noted Guerillas*, 333–335. The doctor who treated Jesse's wound, Dr. Joseph M. Wood, provides interesting details about his patient in an interview in the *St. Louis Globe-Democrat*, Apr. 6, 1882. An account by a Third Wisconsin veteran who claimed to have fired the shot that wounded Jesse is in the *Columbus Journal*, Columbus, NE, Mar. 2, 1904.

The Frank James "we were outlaws" quote is from the *Pittsburgh Press*, Mar. 21, 1915.

48 Cole Younger's comments about the "vigilant committees" is from "Cole Younger's Career as Reviewed by Himself."

The Iron Clad Oath is quoted from Article 2, Section 3 of the Missouri Constitution of 1865.

49 For the robbery of the Clay County Savings Association, Liberty, see the *Liberty Tribune*, Feb. 16, 1866; Robert J. Wybrow, *"Horrid Murder & Heavy Robbery": The Liberty Bank Robbery, 13 February 1866* (London: The English Westerners' Society, 2003); and Yeatman, 85–86.

For the robbery of the Daviess County Savings Association, Gallatin, see *The History of Daviess County*,

Missouri (Kansas City: Birdsall & Dean, 1882), 498–502; *Freeport Journal,* Illinois, Dec. 15, 1869; *Chillicothe Weekly Constitution,* Missouri, Feb. 14, 1901; Jim Muehlberger, "Showdown with Jesse James," *Wild West* 22 (Feb. 2010): 50–53; and Yeatman, 95–97. It is not a given that Frank James was the second robber at Gallatin. John Newman Edwards told journalist Hugh W. Sawyer that it was Jim Anderson, brother of Bloody Bill, who participated in the holdup with Jesse. Edwards also related that the pair had gone to Gallatin specifically to murder Samuel P. Cox. Considering the degree to which revenge was a part of the makeup of the bushwhackers—and especially Jesse—this makes sense. See Hugh W. Sawyer, "Gallatin Trial," typescript, folder 2, Homer Croy Papers, Western Historical Manuscript Collection, Columbia, MO.

50 "They are outlaws, but they are not criminals," is from *Noted Guerillas,* 451.

For the 1875 amnesty bill for the Jameses and the Youngers, see the *Daily Inter-Ocean,* Chicago, Mar. 25, 1875.

51 The best source for Clelland D. "Clell" Miller and his family is Ruth Coder Fitzgerald, *Clell and Ed Miller: Members of the James Gang* (Fredericksburg, VA: privately printed, 1987).

For Clell at the "Battle of Albany," Oct. 27, 1864, see the *Atchison Daily Champion,* May 25, 1886; and *Noted Guerillas,* 326. The story of Colonel Cox saving

Miller's life is from Henry Clay McDougal, *Recollections, 1844–1909* (Kansas City, MO: Franklin Hudson Publishing Co., 1910), 30–31.

52 Clell's capture after the Corydon bank robbery was reported in the *Liberty Tribune,* Mar. 8, 1872. The subsequent trial is well covered by Fitzgerald, *Clell and Ed Miller.* Wayne County, IA, District Court Record Book D, p. 38, records the $150 award to Miller for his witnesses. A transcript is in the Clell Miller File, Milton F. Perry Library, James Farm, Kearney, MO.

Newspaper accounts of the 1874 Muncie train robbery are in the *Leavenworth Weekly Times,* Dec. 10 and 17, 1874.

The botched attempt to capture Clell near Carrollton, MO, is chronicled in a colorful article, "Fooling with a Desperado!," from the *Carrollton Journal,* Apr. 2, 1875; clipping in box 7, folder 17, Records of Charles Henry Hardin, 1875–1877 (RG 3.22), Missouri State Archives, Jefferson City.

53 For Charlie Pitts (Samuel Wells), see Shirley Wells, "The Real 'Charlie Pitts,'" *James-Younger Gang Journal* 17 (Summer 2010): 6–7.

Cole Younger is the source for Margaret Wells and her son Sam (Charlie Pitts) discovering the body of Henry Washington Younger. See *The Story of Cole Younger by Himself,* 8–9.

The death of Charlie's father, George Washington "Wash" Wells, is described in Petersen, *Quantrill of Missouri,* 187–188; and the *Liberty Tribune,* Oct. 20, 1876.

54 Charlie's wife, Jennie, describes their life while working with the Missouri-Kansas-Texas Railroad in a WPA interview from 1937. See Jennie Lamar interview, #7631, Vol. 52, Indian-Pioneer Papers, Western History Collections, University of Oklahoma Library, Norman.

The physical description of Pitts is from the *St. Paul Dispatch*, Sept. 25, 1876, and surviving photographs, one of which is from the famous postmortems, illustrated in this book.

Pitts's relationship with the widow Beemer is from a lengthy interview she gave to a *Kansas City Times* reporter. In addition to the *Times*, the interview was published in the *St. Louis Globe-Democrat*, Aug. 7, 1876. Beemer subsequently penned a letter to the *Times*, dated Aug. 16, in which she desired to "correct a few statements" made in the original *Times* interview. Contradicting what she told the *Times* reporter, Beemer denied having any knowledge of Pitts's activities as a bank and train robber. "Pitts and Chadwell may both be very bad men," she wrote, "but I have no evidence of this fact, outside of rumor; and I must have more evidence than I have at present before I believe all I have heard against them." I do not believe that the widow Beemer was truly this naive. Her letter is printed in the Aug. 18, 1876, edition of the *Kansas City Times*.

55 Charlie's brothers, Robert and Charles E. Wells, are both found in Wyandotte County, KS (about 125 miles north of Cherokee), in the 1875 Kansas State census.

Robert was living with his mother and sisters in Wyandotte Township, and Charles, a merchant, was residing in the Quindaro Township. Samuel Wells (Charlie Pitts), his wife, Virginia, and daughter, Mary, are enumerated in the 1870 U.S. census in the very same Quindaro Township, Wyandotte County.

For the mules, harnesses, and wagons purchased by Charlie Pitts with his Rocky Cut money, see the *St. Louis Globe-Democrat*, Aug. 17, 1876; and the *Sedalia Daily Democrat*, Sept. 9 and Oct. 10, 1876. The *Sedalia Daily Democrat* of Sept. 9 reported that this property was captured near Fort Scott, KS, under the care of Robert Wells.

56 For the portrait of Charlie Pitts in the possession of Lillie Beemer, see the *Sedalia Daily Democrat*, Oct. 4, 1876.

William Chadwell, age seven, is enumerated in the 1860 U.S. census for the Eastern Precinct, Greene County, IL, in the household of Margaret Chadwell, his mother. Significantly, Cole Younger remembered that Chadwell was "a young fellow from Illinois." See his *The Story of Cole Younger by Himself*, 77. Bill Chadwell does not appear in subsequent Kansas censuses, but brothers Matterson (Madison), Samuel, and James do. His mother died in Joplin, MO, in 1878.

My description of the teenage Chadwell comes from the account of an unknown Crawford County, KS, woman in whose home Chadwell lived for several months in 1871. See the *Faribault Republican*, Oct. 25, 1876.

57 The story of Chadwell grabbing the blasting powder out of the fire is from the *Burlington Hawk-Eye* (Iowa), Nov. 23, 1876, which was copying an article that originally appeared in the *California Democrat* (Missouri).

For the robbery of the Baxter Springs, Kansas, bank, see the *St. Louis Globe-Democrat,* Apr. 20, 1876.

The Kansas manhunts for Pitts and Chadwell are detailed in the *St. Louis Globe-Democrat,* Aug. 7 and 17, 1876. The Aug. 7 article carried the sensational report that Pitts had been captured while eating dinner in a house on Spring Creek and that a wad of $1,800 in cash was found on him. This same article contains the story of the posse surrounding Chadwell in a cornfield. However, the Aug. 17 news item fails to mention either of these episodes and states that Pitts and Chadwell rode away from the home of Chadwell's father-in-law a few days before the arrival of the posse.

58 Cole's comparison of Frank and Jesse is from the *Winona Daily Republican,* Oct. 13, 1883.

For one version of Cole's near shoot-out with Jesse, see his *The Story of Cole Younger by Himself* (Chicago: The Henneberry Co., 1903), 92–93.

59 My description of Frank James comes from the following contemporary sources: *St. Louis Dispatch,* Nov. 23, 1873; *Dolores News,* Rico, Colorado, Oct. 14, 1882; *St. Louis Missouri Republican,* Oct. 6, 1882; *Kansas City Weekly Journal,* Jan. 1, 1883; *Kansas City Journal,* Oct. 9, 1882, and June 18, 1897; and *St. Louis Globe-Democrat,* Oct. 11, 1882.

There is considerable confusion over the heights of Frank and Jesse James, as well as the difference in height between the two. John Newman Edwards, who had met the brothers, wrote that "Frank was a little older and taller than Jesse." Morris Langhorn, editor of the *Independence Herald,* met Frank in 1874 and later said, "It was a mistake to think Jesse James is the taller of the two; he is not; Frank bears that distinguished mark." Upon Frank's surrender to the Missouri governor in 1882, his height was given by reporter Frank O'Neil as "exactly five feet nine inches." Bob Ford said Frank was five feet, eleven and a half inches, and Langhorn said the outlaw was "about six feet tall." Oddly, no effort appears to have been made to get an official measurement of Jesse's body after his assassination on Apr. 3, 1882. A reporter for the *Western News,* a St. Joseph newspaper, described Jesse's body, apparently from personal inspection, and gave the outlaw's height as "about five feet eight inches." Jesse's brother-in-law told a *Kansas City Journal* reporter that Jesse was "about" five feet, eleven inches tall. Other contemporary newspapers provide heights ranging from five feet, eight to six feet, one-half inches. See *Noted Guerillas,* 168; *Sedalia Weekly Bazoo,* Sept. 20, 1881, and Apr. 11, 1882; *St. Louis Missouri Republican,* Oct. 6, 1882; *Kansas City Journal,* Apr. 5 and Oct. 9, 1882; *Western News,* Apr. 7, 1882; *St. Joseph Weekly Gazette,* Apr. 5, 1882; and the *County Paper,* Oregon, Missouri, Apr. 14, 1882.

My description of Jesse James comes from several sources, but see particularly *Noted Guerillas,* 167–168;

the *St. Louis Dispatch,* Nov. 23, 1873; and the *St. Joseph Weekly Gazette,* Apr. 5, 1882.

The quote about Jesse sitting straight in the saddle is from Elmer Pigg to Homer Croy, Jefferson City, MO, Oct. 30, 1948, folder 742, Homer Croy Papers, Western Historical Manuscript Collection, Columbia, MO.

Charley Ford's recollections of Jesse's sense of humor are found in "Jesse on a Lark," *Sedalia Weekly Bazoo,* Apr. 18, 1882.

60 Thomas Mimms, the brother of Jesse's wife, Zee, is quoted from the *Kansas City Journal,* Apr. 5, 1882.

George Hite Jr. was the cousin Jesse cautioned not to believe any stories of his capture. Hite is quoted from the *Weekly Missouri Republican,* Apr. 13, 1882.

Charley Ford's story of the "ball of fire" is from the *Liberty Weekly Tribune,* Apr. 21, 1882.

61 Charles S. Murray's characterization of Jesse as a "queer combination" is as quoted in Robertus Love, *The Rise and Fall of Jesse James* (New York: G. P. Putnam's Sons, 1926), 108.

My description of the Younger brothers comes mostly from the reporting of journalists following the capture of the Youngers in Minnesota. See especially the *St. Paul Dispatch,* Sept. 22, 1876; the *St. Louis Republican,* Sept. 25, 1876; and the *St. Louis Globe-Democrat,* Sept. 28, 1876.

62 Cole's quote on Jim Younger's mood swings is from the *Saint Paul Globe,* Oct. 20, 1902.

The Bob Younger quote—"I might have been something"—is from the *St. Louis Globe-Democrat*, Sept. 26, 1876.

63 The Jesse James letters of August 14 and 18 were published in the *Kansas City Times* of Aug. 18 and 23, 1876, respectively. The originals of these letters have not survived, so one cannot say absolutely that the letters were penned by Jesse, but they were accepted as such at the time, and James scholars have since concurred.

Three: Tigers on the Loose

65 The locust damage in Minnesota in 1876 is well documented in F. V. Hayden, *Ninth Annual Report of the United States Geological and Geographical Survey of the Territories . . .* (Washington: Government Printing Office, 1877), 617–621.

66 Literature on the Centennial International Exposition of 1876 is abundant. For information on the Yale Lock Manufacturing Company's exhibit, see *The Great Centennial Exhibition, Critically Described and Illustrated*, by Phillip T. Sandhurst et al. (Philadelphia: P. W. Ziegler & Co., 1876), 316.

67 For descriptions of the Yale chronometer lock, see *The Masterpieces of the Centennial International Exposition*, Vol. 3: *History, Mechanics, Science*, by Joseph M. Wilson (Philadelphia: Gebbe & Barrie: 1876), 229–230; *The Encyclopaedia Britannica*, Vol. 14 (Edinburgh: Adam and Charles Black, 1882), 751; and the *Daily Tribune*, Salt Lake City, Dec. 20, 1876.

The term "bulldozing" is related in C. B. Berry, *The Other Side, How It Struck Us* (London: Griffith and Farran, 1880), 155.

News of the planned installation of a chronometer lock in the First National Bank of Northfield first appeared in the *Rice County Journal,* Aug. 9, 1876. A follow-up article appeared in a later issue of the *Journal,* which I have been unable to locate. However, the follow-up article was reprinted in the *Minneapolis Tribune* of Sept. 11, 1876.

68 Cashier Phillip's departure for Philadelphia was reported in the *Rice County Journal,* Sept. 7, 1876.

69 Evidence of Samuel Hardwicke's significant role in the planning and implementation of the raid on the James farm is found in the letters of Allan Pinkerton. See particularly Pinkerton's letter to Hardwicke of Dec. 28, 1874, reproduced in Ted P. Yeatman, *Frank and Jesse James: The Story Behind the Legend* (Nashville, TN: Cumberland House, 2000), 129–131. Former Clay County sheriff George E. Patton commented on Hardwicke's role in the raid in a letter to his family: "He [Hardwicke] was the prime mover of the whole affair and the getter-up of the plan of operations and helped to execute [it] to my certain knowledge." Patton to M. D. Scruggs, Liberty, MO, Feb. 21, 1875, Culbertson Collection, Watkins Woolen Mill State Historic Site, Lawson, MO. Gallatin, MO, attorney Henry Clay McDougal claimed to have been the "middleman" between Hardwicke and Pinkerton: "[A]ll their

correspondence was through me." See Henry Clay McDougal, *Recollections, 1844–1909* (Kansas City, MO: Franklin Hudson Publishing Co., 1910), 29.

For my description of Hardwicke, I have relied upon *History of Clay and Platte Counties, Missouri* (St. Louis: National Historical Company, 1885), 336–339; *Liberty Tribune*, Feb. 17, 1860; and *Liberty Advance*, July 19, 1895.

70 For Hardwicke's move from his farmstead south of Liberty to the town square, see George E. Patton to M. D. Scruggs, Feb. 21, 1875; the *Kansas City Times*, Apr. 3, 1875; and *Semi-Weekly Wisconsin*, Milwaukee, May 1, 1875.

As far as is known, the letters Hardwicke wrote to Jesse have not survived, but Jesse discusses them in his letter to Dr. Reuben Samuel of Mar. 23, 1875. In this letter, Jesse wrote that Hardwicke had asked that his letters to the outlaw be burned, a request Jesse did not honor. Hardwicke, Jesse wrote, "knows they are too valuable to me." Jesse's letter to Dr. Samuel remained in private hands, unknown to scholars, for nearly 130 years. It was auctioned by Christie's on Dec. 16, 2004, for $175,500 (Sale 1450, Lot 397).

71 For the Clay County grand jury inquiry into the Pinkerton raid, see the *Liberty Tribune*, Apr. 9, 1875; and Robert J. Wybrow, *"My Arm Was Hanging Loose": The Pinkerton Attack on the James' Family Home* (London: The English Westerners' Society, 2005), 25.

72 For the murder of Daniel Askew and the subsequent inquest, see the *Liberty Tribune*, Apr. 16, 1875; *Leavenworth Weekly Times*, Apr. 22, 1875; and the *Troy Herald*, Troy, MO, Apr. 28, 1875. Gang member Dick Liddil claimed that Clell Miller was with Jesse when Askew was killed, but a story passed down in one branch of the James family has Frank and Jesse as the killers. See *Sedalia Weekly Bazoo*, Sept. 18, 1883; and Yeatman, 145.

The *Kansas City Times* quote referring to a "tiger" on the loose in Clay County is as quoted in the *Troy Herald*, Apr. 28, 1875.

For the report of the five men, enemies of the James boys, marked for death, see the *Semi-Weekly Wisconsin*, May 1, 1875. The *Daily Inter-Ocean*, Chicago, of May 15, 1875, in an article titled "A Reign of Terror," claimed that fifteen men had been ordered to leave Clay County. In what was surely an exaggeration, one report claimed that Hardwicke went from his house to his office "armed with two revolvers, a dirk-knife and a shotgun." See the *Iola Register*, Iola, KS, June 19, 1875.

73 Hardwicke's imminent move to St. Paul, Minnesota, was reported in the *Liberty Tribune*, Apr. 28 and May 12, 1876. In 1879, George E. Patton wrote that in the aftermath of the Pinkerton raid, "Samuel Hardwicke had to leave the country, forsake a good home, a lucrative practice and move his family to a distant State." *Sedalia Daily Democrat*, Dec. 18, 1879. See also the Samuel Hardwicke file, Milton Perry Library, James Farm, Kearney, MO.

There are numerous newspaper reports chronicling the widespread hunt for the Rocky Cut robbers. Chief James McDonough eventually sent men to Denison, Texas, to stake out a house that he understood was a gang refuge. See his letter to Governor Charles Hardin of Sept. 12, 1876, Records of Charles Henry Hardin, 1875–1877 (RG 3.22), Missouri State Archives, Jefferson City, MO.

The *Sedalia Weekly Bazoo* of Apr. 18, 1882, mentions the death threats Hobbs Kerry received while in the Cooper County jail.

Many locations have been put forward as the meeting place of the James-Younger gang in mid-August 1876, where they made the decision to travel to Minnesota, including the ranch house of outlaw Calvin "Cal" Carter east of Denison, Texas; the home of Moses and Emeline Miller in Clay County, MO; an undisclosed Kansas City, MO, location; and a remote spot in eastern Kansas. See James McDonough to Governor Hardin of Sept. 22, 1876, Records of Charles Henry Hardin; Henry S. Miller interview in *Kansas City Daily Journal*, Sept. 5, 1896; Marley Brant, *The Outlaw Youngers: A Confederate Brotherhood* (Lanham, MD: Madison Books, 1992), 164; and J. W. Buel, *The Border Outlaws . . .* (St. Louis, MO: Historical Publishing Co., 1882), 217.

74 Samuel Hardwicke's letter to the editor of the *Liberty Tribune*, mailed from St. Paul, appeared in the issue of July 21, 1876. Jesse, an avid newspaper reader, may

have discovered this himself, or, and this seems more likely, he was alerted to the piece by family or friends in Clay County.

Most writers and historians have missed Hardwicke as a major motivation for the James-Younger gang's Minnesota expedition. However, the contemporary press did not miss the story. An Oct. 15, 1876, letter by a visitor to the James farm (originally published in the *Chicago Times*) gave the Liberty attorney as "the real cause of the robbers going to Minnesota," as did an article originally published in the *Boonville Advertiser* titled "Why It Was the James Boys went to Minnesota." These articles were also published in the *Saint Paul Dispatch*, Oct. 19, 1876, and *The State Journal*, Jefferson City, MO, Oct. 27, 1876. Clay County locals also knew about the Hardwicke connection. Dr. Robert Sheetz, son of Dr. Samuel Sheetz, who treated the wounded Zerelda Samuel in the aftermath of the Pinkerton raid, said that "one of the reasons that the James' went to Minnesota was to kill a certain lawyer from Liberty who had gone to St. Paul to get away from the boys." See Elmer Pigg to Homer Croy, Jefferson City, MO, no date, folder 740, Homer Croy Papers, Western Historical Manuscript Collection, Columbia, MO.

Bob Younger's enthusiasm for Jesse's plan is detailed in a letter Jim Younger purportedly wrote to former sweetheart Cora McNeill in August of 1898. The private letters of Jim and Cole Younger, written from Stillwater in the late 1890s, present a problem in that they are not publicly accessible. I have not seen the letters, only excerpts by those who claimed to have access to them. The letters were last in the possession of James-Younger collector Wilbur Zink, who died in 2010, and they are said to remain with Zink's family at present. Marley Brant quotes the Jim Younger letter of August 1898, in her letter to John J. Koblas, Los Angeles, CA, Nov. 22, 1982, box 1, John J. Koblas Collection, Northfield Historical Society, Northfield, MN. Wilbur Zink quotes from the letters of both Jim and Cole in his letter to Koblas, Appleton City, MO, Nov. 11, 1982, *ibid.*

For Cole's opposition to the Minnesota expedition, see "Cole Younger's Career as Reviewed by Himself," the *Minneapolis Journal,* Mar. 4, 1903; and Todd M. George to Homer Croy, Lee's Summit, MO, Oct. 31, 1956, folder 33, B. James George Collection, Western Historical Manuscript Collection.

75 The James-Younger gang's mode of transportation to Minnesota has generated much speculation, all due to the confusing and conflicting accounts left by Cole and Jim Younger. The private letters from the pair referenced above indicate the gang traveled to Minnesota horseback, a long and tiresome journey to be sure—and one that makes little sense. The gang had plenty of money after the Rocky Cut robbery, and the boys never hesitated in spending their ill-gotten gains on luxuries. Although Cole's statements and writings should be used with caution, I believe he spoke the truth when he told a newspaper reporter in 1903,

"The eight of us took the same train at St. Joseph, or points south, and went by rail to Mankato and then to St. Paul and Minneapolis." Cole also wrote of the gang traveling by rail in his autobiography. See "Cole Younger's Career as Reviewed by Himself"; and *The Story of Cole Younger by Himself*, 77.

76 My description of Minnesota's Big Woods is taken from Warren Upham, *The Geology of Central and Western Minnesota* (St. Paul: The Pioneer Press Co., 1880), 26–28; and Boston W. Smith, *Spicy Breezes from Minnesota Prairies* (Philadelphia: American Baptist Publication Society, 1885), 102–104.

77 The stay of some of the James-Younger gang at the Nicollet House was later reported in the *Minneapolis Tribune*, Sept. 9, 1876. The newspaper stated that one gang member was sick during the stay and did not leave his room. Cole Younger identified the sick man as Bill Chadwell in a statement in the *St. Louis Globe-Democrat*, Apr. 6, 1882.

My description of the linen dusters worn by the James-Younger gang is based on an original duster that was left behind in the Northfield bank during the Sept. 7 raid. This duster, forty-four inches in length, is now part of the collections of the Minnesota Historical Society. Unlike modern dusters, the Northfield duster has no sleeves. Instead, an attached loose cape protected the arms.

78 The prostitute Mollie Ellsworth was reported to have been a native of Buffalo, New York, although the

1875 Minnesota state census (Minneapolis 5th Ward) gives her birthplace as Ireland. That same census records her name as "Kittie Traverse alias Mollie Ellsworth." Her obituary, which gives her "real name" as Kate Traverse, states that she pursued "her life of shame" first in St. Louis and later Omaha. The *St. Louis Globe-Democrat* of Oct. 30, 1875, lists a Mollie Ellsworth as one of several "frail ones" fined $25 each for "being inmates of houses of ill fame." Mollie failed to appear before the court in answer to the charge. Mollie's obit appears in the *Minneapolis Tribune*, Oct. 28, 1876. My thanks to Donna Tatting for providing me with a copy of the obit.

Mollie's story of her encounter with Jesse James was published in the *St. Paul and Minneapolis Pioneer Press and Tribune*, Sept. 20, 1876.

80 Chinn & Morgan's, "one of the most elegant gambling houses in the Northwest," is described in the *St. Paul Daily Globe*, Apr. 4, 1883. The casino closed its doors in 1887 when there was a crackdown on gambling in St. Paul. Chinn and Morgan opened a gambling hall in New York City in 1890, but it was short-lived. Chinn became quite famous as a breeder and racer of American thoroughbreds. His horse, Leonatus, won the Kentucky Derby in 1883, and a horse foaled on Chinn's stock farm, George Smith, won the 1916 Kentucky Derby. Although Chinn is not well known today, there is considerable information on him (and his various knife fights) in contemporary newspapers and magazine articles. See the *St. Paul Daily News*,

Nov. 16, 1892; the *St. Paul Daily Globe*, Oct. 15, 1888; and *Seen and Heard* 2 (Aug. 13, 1902): 1025–1039. An obituary for Chinn is in the *Central Record*, Lancaster, KY, Feb. 5, 1920.

81 The James brothers' cousin, George Hite Jr., said that Frank and Jesse made trips to Kentucky almost yearly beginning in about 1865. See the *Weekly Missouri Republican*, Apr. 13, 1882.

The story of the outlaws removing their dusters in the gambling house is from the *Saint Paul Dispatch*, Sept. 9, 1876; and the *Pioneer Press and Tribune*, Sept. 9, 1876. Cole Younger describes his and Chadwell's visit to Chinn & Morgan's in *The Story of Cole Younger by Himself*, 77–78.

82 The street address of the Hardwicke & Barnum St. Paul law office is given in John J. Koblas, *Jesse James Ate Here: An Outlaw Tour and History of Minnesota at the Time of the Northfield Raid* (St. Cloud, MN: North Star Press of St. Cloud, 2001), 43.

83 George Hite Jr.'s recollection about Jesse going to Chicago to kill Allan Pinkerton is from the *Weekly Missouri Republican*, Apr. 13, 1882. This episode is yet another example of the degree to which revenge was a part of Jesse's makeup.

84 Eyewitness testimony of the gang's presence in Red Wing was recounted later in the *Red Wing Argus*, Sept. 14, 1876; the *Pioneer Press and Tribune*, Sept. 9, 1876; and the *Saint Paul Dispatch*, Sept. 16, 1876. The four gang members checked in to Red Wing's National

Hotel, giving their names as J. C. Horton, Nashville; H. L. Nest, Nashville; Charles Wetherby, Maryland; and Ed Everhard, Maryland.

85 Bob Younger and Bill Chadwell's St. Paul shopping spree is described in the *Pioneer Press and Tribune,* Sept. 9, 1876; and the *Saint Paul Dispatch,* Sept. 9, 1876.

86 The activities of Cole Younger and Charlie Pitts in St. Peter were later reported in the *Saint Peter Tribune,* Sept. 13, 1876; and the *Pioneer Press and Tribune,* Sept. 9, 1876. The pair first lodged at St. Peter's Nicollet House, where Cole registered as J. C. King and Pitts as J. Ward, both of Virginia. The identity of the outlaw who quizzed the American House clerk about St. Peter having a bank is not given in the newspaper account, but Cole seems more likely than Pitts.

87 The story of Cole and Pitts tossing coins to the local boys is from Homer Croy, *Last of the Great Outlaws: The Story of Cole Younger* (New York: Duell, Sloan and Pearce, 1956), 110.

Cole apparently paid for Pitts's horse, as well as his own. See "Cole Younger's Career as Reviewed by Himself."

Cole's account of his experiences in St. Peter, including his acquaintance with Horace Greeley Perry, is in *The Story of Cole Younger by Himself,* 78–79.

88 Cole tells of his concerns for the whereabouts of Bob and Chadwell and the possibility that they had been arrested in *The Story of Cole Younger by Himself,* 78.

Bob Younger and Bill Chadwell's activities in St. Peter are found in the *Saint Peter Tribune*, Sept. 13, 1876.

89 My information on the town of Mankato comes primarily from the *Minnesota State Gazetteer and Business Directory, 1878–9* (Detroit, MI: R. L. Polk & Co., 1878); and Koblas, *Jesse James Ate Here*, 190–198.

For the gang's activities in Mankato, including the planned bank robbery of Sept. 4, 1876, I have relied upon John Jay Lemon, *The Northfield Tragedy* (1876; reprint, London: Westerners Publications Ltd., 2001), 3–5; *The Mankato Review*, Sept. 12 and 26, 1876; *Saint Peter Tribune*, Sept. 13, 1876; *Saint Paul Dispatch*, Sept. 11, 1876; and George Huntington, *Robber and Hero: The Story of the Northfield Raid on the First National Bank of Northfield, Minnesota, by the James-Younger Band of Robbers, in 1876* (1895; reprint, Minneapolis: Ross & Haines, 1962), 5–7.

91 The assistant cashier of Mankato's First National Bank, George T. Barr, left an important account of his encounter with Cole Younger in the bank, and also of a conversation with Cole in the Stillwater Prison in 1895. Cole told Barr in 1895 that "the original plan of the raiders had fixed on Mankato as the point they would strike." The reason for aborting the Mankato plan, he explained, was "because of so many men being at work near each of the two banks there, making the chances of a safe get away very uncertain." George T. Barr, "Account of Northfield Bank Robbery in 1876," typescript, box 2, folder 25, John J. Koblas Collection, Northfield Historical Society, Northfield, MN.

I have been unable to find any biographical information on Charles Robinson, the man who said he recognized Jesse, that would confirm his story of having
once lived in Missouri. Some contemporary newspaper accounts reported that after Robinson encountered Jesse, he told his boss, an Ed O'Leary, and it was
O'Leary who "notified the several banks and police."
See the *Mankato Review,* Sept. 12, 1876.

93 Cole mentions his visit to Madelia with Charlie Pitts
in *The Story of Cole Younger by Himself,* 79. The
owner of the Madelia hotel where the pair lodged,
T. L. Vought, discusses their visit in "Capture of
the Younger Brothers," *Northfield News,* Sept. 18,
1897.

I believe that Jesse and Clell were the two robbers
who visited Northfield a week to ten days before the
robbery because (1) the article describing the First
National Bank's new safe and chronometer lock,
from Northfield's *Rice County Journal,* was found
on Clell's dead body in the aftermath of the Raid, (2)
Clell's companion was described as "one of the leaders of the gang," (3) Clell and Jesse's movements
during this period allow for a visit to Northfield,
whereas Cole, Pitts, Bob, and Chadwell are known to
have been in St. Peter and St. Paul, and (4) Jesse and
Clell, good friends, often traveled together. See the
Saint Paul Dispatch, Sept. 8, 1876; the *Winona Daily
Republican,* Sept. 8, 1876; the *Minneapolis Tribune,*
Sept. 11, 1876; and the *St. Louis Globe-Democrat,*
Sept. 11, 1876.

94 Jesse and Clell's conversation regarding the peace-loving tendencies of the Northfield people was conducted with John Mulligan, who lived near Brush Prairie, two and a half miles west of Northfield. They also asked Mulligan about the local roads and had him go over a map one of the outlaws carried. This episode was reported in the *Rice County Journal*, Sept. 14, 1876.

When interviewed shortly after his capture, Bob Younger told a *Minneapolis Tribune* reporter that "the raid in Minnesota was not intentional. They came for pleasure, but learned ex-Governor Ames, of Mississippi, had money in the Northfield bank; one of the boys had a spite against him, and so the robbery was planned, and to pay expenses." See the *Minneapolis Tribune*, Sept. 25, 1876. T. J. Stiles, in his 2002 biography of Jesse James, excerpts a fragment of the above quote and uses it out of context to assert that Adelbert Ames was the "bandits' purpose in coming to Minnesota." As the full quote makes clear, Younger is saying that the Northfield bank did not become a target until *after* the gang's arrival in Minnesota. Cole Younger made a nearly identical statement to a *Faribault Republican* reporter: "[H]e said they came up here on a pleasure excursion, and got short of money. He stated that they selected the Northfield bank for their operations in preference to others for the reason that the Ames were interested in it, especially Gov. Ames of Mississippi, against whom one of the band had a grudge." *Faribault Republican*, Oct. 4, 1876. A

Saint Peter Tribune reporter also asked Bob Younger why the Northfield bank was selected, and he replied that "they thought there was more money to be had there—that in Mankato there were three banks, and the money was too much divided." See the *Saint Peter Tribune,* Sept. 27, 1876. I agree with Stiles that the gang member described as having a "spite" against Adelbert Ames was undoubtedly Jesse James. See Stiles, *Jesse James: Last Rebel of the Civil War* (New York: Alfred A. Knopf, 2002), 324–325.

95 For Ames's political troubles and resignation as governor of Mississippi see the *Daily Inter-Ocean,* Chicago, Feb. 26, 1876; *St. Louis Globe-Democrat,* Mar. 30, 1876; and Richard Nelson Current, *Those Terrible Carpetbaggers: A Reinterpretation* (New York: Oxford University Press, 1988), 324–325.

96 The *Faribault Democrat,* Sept. 15, 1876, reported that the gang had spent the night of Sept. 6 at Millersburg and Cannon City, which is confirmed by Cole Younger in *The Story of Cole Younger by Himself,* 80. The names of the outlaws at Millersburg and Cannon City were determined by Elias Hobbs, former Northfield chief of police, after interviews with several individuals who saw the gang members on Sept. 5 and 6. "Witnesses will describe men & horses at every point," Hobbs wrote. His statement is found in File No. 5665: *State vs. Cole, Jim, and Bob Younger,* 1876, Rice County case files and miscellaneous court papers, State Archives, Minnesota Historical Society, St. Paul.

Jim Younger's thoughts of abandoning the gang was reported in the *Minneapolis Tribune,* Nov. 15, 1876.

Four: The Hottest Day Northfield Ever Saw

97 Northfield's *Rice County Journal* of Sept. 7, 1876, carried the announcement of Professor Lingard's scheduled performance that evening. Additional details for Lingard's show are in an advertisement for "The Great Lingard" in the *Dubuque Herald,* Sept. 19, 1876.

98 Heywood's biography is given in the *Rice County Journal,* Sept. 14, 1876; and George Huntington, *Robber and Hero: The Story of the Northfield Raid on the First National Bank of Northfield, Minnesota, by the James-Younger Band of Robbers, in 1876* (1895; reprint, Minneapolis: Ross & Haines, 1962), 79–83. Heywood's Civil War career is treated in detail in Gerald D. Otis, *Joseph Lee Heywood: The Humble Hero* (Northfield, MN: Northfield Historical Society, 2006).

100 The Detroit Safe Company was identified in the *Rice County Journal,* Aug. 9, 1876, as the manufacturer of the safe and the vault doors at the First National Bank. The original Detroit Safe Company vault doors are in place in the restored bank museum in Northfield today.

The calendar clock in the bank was the No. 4 Hanging Office model, manufactured by the Ithaca Calendar Clock Co. of Ithaca, New York.

101 Biographies for Frank Wilcox, assistant bookkeeper, and Alonzo Bunker, teller, are found in *Robber and Hero*, 84–88.

102 Heywood's conversation with President Strong about the St. Albans Raid was reported in the *St. Louis Globe-Democrat*, Sept. 29, 1876, and other newspapers.

103 Cole Younger claimed to have gone into the First National Bank on Sept. 7 prior to the robbery and gotten a twenty-dollar bill changed. See the *Faribault Democrat*, Dec. 1, 1876.

For my reconstruction of the Northfield Raid, I have relied almost entirely on the accounts left by eyewitnesses. These include the depositions of Elias Hobbs and J. S. Allen, Sept. 8, 1876, in File No. 5665: *State vs. Cole, Jim, and Bob Younger*, 1876, Rice County case files and miscellaneous court papers, State Archives, Minnesota Historical Society, St. Paul; Henry Wheeler's account in the *Northfield News*, Sept. 10, 1926; Anselm Manning's account in the *Saint Paul Globe*, July 11, 1897; Adelbert Ames's letters in Blanche Butler Ames, ed., *Chronicles from the Nineteenth Century: Family Letters of Blanche Butler and Adelbert Ames*, 2 vols. (Clinton, MA: Privately Printed, 1957), 2: 403–406; Adelbert Ames's account in the *Northfield News*, Aug. 2, 1929; Theodore Miller's account in Early Northfield history scrapbook, Northfield Public Library; the several accounts contained in *The Northfield Bank Raid: Fiftieth Anniversary*

Finds Interest Undimmed in Oft-told Tale of Repulse of James-Younger Gang, 10th edition (Northfield: Northfield News, 2008); and Cole Younger's accounts in the *Saint Paul Globe*, July 4, 1897, *The Story of Cole Younger by Himself* (Chicago: The Henneberry Co., 1903), 79–85, and W. C. Heilbron, *Convict Life at the Minnesota State Prison, Stillwater, Minnesota* (1909; reprint, Stillwater, MN: Valley History Press, 1996), 137–143. Equally important is the July 10, 1897, issue of the *Northfield News*, which prints interviews with sixteen Northfield residents who witnessed or participated in some aspect of the raid. Additionally, George Huntington's *Robber and Hero*, a seminal narrative published in Northfield in 1895, is based on his interviews and correspondence with eyewitnesses. I have also drawn heavily from those Minnesota newspaper reports that are derived from eyewitness testimony. These include the *Rice County Journal*, Sept. 14, 1876; the *Minneapolis Tribune*, Sept. 8, 1876; the *St. Paul and Minneapolis Pioneer Press and Tribune*, Sept. 9, 1876; the *Saint Paul Dispatch*, Sept. 8 and 9, 1876; and the *Saint Peter Tribune*, Sept. 13, 1876. A reporter for the *Pioneer Press and Tribune*, Joseph Have Hanson, wrote the first book on the raid and the subsequent manhunt. Published in St. Paul, Hanson's *The Northfield Tragedy* appeared before the year was out. For whatever reason, Hanson did not give his name as author, using instead the pseudonym John Jay Lemon.

While there is no lack of primary source material for the raid, it is important to note that no two eyewitness accounts completely agree with each other. There are more than a few conflicting details that simply cannot be reconciled, a subject I will come to again in these notes. The Northfield Raid was seven minutes of high excitement, heart-pounding action, and—confusion. Dramatic episodes played themselves out simultaneously, both inside and outside the bank. It is understandable that people would not only have trouble making sense of what they were seeing, but that they would commit errors in relating what transpired—it all happened so fast. It is also understandable that the Younger brothers would lie to protect themselves and their comrades.

106 Identifying the robbers inside the bank and those guarding on the street has been a source of considerable debate for the last 136 years. It seems like it should be fairly straightforward. As for those in the bank, bank employees Bunker and Wilcox were in agreement in identifying Charlie Pitts and Bob Younger as two of the three inside men. Bunker named these two in his accounts published in the *Saint Paul Dispatch*, Sept. 27, 1876; the *Madelia Times*, Nov. 20, 1896; and the *Buckeye Informer*, Milo, OH, Nov. 15, 1896. Wilcox identified Pitts as one of the inside men in the *Minneapolis Tribune*, Sept. 26, 1876. Author T. J. Stiles, in his *Jesse James: Last Rebel of the Civil War* (New York: Alfred A. Knopf, 2002), 461 n. 68, claims that "Wilcox never said that Bob was in the bank." This is incorrect, for Wilcox stated in 1897 that the "three who came in were Bob Younger, Pitts and as I

believe, Frank James." See the *Northfield News,* July 10, 1897. Furthermore, Bob Younger later admitted to a reporter, "I was one of the number who went into the bank." Younger's statement appears in the *Minneapolis Tribune,* Sept. 23, 1876. But it is the identification of the third inside man, the robber who shot and killed Joseph Lee Heywood, that has been the source of so much speculation and argument. The Youngers refused to provide the authorities with the name of this man, at the same time denying that the James brothers were ever part of the raid. Modern authors and historians love to name Jesse James as the third man. The impulse killing of Heywood fits with what many believe to be Jesse's volatile personality, his supposed hotheadedness, and, of course, his revengefulness. But, Wilcox, an eyewitness to the shooting, believed Heywood's killer to be Frank James. In fact, Wilcox came to this conclusion after making a personal visit to the Jackson County, Missouri, jail to see Frank James after the outlaw's surrender in 1882. So, if Frank, Bob, and Charlie were in the bank, that leaves Jesse, Cole, Jim, Clell Miller, and Bill Chadwell outside. Cole wrote that he and Miller were the two who followed the inside men to Division Street, which leaves Jesse, Jim, and Chadwell as the robbers who were guarding the escape route at the bridge in Mill Square.

110 For what transpired in the bank, we have only the accounts of Frank Wilcox and Alonzo Bunker, and a brief statement by Bob Younger regarding Joseph Heywood. Because Bunker fled the bank before the robbers exited,

we must rely upon Wilcox's accounts for the events immediately preceding the murder of Heywood. Wilcox was interviewed by more than one reporter shortly after the raid. See his statements in the *Saint Paul Dispatch,* Sept. 8, 1876, and the *St. Paul and Minneapolis Pioneer Press and Tribune,* Sept. 9, 1876. Wilcox also testified before the coroner's inquest on Sept. 8. His deposition is in File No. 5665: *State vs. Cole, Jim, and Bob Younger,* 1876, Rice County case files and miscellaneous court papers, State Archives, Minnesota Historical Society, St. Paul. Last, Wilcox gave a detailed account twenty-one years later to a reporter for the *Northfield News,* published in the July 10, 1897, edition.

121 Some accounts place the value of the cash in the bank's till—the one Bob Younger missed—at $3,000. But Bunker, in his first interview after the raid, stated that it amounted to $2,000. See the *Saint Paul Dispatch,* Sept. 27, 1876.

122 Alonzo Bunker would later claim that his purpose in fleeing the bank was to raise the alarm "so that the citizens could come to the rescue." It seems more likely, however, that he fled out of absolute fear for his life. Wilcox said more than once that Bunker bolted immediately after Frank James fired the shot to intimidate Heywood. More significantly, Bunker seems to have made no attempt to warn anyone after escaping the bank. When Nellie Ames encountered him on Fifth Street and asked him what was the matter, Bunker replied only that he had been shot and hurried on to the residence of a doctor.

Bunker tells of running over undertaker Theodore Miller in "Northfield Raid," *Ironwood News Record,* Ironwood, MI, Sept. 21, 1895. His description of the pain he felt when Pitts's bullet struck him is from the *Madelia Times,* Nov. 20, 1896.

129 Ellen M. "Nellie" Ames's recollections of her experiences during the raid are found in a July 10, 1897, affidavit in files 85 and 86, Minnesota Board of Pardons, Pardon Applications, State Archives, Minnesota Historical Society, St. Paul; and in an expanded version of her July 10 testimony published in the *Saint Paul Globe,* July 11, 1897.

132 Which robber or robbers exited the bank first, or whether all three exited together, has often been a source of confusion. No less than three accounts from Cole Younger have Bob as the first one to answer the call to come out, after which Bob gets into his brief duel with Anselm Manning at the Scriver corner. Jesse James biographer T. J. Stiles, who would very much like to have Jesse in the bank in place of Bob, states that "No witnesses inside or outside of the bank testified to anyone exiting separately." Stiles was apparently unaware of Frank Wilcox's account published in the *Northfield News,* July 10, 1897: "The call [to come out] was responded to quickly by Pitts and Bob Younger and they were outside *before the third one started*" (emphasis added). This is consistent with Wilcox's statements from shortly after the raid. He told a reporter for the *Pioneer Press and Tribune* that "Almost immediately they took the alarm and

somehow jumped over the counter, making their exit. *The small man was last to go*" (emphasis added). This same scenario is also suggested in Wilcox's testimony at the coroner's inquest of Sept. 8, 1876. Wilcox stated that "two sprung over counter to run out of bank the 3ᵈ followed pushed Heywood from him and fired at Heywood hitting him in the head." A previously unknown interview with Cole from 1889 agrees with the Wilcox version of events: "I called to the men inside to come out and *Bob and one other came out together*" (emphasis added). Clearly, Frank James was still engaged with Heywood when Bob and Charlie fled. See Stiles, *Jesse James: Last Rebel of the Civil War* (New York: Alfred A. Knopf, 2002), 333; *Pioneer Press and Tribune*, Sept. 9, 1876; Frank Wilcox deposition, Sept. 8, 1876, cited above; and "Dying at Stillwater," *St. Paul Daily Globe*, June 23, 1889.

The men throwing rocks at the robbers are mentioned in several accounts. It was a foolhardy and dangerous undertaking. Truman Streeter would later state that he was shot at six times by the robbers. See the *Pioneer Press and Tribune*, Sept. 12, 1876.

133 Cole Younger would later state that the reason Bob ran toward Anselm Manning at the stairs was "in order to get his (Bob's) horse, which was tied down near the corner." This is possible, but we are left wondering why Bob was without a horse at the end. We know that one horse was killed by Manning and two horses escaped. Either Bob's horse was the one killed or it was one of the two that ran off. It seems more likely

that his was the one killed, although Cole would always claim that Manning killed Charlie Pitts's mount. See the *Faribault Democrat,* Dec. 1, 1876; the *Saint Paul Globe,* July 4, 1897; and *The Northfield Bank Raid,* 9.

Henry Wheeler's account of shooting Bob Younger is in the *Northfield News,* Sept. 10, 1926; and *The Northfield Bank Raid: Fiftieth Anniversary Finds Interest Undimmed in Oft-told Tale of Repulse of James-Younger Gang,* 10th edition (Northfield: Northfield News, 2008), 15–16. A slightly different version by Wheeler, from an 1897 issue of the *Grand Forks Plaindealer,* is reprinted in a *Grand Forks Herald* column by Jack Hagerty, an undated clipping of which is in box 3, folder 58, John J. Koblas Collection, Northfield Historical Society. In this 1897 version, Wheeler says that the hotel clerk handed him only three cartridges to begin with and that it was the third cartridge that fell and broke open upon the floor. Just then, the clerk gave Wheeler more cartridges, after which Wheeler made the shot that wounded Bob Younger.

Wheeler's bullet fractured Bob's elbow joint, making an ugly and painful wound. Early accounts of the raid stated that Wheeler's shot struck Younger in the thigh or leg, because Bob "at once changed hands with his pistol, grasping the wounded leg as if in pain." However, Bob Younger later explained to a reporter that the act of his arm falling limp after being struck gave the impression that he was grabbing his leg. See the *Rice County Journal,* Sept. 14, 1876; the *Northfield*

News, July 10, 1897; and the *Saint Paul Dispatch*, Sept. 22, 1876.

135 All descriptions of Heywood's death come from Frank Wilcox. Wilcox was generally consistent in stating that Frank James fired one shot at the acting cashier as he climbed over the counter to exit the bank. However, in his statement appearing in the *Pioneer Press and Tribune*, Sept. 9, 1876, Wilcox described Heywood's killer as firing two shots from the counter, the first one "I do not think is the one that took effect."

136 Cole's rescue of his brother Bob presents another conundrum in regard to robber identities. In an interview given before Cole was transferred from Faribault to Stillwater, Cole claimed that the two who rode double out of Northfield were the two who escaped Minnesota, meaning Frank and Jesse. When Cole recounted the raid years later, however, he wrote in much detail about how he pulled a man up behind him, but he said that man was Charlie Pitts, not Bob. Eyewitness testimony and subsequent information, however, make it clear that it was Bob who was the wounded man left on foot and who called to his cohorts not to leave him. It is hard to imagine what advantage Cole would have gained by lying about the matter. So why did he? See the *Faribault Democrat*, Dec. 1, 1876; and the *Saint Paul Globe*, July 4, 1897.

137 Albert H. Taisey's story of just missing the raid is from the *Pioneer Press and Tribune*, Sept. 8, 1876.

The story of the Carleton women arming themselves with axes is from "Reminiscences of Carleton's first Dean of Women, Margaret Evans Huntington, made on June 19, 1916," Carleton College Archives, Northfield, MN.

138 Dwight Lockerby's recollections of his teacher, Mrs. Nettie Bunker, and the Northfield Raid, are in "Councilman D. D. Lockerby in Northfield, Minn., Day James Bros. Raided the Bank There," *Eau Claire Leader*, Eau Claire, WI, Feb. 21, 1915. A similar account by a fellow classmate of Lockerby's is Harold B. Kildahl Sr., *Westward We Came: A Norwegian Immigrant's Story, 1866–1898*, ed. Erlinge E. Kildahl (West Lafayette, IN: Purdue University Press, 2008), 57–58.

139 For Nettie Bunker's search for her husband, see George Huntington, *Robber and Hero: The Story of the Northfield Raid on the First National Bank of Northfield, Minnesota, by the James-Younger Band of Robbers, in 1876* (1895; reprint, Minneapolis: Ross & Haines, 1962), 39; and the *Madelia Times*, Nov. 20, 1896.

140 Harold B. Kildahl's sister, Matilda, was the woman helping Lizzie Heywood with the dressmaking the afternoon of the robbery. Kildahl relates, in *Westward We Came*, 58, how Lizzie first heard the news of her husband's death. Huntington also tells this story in *Robber and Hero*, 39–40. The relationship between Heywood's first and second wives is from a letter of

Adelbert Ames to his wife, Blanche, Sept. 13, 1876, in
Blanche Butler Ames, ed., *Chronicles from the Nineteenth Century: Family Letters of Blanche Butler
and Adelbert Ames,* 2 vols. (Clinton, MA: Privately
Printed, 1957) 2: 412.

141 Details on Nicolaus Gustavson after being shot and his
subsequent death are from *The Northfield Tragedy,*
23; the *Northfield News,* July 10, 1897; and the *Pioneer Press and Tribune,* Sept. 12, 1876.

142 The Adelbert Ames quote referring to the women and
children viewing the bodies of the robbers is from
his letter dated Sept. 8, 1876, in *Chronicles from the
Nineteenth Century,* 404.

The Pittsburgh traveling salesman was Albert V.
Dutcher, who worked for J. P. Smith, Son & Co., a
manufacturer of table glassware. Dutcher's account
was published in the *Saint Peter Tribune,* Sept. 13,
1876.

The wounded Alonzo Bunker insisting on being
driven through Division Street is from his account in
the *Madelia Times,* Nov. 20, 1896.

143 The story of George Bates and his souvenir bullet is
from *The Northfield Tragedy,* 17.

144 The rumor that the robbers were headed to John T.
Ames's home and Adelbert Ames's efforts to calm
his brother are from Adelbert's letter to his wife of
Sept. 9, 1876, in *Chronicles from the Nineteenth Century,* 405.

145 The telegraphic messages John T. Ames sent to Minneapolis and St. Paul were published in the *Pioneer Press and Tribune,* Sept. 8, 1876. This issue also reported the rapid response to Ames's call for help.

146 The original telegram to George M. Phillips informing him of the raid and Heywood's death is in the General Ledger, First National Bank of Northfield. A photocopy is in box 2, folder 26 of the Koblas Collection.

Five: And Then There Were Six

147 Various figures are given for the money stolen from the Northfield bank. The figure I offer ($8 in coin and $18.60 in scrip) is from the robbery indictment against the Youngers as published in the *Saint Paul Dispatch,* Nov. 15, 1876.

Cole related in an 1880 interview with J. W. Buel that Jim had received four wounds in Northfield and that he had received eleven. In one account, Cole stated that the wound in his hip was from a pistol ball and not Manning's rifle, but in another he gave credit to Manning's Remington. Cole would also contradict himself as to the location of his wound, claiming at one point that Manning wounded him in the thigh instead of the hip. When Charlie Pitts was killed on the Watonwan, he had, in addition to a fatal bullet wound in his chest, wounds to his right arm and right hip. One or both of these wounds may have been inflicted at Northfield. As for the James brothers, Cole indicated that neither Jesse nor Frank had been wounded during the raid. But

Frank would later tell Dr. Mosher, whom the brothers would encounter during their flight through Iowa, that he had received his leg wound at Northfield. See James W. Buel, *The Border Outlaws*... (St. Louis, MO: Historical Publishing Co., 1882), 256; the *Saint Paul Globe*, July 4, 1897; Cole Younger, *The Story of Cole Younger by Himself* (Chicago: The Henneberry Co., 1903), 81 and 87; the *Northfield News*, July 10, 1897; the *Mankato Review*, Sept. 26, 1876; the *Mankato Record*, Sept. 30, 1876; the *Minneapolis Tribune*, Sept. 22, 1876; the *St. Paul and Minneapolis Pioneer Press and Tribune*, Sept. 24, 1876; the *Faribault Democrat*, Oct. 6, 1876; and the *Sedalia Weekly Bazoo*, May 28, 1878.

148 Cole wrote that the gang intended to "wreck" the Northfield telegraph office in *The Story of Cole Younger by Himself*, 80.

The gang forcing the elderly farmer off the road outside of Northfield is from John Jay Lemon, *The Northfield Tragedy* (1876; reprint, London: Westerners Publications Ltd., 2001), 25.

149 The Northfield telegraph operator's numerous attempts to reach the operator at Dundas is mentioned in *The Northfield Tragedy*, 11. The gang's encounters with the Dundas hardware store owner, George A. Sexton, and the St. Paul traveling salesman were reported in the *Saint Peter Tribune*, Sept. 15, 1876; and the *Faribault Democrat*, Sept. 15, 1876.

The commandeering of one of the horses from the team pulling the wagon of hoop poles was reported in the *Saint Paul Dispatch*, Sept. 8, 1876; and the *Minneapolis Tribune*, Sept. 8, 1876. Some accounts have this episode occurring just prior to the gang reaching Dundas. The two Northfield men who caught up to the gang as they were taking the horse were Jack Hayes and Dwight Davis. See the *Saint Paul Dispatch*, Sept. 8 and 9, 1876; and *The Northfield Tragedy*, 11.

151 The blood trickling from Bob's fingers was reported in the *Minneapolis Tribune*, Sept. 8, 1876; and the *Saint Paul Dispatch*, Sept. 8, 1876.

The pail of water to wash Bob's arm was obtained from farmer Robert Donaldson. See the *Faribault Democrat*, Sept. 15, 1876, which also contains the quote of the gang claiming they had killed a "blackleg" in Northfield. "Blackleg" is defined in John Camden Hotten, *The Slang Dictionary* (London: John Camden Hotten, 1864), 75.

The "borrowing" of the saddle for Bob was reported in the *Pioneer Press and Tribune*, Sept. 9, 1876.

The account of the hotel owner, Samuel Cushman, recognizing the gang as they fled through Millersburg is in *The Northfield Tragedy*, 25–26.

152 For the gang's arrival in Shieldsville and their encounter with the Faribault posse in front of Hagerty's saloon, see the *Pioneer Press and Tribune*, Sept. 9, 1876; the *Minneapolis Tribune*, Sept. 9, 1876; the *Saint Paul Dispatch*, Sept. 9, 1876; the *Farmington Press*, Sept. 14, 1876; the *Faribault Democrat*, Sept. 15, 1876; *The Northfield Tragedy*, 26; and John J.

Koblas, *Faithful Unto Death: The James-Younger Raid on the First National Bank, Northfield, Minnesota, September 7, 1876* (Northfield, MN: Northfield Historical Society Press, 2001), 103.

154 The posse's long-range fight with the gang four miles from Shieldsville is from the *Saint Paul Dispatch*, Sept. 9, 1876; the *Pioneer Press and Tribune*, Sept. 9, 1876; the *Faribault Democrat*, Sept. 15, 1876; *The Northfield Tragedy*, 27; and *The Story of Cole Younger by Himself*, 86. It is important to note that the *Pioneer Press and Tribune* reported that the man who fell from the horse during the skirmish "had a wounded arm." That would be Bob Younger.

156 Cole wrote of being "practically lost" in the Big Woods in *The Story of Cole Younger by Himself*, 86.

The gang's encounter with Levi Sager is from the *Pioneer Press and Tribune*, Sept. 10, 1876; the *Minneapolis Tribune*, Sept. 9, 1876; the *Faribault Democrat*, Sept. 15, 1876; and *The Northfield Tragedy*, 27. Accounts vary as to the direction the gang traveled with Sager and where he left them the night of Sept. 7. I have followed the report in the *Pioneer Press and Tribune* of Sept. 10, which represented the latest information from Waterville locals.

157 Another account places the gang in the barn of Daniel Walsh, just west of Kilkenny, on the night of the robbery. However, contemporary newspapers reported that the gang's stay with Lord Brown came from an eyewitness. A report later appeared in the

Minneapolis Tribune that one of the two men killed
in Northfield was believed to be one of Lord Brown's
sons. Although false, there has been speculation that
Lord Brown's son, Edward, had some connection to
the robbery. Twenty-eight years old in 1876, he had
recently been released from Stillwater Prison after
serving time for horse stealing. See Koblas, *Faithful
Unto Death*, 105–106; the *Saint Paul Dispatch*, Sept.
9, 1876; the *Pioneer Press and Tribune*, Sept. 10, 1876;
the *Minneapolis Tribune*, Sept. 9 and 11, 1876; and
Chip DeMann to Mark Lee Gardner, Dundas, Minn.,
Sept. 16, 2011.

158 For Sheriff Ara Barton's nightlong efforts to contain
the outlaws, see *The Northfield Tragedy*, 28.

There are contradictory accounts as to where Ira
Sumner photographed the dead outlaws. Elise Ytterboe, a teenager at the time of the robbery, claimed
she visited Tschann's Meat Market the morning after
the raid and saw "the two dead robbers propped up
in a sitting position between two buildings near the
market having pictures taken of them." Tschann's
Meat Market was on the south side of Mill Square,
the same side of the square that contained the vacant
store where the bodies were stored. Ira Sumner's
daughter, on the other hand, wrote that the bodies were taken up to her father's studio to be photographed. Sumner's daughter was not yet born in 1876,
so she was no eyewitness, but Elise Ytterboe's account
was not written until sixty-two years after the raid. A
close examination of the photos themselves indicates

that the bodies were photographed indoors. See Elise
Ytterboe, *Ole Voices No. 1, Reminiscenses,* ed. by
Jeff M. Sauve (St. Olaf College: Shaw-Olson Center
for College History, 2009), 4–5; and Grace Sumner
Northrop to Emith Buth, Sun City, AZ, July 18, 1978,
Rice County Historical Society, Faribault, MN. My
thanks to Quinn Jacobson, Denver wet-plate photo-
graphic artist, for his comments on the postmortem
images.

160 The 11:00 A.M. coroner's inquest is mentioned in the
Pioneer Press and Tribune, Sept. 9, 1876.

The account of the bodies being displayed in Mill
Square on Sept. 8 is from George Huntington, *Robber and Hero: The Story of the Northfield Raid on
the First National Bank of Northfield, Minnesota, by
the James-Younger Band of Robbers, in 1876* (1895;
reprint, Minneapolis: Ross & Haines, 1962), 40.

The quote of the *Minneapolis Tribune*'s correspondent
regarding the "floodgates of information" is from the
Tribune issue of Sept. 8, 1876.

Several newspapers printed descriptions of the dead
robbers' clothing and personal effects, but see the
Saint Paul Dispatch, Sept. 8, 1876; the *Minneapolis
Tribune,* Sept. 8, 1876; the *Pioneer Press and Tribune,*
Sept. 9, 1876; and *The Northfield Tragedy,* 12–15.
The Arab Horse Maxims were printed periodically
in newspapers as filler throughout the late nineteenth
century. I have quoted the first maxim from the *Indiana Progress,* Indiana, Pennsylvania, Feb. 24, 1876.

163 The *Saint Paul Dispatch* of Sept. 9, 1876, initially
reported that Chadwell's body had been identified by
Peterman as Bill Yates, "a former resident of Minneapolis," but later corrected the name to Stiles in its
issue of Sept. 11, claiming that Yates and Raymond
were Stiles's aliases. The response of Bill Stiles's father,
Elisha, to the news (false) that his son had been killed
in Northfield, is quoted from the *Pioneer Press and
Tribune*, Sept. 26, 1876. The several articles pointing
out the many problems with the Stiles identification
are found in the *Saint Paul Dispatch*, Sept. 16, 1876;
the *Wright County Times*, Monticello, MN, Sept. 28,
Oct. 26, and Nov. 30, 1876; and the *Faribault Republican*, Oct. 25, 1876. Bob Younger is quoted from the
Mankato Review, Nov. 28, 1876.

William "Bill" Stiles is enumerated in the household of
Elisha Stiles in the 1857 Minnesota territorial census,
the 1860 U.S. census for Minnesota, and the 1870 U.S.
census for Minnesota. In the 1857 and 1860 censuses,
the Stiles family is living in the town of Monticello,
Wright County. In the 1870 census, they are found
living in the town of Santiago, Shelburne County. In
each census, Bill Stiles's birthplace is given as New
Brunswick, Canada. Stiles's mother appears to have
died sometime before 1860, and his youngest sister,
Minnie May, was adopted by Reverend Elijah W. and
Mary C. Merrill. Minnie May wed Caleb H. Peterman
at Cannon Falls, MN, on Aug. 10, 1875. According to
the contemporary newspapers, Peterman was no longer living with his wife at the time of the raid. See the

Elijah W. Merrill household in the 1870 U.S. census for the Cannon Falls Township, Goodhue County, MN; Goodhue County, MN, marriage records for 1875; and *The Northfield Tragedy*, 14.

In 1897, Norman Van Buskirk, a Northfield resident, claimed he took Caleb Peterman and another Cannon Falls man to see the bodies of the robbers the day after the raid. According to Buskirk, as they were viewing the corpse of Chadwell, Peterman said, "For God's sake, Norm, don't you know that man? Why that's Bill—Bill Stiles, my brother-in-law." Buskirk did not explain why Peterman thought he should recognize Stiles, and I have my doubts about the story. See the *Saint Paul Globe*, July 11, 1897.

166 Governor Pillsbury's reward proclamations are printed in the *Minneapolis Tribune*, Sept. 9 and 13, 1876, as well as several other Minnesota newspapers. The reward offer of the First National Bank is explained in the *Rice County Journal*, Sept. 14, 1876. The criticism of the initial $500 reward is found in the *Saint Paul Dispatch*, Sept. 9, 1876.

167 For Detective Larry M. Hazen in St. Paul and Northfield, see the *Saint Paul Dispatch*, Sept. 9 and 11, 1876; and the *Rice County Journal*, Sept. 14, 1876. My description of Hazen is from the *Rocky Mountain News*, Dec. 10, 1875. A history and profile of Hazen's detective agency is found in *Leading Manufacturers and Merchants of Cincinnati and Environs* (Boston: International Publishing Co., 1886), 134.

Kansas City chief of police Speers received the photographs of the two dead robbers on September 15, and from "the unqualified statements made to him by a number of persons yesterday who saw the photographs and knew the men, Capt. Speers is confident, he says, that one of the pictures is that of Cell Miller . . . and the other that of Bill Chadwell." See the *Kansas City Times*, Sept. 16, 1876. Former gang member Hobbs Kerry later confirmed these identifications after viewing the photographs. See the *Saint Paul Dispatch*, Sept. 28, 1876.

169 Chief of Police McDonough is quoted from his letter to Governor Charles H. Hardin of Sept. 12, 1876, Records of Charles Henry Hardin, 1875–1877 (RG 3.22), Missouri State Archives, Jefferson City, MO.

The fate of the bodies of Miller and Chadwell is well covered in Koblas, *Faithful Unto Death*, 87–88. That the bodies were buried following the inquest is confirmed in the *Saint Paul Dispatch*, Sept. 9, 1876. The story of the Northfield mayor intimating that the bodies would not be deeply buried is from "He Shot the Youngers," the *Macon Telegraph*, Georgia, July 25, 1897. See also Francis F. McKinney, "The Northfield Raid, and Its Ann Arbor Sequel," *Michigan Alumnus: A Journal of University Perspectives* 61 (Dec. 1954): 38–45.

Six: The Great Manhunt

173 The gang's encounter with George James at the ford of the Cannon River is chronicled in the *Saint Paul Dispatch*, Sept. 9, 1876; the *Minneapolis Tribune*, Sept. 9,

1876; the *Pioneer Press and Tribune,* Sept. 10, 1876; and *The Northfield Tragedy,* 29. For the gang's visit to the Rosnau farm and Wilhelm Rosnau as guide, see the *Saint Paul Dispatch,* Sept. 9, 1876; the *Pioneer Press and Tribune,* Sept. 10 and 13, 1876; the *Mankato Review,* Sept. 12, 1876; and *The Northfield Tragedy,* 30–31. Various spellings are given for Rosnau's surname in the contemporary accounts. His large household, including son Wilhelm, is enumerated in the 1875 Minnesota state census and the 1880 federal census, Elysian Township, Le Sueur County.

177 The last sighting of the gang on Friday, Sept. 8, is mentioned in the *Saint Paul Dispatch,* Sept. 11, 1876; and *The Northfield Tragedy,* 30.

The special train patrolling on the Winona & St. Peter line is mentioned in the *Mankato Review,* Sept. 12, 1876.

The "hog pen of the state" is from the *Pioneer Press and Tribune,* Sept. 10, 1876.

For the fear felt by posse members and local citizens alike, see the *Pioneer Press and Tribune,* Sept. 10 and 20, 1876. The lack of adequate weapons for some posse members is from the *Pioneer Press and Tribune,* Sept. 9 and 20, 1876.

178 The price gouging by the Big Woods locals is mentioned in the *Mankato Review,* Sept. 12, 1876.

179 The large state atlas carried by many posse members was *An Illustrated Historical Atlas of the State of Minnesota* by A. T. Andreas (Chicago: A. T. Andreas,

1874). One reporter claimed that "hundreds carried maps taken from the books." See the *Pioneer Press and Tribune*, Sept. 20, 1876.

180 The problems with leadership and lack of coordination, especially between the Minneapolis and St. Paul contingents, was reported in the *Pioneer Press and Tribune*, Sept. 10, 12, and 20, 1876; the *Saint Paul Dispatch*, Sept. 11, 1876; and the *Minneapolis Tribune*, Sept. 11, 1876.

Biographical information on Detective Michael Hoy is found in his obituary, published in the *Saint Paul Daily Globe*, Mar. 21, 1895. Biographical information on Detective John B. Bresette (also spelled Bresett) is in his obituary, published in the *Saint Paul Daily Globe*, Mar. 18, 1892; and *Pen Pictures of St. Paul, Minnesota, and Biographical Sketches of Old Settlers*, by T. M. Newson (Saint Paul, MN: Published by the author, 1886), 574.

181 Mike Hoy's hanging of the ex-con Dolan is reported in the *Saint Paul Dispatch*, Sept. 12, 1876; the *Minneapolis Tribune*, Sept. 12, 1876; and the *Pioneer Press and Tribune*, Sept. 13, 1876.

183 The false report of the robbers crossing the Cannon River bridge was published in several newspapers. See the *Saint Paul Dispatch*, Sept. 11, 1876; the *Minneapolis Tribune*, Sept. 11, 1876; the *Pioneer Press and Tribune*, Sept. 12 and 13, 1876; and the *Mankato Review*, Sept. 12, 1876. See also *The Northfield Tragedy*, 34–35. The special train from St. Paul carrying Chief

of Police King and private detective Larry Hazen is mentioned in the *Minneapolis Tribune*, Sept. 11, 1876; the *Pioneer Press and Tribune*, Sept. 12, 1876; and the *Saint Peter Tribune*, Sept. 13, 1876.

184 The report of the discovery of the "false grave" is in the *Minneapolis Tribune*, Sept. 11, 1876; the *Mankato Review*, Sept. 12, 1876; the *Pioneer Press and Tribune*, Sept. 12, 1876.

Joseph Lee Heywood's funeral is described in considerable detail in the *Rice County Journal*, Sept. 14, 1876.

185 The quote arguing that it was not Heywood's duty to give his life for the First National Bank is from the *Western Progress*, Spring Valley, MN, Sept. 13, 1876.

Adelbert Ames explained the reward monies offered and his responsibility for a part of it in his letter to Blanche Ames, Sept. 22, 1876, in Blanche Butler Ames, ed., *Chronicles from the Nineteenth Century: Family Letters of Blanche Butler and Adelbert Ames* (Clinton, MA: Privately printed, 1957), 2: 425.

For the Heywood Fund, see George Huntington, *Robber and Hero: The Story of the Northfield Raid on the First National Bank of Northfield, Minnesota, by the James-Younger Band of Robbers, in 1876* (1895; reprint, Minneapolis: Ross & Haines, 1962), 101–119.

187 The shotgun accident of the two boys of Henderson, MN, "playing robbers" was reported in the *New Ulm Herald*, Sept. 15, 1876; and the *Saint Peter Tribune*,

Sept. 20, 1876. The Owatonna boy accidentally shooting his mother is from the *Saint Paul Dispatch,* Sept. 16, 1876.

The robbers' camp of Friday night, September 8, is described in the *Pioneer Press and Tribune,* Sept. 13, 1876; and *The Northfield Tragedy,* 31–32. Cole referred to the fact that the gang had worn out their horses in *The Story of Cole Younger by Himself* (Chicago: The Henneberry Co., 1903), 86.

Local folklore has the gang's Friday night camp located on a well-known wooded peak known as Klondike Hill just north of Lake Francis, but it's just that, folklore (one version even has the outlaws hiding in a cave somewhere on the peak). No contemporary accounts and newspaper reports I have examined mention Klondike Hill. The various theories on Klondike Hill are summarized in Earl Weinmann, ed., *Caught in the Storm: A Field Guide to the James & Younger Gang Escape Trail* (Northfield, MN: Northfield Historical Society Press, 2008), 66–68.

190 For the food the gang subsisted on during their flight, see *The Northfield Tragedy,* 33. The story of the gang stealing a woman's baking is from the *Saint Paul Dispatch,* Sept. 11, 1876. Their failed attempts to kill a calf and hog are mentioned in the *Minneapolis Tribune,* Sept. 23, 1876; and *The Northfield Tragedy,* 32.

For the gang's camp north of Marysburg, see the *Pioneer Press and Tribune,* Sept. 12 and 23, 1876; and *The Northfield Tragedy,* 32. Mike Hoy's scoffing at the report of the two boys who claimed to have seen the robbers near Marysburg is from the *Pioneer Press and Tribune,* Sept. 12, 1876.

191   The gang's day camp on Madison Lake and the nine-mile march of that night is mentioned in *The North-field Tragedy,* 32–33; and *The Story of Cole Younger by Himself,* 86.

The discovery of the robbers' abandoned horses on Tuesday, Sept. 12, was big news, so it was reported in numerous Minnesota newspapers, but see the *Pioneer Press and Tribune,* Sept. 13, 1876; and *The Northfield Tragedy,* 35. The telegraph advising that the robbers were on foot is reproduced in the *Minneapolis Tribune,* Sept. 12, 1876.

193   The quotes stating that the outlaws had escaped and that the manhunters were "baffled" are from the *Minneapolis Tribune,* Sept. 12, 1876; and the *Pioneer Press and Tribune,* Sept. 12, 1876.

Faribault County sheriff A. B. Davis's sighting of five strange men near Indian Lake was reported in the *Mankato Review,* Sept. 19, 1876, and other newspapers. However, these men were not the robbers. It was later learned that they were a party of five "Scandinavians" from the town of Albert Lea. Cole Younger also stated later that the gang was never at Indian Lake. See the *Minneapolis Tribune,* Sept. 13, 1876; and the *Mankato Review,* Sept. 26, 1876.

The departure of the manhunters for Minneapolis and St. Paul on the morning of Sept. 13 is noted in the *Saint*

Paul Dispatch, Sept. 14, 1876; the *Mankato Review,* Sept. 19, 1876; and *The Northfield Tragedy,* 37.

194 I have based my narrative on the gang's kidnapping of Thomas Jefferson Dunning on the accounts in the *Mankato Union,* Sept. 15, 1876; the *Mankato Record,* Sept. 16, 1876; the *Mankato Review,* Sept. 19, 1876; the *Saint Paul Dispatch,* Sept. 13, 1876; the *Minneapolis Tribune,* Sept. 13, 1876; the *Pioneer Press and Tribune,* Sept. 14, 1876; the *Faribault Democrat,* Dec. 12, 1876; *The Northfield Tragedy,* 37–38; the *Saint Paul Globe,* July 4, 1897; and *The Story of Cole Younger by Himself,* 86–87. Cole later stated that their meeting with Dunning was entirely accidental. See the *Mankato Review,* Sept. 26, 1876.

197 Some newspapers reported that after the release of Dunning, the gang had breakfast at the home of a German named Graf Stoltzberg (also Solberg). This report proved to be false. See the *Pioneer Press and Tribune,* Sept. 14, 1876; and the *Mankato Review,* Sept. 19, 1876.

198 The telegram giving the news of the Dunning capture was printed in the *Saint Paul Dispatch,* Sept. 13, 1876.

Hoy and Bresette receiving the news of the Dunning capture and their return to Mankato was reported in the *Minneapolis Tribune,* Sept. 13, 1876; and the *Saint Paul Dispatch,* Sept. 14, 1876. See also *The Northfield Tragedy,* 38.

199 The Mike Hoy quotes are from the *Pioneer Press and Tribune,* Sept. 14, 1876.

200 The quote from the *Saint Paul Dispatch* about the excitement in the streets of Mankato is from the issue of Sept. 14, 1876.

For the selection of General Edmund Mann Pope to direct the manhunt, see the *Pioneer Press and Tribune,* Sept. 14, 1876; and *The Northfield Tragedy,* 38–39.

201 The quote remarking that the preparations in Mankato seemed that the manhunters were expecting an attack from Sitting Bull is from *The Northfield Tragedy,* 39.

For the gang's movements through Mankato and their crossing of the Blue Earth River the night of Wednesday, Sept. 13, see the *Mankato Review,* Sept. 26, 1876; the *Mankato Record,* Sept. 30, 1876; the *Minneapolis Tribune,* Sept. 14 and 23, 1876; the *Pioneer Press and Tribune,* Sept. 15, 1876; and *The Northfield Tragedy,* 40.

Several newspaper accounts reported that suspicious whistling was heard in Mankato the night the gang passed through town, the supposition being that these were signals used by the robbers. There were also reports that rocks had been thrown near the two bridges over the Blue Earth River, supposedly tossed by the gang to see if the bridges were guarded. However, the Younger brothers later stated that they did not whistle or use other signals because they were always together. They also denied throwing any rocks near the bridges. In fact, they did not even approach the county wagon bridge. See the *Mankato Review,* Sept. 26, 1876.

204 For the gang robbing the melon patch and, later, the chicken coop, see the *Mankato Record,* Sept. 16 and 30, 1876; and the *Mankato Review,* Sept. 26, 1876.

The robbers' Pigeon Hill camp is described in the *Pioneer Press and Tribune,* Sept. 15, 1876; and *The Northfield Tragedy,* 41. Cole's claim that he did not approve of the location of the camp is from the *Mankato Review,* Sept. 26, 1876.

205 For Mike Hoy at Pigeon Hill, see *The Northfield Tragedy,* 40–41; and the *Saint Paul Dispatch,* Sept. 14 and 18, 1876. George Tinsley, a member of Hoy's party, gave a very positive report on his commander's actions in the *Minneapolis Tribune,* Sept. 15, 1876. The Youngers mentioned hearing the hooting and hollering of Hoy's squad, as well as Hoy's orders, in interviews reported in the *Mankato Review,* Sept. 26, 1876; and the *Mankato Record,* Sept. 30, 1876.

206 Hoy's telegram announcing that he had captured the blankets, bridles, and coats of the robbers appeared in the *Minneapolis Tribune,* Sept. 14, 1876.

That Hoy had been cautioned not to act rashly in his pursuit of the robbers the morning of Sept. 14 was reported in the *Mankato Review,* Sept. 26, 1876. This issue also contains the quote blaming Hoy for the failure at Pigeon Hill.

207 For the gang fleeing southeast from Pigeon Hill to the Blue Earth River, see *The Northfield Tragedy,* 42. The possemen overhearing the gang in the thicket is

from the *Minneapolis Tribune*, Sept. 15, 1876; and
The Northfield Tragedy, 42.

209 Much has been written about the decision of the gang
to separate. Cole would state shortly after his capture that "We parted in peace." However, he makes
it clear in his memoir that Jesse and Frank were not
happy with the way the Dunning situation had been
handled and that the brothers were very concerned
about their slow pace. Some of the more outlandish
accounts of the separation claim that Jesse wanted to
kill Bob so that the gang could travel faster; this claim
is ludicrous. (Interestingly, many of these tales confuse
Bob with Jim, but there is ample evidence that it was
Bob's wound that was slowing the gang down.) That
Jesse wished to abandon Bob, however, and that there
had been hard feelings surrounding the separation, is
revealed in interviews with Cole from 1882 and 1887.
Cole would contradict himself (of course) on his deathbed in March 1916, telling Jesse James Jr. and Harry
Hoffman that Jesse and Frank had gone out looking
for horses but had only found two. Jesse suggested
that Cole and Bob take the two horses and escape, but
because Bob's arm "had taken a turn for the worse,"
Cole told Jesse and Frank to mount the horses and go.
See the *Mankato Review*, Sept. 26, 1876; *The Story of
Cole Younger by Himself*, 87; J. W. Buel, *The Border Outlaws . . .* , 371; the *St. Louis Globe-Democrat*,
Apr. 6, 1882, and Jan. 25, 1887; and Harry C. Hoffman, "The Fog Around the Rumors Cleared Away,"
typescript, Harry Hoffman Donations Accession File,

Missouri State Museum, Jefferson City, MO. Former gang member George Shepherd would claim that Frank, not Jesse, wanted to kill Bob. Where Shepherd got his information is unknown, but it is false, nevertheless. See the *Liberty Tribune*, Feb. 27, 1880.

Just a day after his capture, Cole Younger told reporter J. Newton Nind that he and his brothers and Pitts had given their valuables to the James boys, "thinking their chances best." A German farmer who encountered Jesse and Frank near Lamberton, Minnesota, shortly after they separated from the Youngers, claimed the Jameses had five watches and a great deal of money on them. But for some reason, the Youngers would later deny giving their watches and money to the Jameses, declaring that the newspapers had misreported the German's account. Instead of "five" gold watches, it should have been "fine" gold watches. However, when the Youngers were captured, they were found to have "but a small amount of money and no watches." See the *Saint Paul Dispatch*, Sept. 18, 1876; the *Faribault Democrat*, Dec. 1, 1876; and the *Mankato Record*, Sept. 23, 1876.

Seven: Last Stand on the Watonwan

211 Pope's headquarters move and new picket line are described in *The Northfield Tragedy*, 43; and the *Pioneer Press and Tribune*, Sept. 15, 1876.

For Richard Roberts's later reminiscences of his encounter with Jesse and Frank at the bridge, see the

Mankato Free Press, Feb. 16, 1931. Contemporary reports are found in the *Pioneer Press and Tribune,* Sept. 16, 1876; the *Saint Paul Dispatch,* Sept. 15, 1876; the *Mankato Record,* Sept. 16, 1876; the *Mankato Review,* Sept. 19, 1876; and *The Northfield Tragedy,* 44–45. For mention of the particular boot prints of the robbers, see the *Minneapolis Tribune,* Sept. 15, 1876; and the *Pioneer Press and Tribune,* Sept. 15, 1876.

213 The robbery of Joseph Rockwood's iron-gray mares was reported in the *Saint Paul Dispatch,* Sept. 15, 1876; the *Pioneer Press and Tribune,* Sept. 16, 1876; and the *Minneapolis Tribune,* Sept. 16, 1876. Several newspapers carried the story that the robbers had assaulted Rockwood when they stole his horses, knocking him in the head with the butt of a pistol. This story later proved to be false. See the *Minneapolis Tribune,* Sept. 18, 1876.

214 The various theories as to what had become of the Younger brothers and Pitts are covered in the *Saint Paul Dispatch,* Sept. 18, 1876.

The raid on Jack O'Neil's Mankato brothel is mentioned in the *Saint Paul Dispatch,* Sept. 16 and 18, 1876; and *The Northfield Tragedy,* 50–51.

216 Judson Jones wrote of the vicious attack of Mike Hoy in an open letter to Hoy published in the *Saint Peter Tribune,* Sept. 20, 1876. The Minneapolis mayor defended his detective, arguing that Jones had insulted Hoy's manhood. A letter from the mayor, along with a rebuttal from Jones, is published in the *Saint Peter*

Tribune, Sept. 27, 1876. Additional coverage of the incident is found in the *Pioneer Press and Tribune,* Sept. 19, 1876; and the *Mankato Union,* Sept. 29, 1876.

218 The quote expressing awe for the James-Younger gang's success in evading the posses, probably written by reporter J. Newton Nind, appeared in the *Pioneer Press and Tribune,* Sept. 20, 1876.

219 Bob Younger told of the movements of the Youngers and Pitts after the separation with the James brothers in an interview published in the *Saint Paul Dispatch,* Sept. 22, 1876. He told a reporter for the *Pioneer Press and Tribune,* Sept. 23, 1876, that the band was "making due west as near as possible." Cole's claim that they were headed for a farm with horses is from his *The Story of Cole Younger by Himself,* 87. That farm belonged to John Doolittle.

220 Cole mentions his homemade cane in *The Story of Cole Younger by Himself* (Chicago: The Henneberry Co., 1903), 87. Bob's problems with his right arm are described in the *St. Paul and Minneapolis Pioneer Press and Tribune,* Sept. 23, 1876. Cole told the story of Bob resting his shattered elbow on Cole's prone body to a reporter for the *Saint Paul Daily Globe,* June 23, 1889, and again in *The Story of Cole Younger by Himself,* 87.

T. L. Vought wrote of his hotel guests, Cole and Pitts, in "Capture of the Younger Brothers by One of the Captors," *Northfield News,* Sept. 18, 1897. Vought's son also wrote of the visit, based on his father's recollections. See "As Boy and Man," the *Webster Journal,* Webster, SD, July 17, 1930; and "Capture of the Youngers Recalled," typescript, box 3, folder 53, John J. Koblas Collection, Northfield Historical Society, Northfield, MN.

221 Vought specifically remembered Cole talking about the bridge near the "head of Armstrong lake." Armstrong Lake is in western Blue Earth County. Today's Omsrud Lake, northwest of Madelia in Brown County is identified as "L. Armstrong" in Andreas's 1874 map of Brown County, and while it is possible that this is the lake Vought was referring to, it is more likely that Omsrud Lake was mislabeled in the atlas.

Sorbel signed an affidavit in 1929 stating that his full name was Asle O. Sorbel. Non-Norwegians clearly had difficulty with its pronunciation and spelling. Newspapers from the time of the raid gave his surname as Suborn, and the 1875 Minnesota state census spelled it Soborn. The 1880 federal census gives it as Sorbol. See the 1875 Minnesota state census, Linden, Brown County; the 1880 U. S. census, Linden, Brown County; and A. O. Sorbel affidavit, Aug. 8, 1929, box 14, folder 219, Koblas Collection.

Colonel Vought's encounter with Oscar Sorbel is mentioned in Vought, "Capture of the Younger Brothers"; George Huntington, *Robber and Hero: The Story of the Northfield Raid on the First National Bank of Northfield, Minnesota, by the James-Younger Band of Robbers, in 1876* (1895; reprint, Minneapolis:

Ross & Haines, 1962), 63–64; and *The Story of Cole Younger by Himself,* 87–88. Huntington claims that Sorbel spent his evenings with Vought and his men, but as it was approximately a ten-mile round-trip from his home to the bridge, this seems unlikely.

223 The best contemporary interview with Oscar Sorbel concerning his role in the spotting of the robbers and his mad ride to Madelia is found in the *Mankato Review,* Sept. 26, 1876. Other accounts are found in the *Pioneer Press and Tribune,* Sept. 22, 1876; the *Saint Paul Dispatch,* Sept. 22, 1876; and the *Saint Peter Tribune,* Sept. 27, 1876. A 1924 account written by Sorbel was published in the *Sioux Falls Argus-Leader,* a photocopy of which is in the Koblas Collection, box 7, folder 87.

227 For my treatment of the pursuit of the Youngers and Pitts by Sheriff Glispin and his posses, as well as the gunfight and capture on the North Fork of the Watonwan, I have relied almost entirely on the accounts from contemporary newspapers: the *Saint Paul Dispatch,* Sept. 22, 1876; the *Pioneer Press and Tribune,* Sept. 22, 23, and 30, 1876; the *Minneapolis Tribune,* Sept. 22 and 23, 1876; the *Mankato Record,* Sept. 23, 1876; the *Mankato Review,* Sept. 26, 1876; the *Saint Peter Tribune,* Sept. 27, 1876; and the *Mankato Union,* Sept. 29, 1876. Later accounts by two of the skirmishers who went into the brush after the robbers are those by T. L. Vought, *Northfield News,* Sept. 18, 1897; and "Geo. A. Bradford Tells Story of Younger Gang," news clipping, 1924, in box 2, folder 12, Koblas Collection.

231 Many modern writers have referred to the capture site as "Hanska Slough." This is incorrect, as Lake Hanska and its outlet or "slough" was nearly three miles north of the capture site.

232 Cole Younger's exchange with Charlie Pitts just before the shoot-out with Glispin's posse is from *The Story of Cole Younger by Himself*, 88–89, and Harry Hoffman, "The Younger Boys Last Stand," the *Norborne Democrat and the Leader*, Missouri, Jan. 3, 1936.

239 Jim Younger waving and cheering to the crowd in Madelia is from the *Saint Peter Tribune*, Sept. 27, 1876. The Luther Pomeroy quote on Cole Younger is from "Old-Timers Remember Younger Gang; Captured Near Here After Robber," Jan. 12, 1939, news clipping, box 2, folder 14, Koblas Collection.

Cole stating that his feet hurt worse than all his wounds and his request for the doctors to "speak up" is from the *Minneapolis Tribune*, Sept. 23, 1876.

240 The removal of a piece of Jim Younger's jaw is from "Dr. Wm. H. Woods," news clipping, Younger Brothers Indictments File, Northfield Historical Society; and *Sedalia Weekly Bazoo*, May 7, 1878. According to the *Mankato Review*, Sept. 26, 1876, both Cole and Jim were given opiates, most likely morphine.

241 Sheriff Glispin telling the crowd he would shoot anyone who touched his prisoners is from the *Minneapolis Tribune*, Sept. 23, 1876; and the *Saint Paul Dispatch*, Sept. 22, 1876. Cole's request for his pistols in the event

of a mob attack is from *The Story of Cole Younger by Himself*, 89–90.

T. L. Vought described the photograph session of the robbers and the Madelia Seven at the Flanders House in "Capture of the Younger Brothers by One of the Captors."

243 Edward Noonan remembered seeing the body of Charlie Pitts laid out in the Madelia jail. See his interview in the *Mankato School Spotlight*, Feb. 14, 1941. The *Saint Peter Tribune*, Sept. 27, 1876, commented that Elias F. Everitt's image of Charlie Pitts did not resemble the living man. Dr. William Wood also noticed the changes in Pitts's face, stating that when he saw the body shortly after Pitts's death, the man had been "strikingly handsome." See the *Mankato Union*, Sept. 29, 1876. Everitt actually made two photographs of Pitts, one with the corpse bare-chested and the other with a checkered shirt.

244 For Bob receiving bouquets of flowers, see the *Minneapolis Tribune*, Sept. 23, 1876. The quote describing the sympathetic tears of the people viewing the outlaws is from the *Saint Paul Dispatch*, Sept. 22, 1876.

245 The exchange between Bob Younger and Mrs. Sorbel is taken from the *Saint Paul Dispatch*, Sept. 23, 1876; and the *Minneapolis Tribune*, Sept. 23, 1876.

247 The attempt by the *Saint Paul Dispatch* reporter to trick Cole into admitting that the James brothers were part of the raid is from the issue of Sept. 22, 1876. The interview with Bob Younger, in which he discusses the

killing of Heywood, is from the *Minneapolis Tribune*, Sept. 23, 1876.

248 The dispute concerning whether the Youngers would be taken to St. Paul or Rice County is from the *Saint Paul Dispatch*, Sept. 22 and 23, 1876; and the *Mankato Review*, Sept. 26, 1876.

249 The Youngers' trip from Madelia to the county jail in Faribault was reported in the *Mankato Union*, Sept. 29, 1876; the *Mankato Review*, Sept. 26, 1876; the *Faribault Democrat*, Sept. 29, 1876; and the *Minneapolis Tribune*, Sept. 23, 1876. The *Faribault Democrat* is the source for the number of people who visited the jail on Sunday, Sept. 24.

252 Chief of Police McDonough's letter of Sept. 22, 1876, to Governor Hardin is in Records of Charles Henry Hardin, 1875–1877 (RG 3.22), Missouri State Archives, Jefferson City, MO. His telegram requesting that the dead robbers not be buried immediately was published in the *Pioneer Press and Tribune*, Sept. 23, 1876.

The visit of Chief McDonough, Officer Palmer, and Calvin Hunn to the capitol and, later, Faribault on Sunday, Sept. 24, was reported in the *Pioneer Press and Tribune*, Sept. 26 and 29, 1876; the *Saint Paul Dispatch*, Sept. 25, 1876; the *Minneapolis Tribune*, Sept. 25, 1876; the *St. Louis Republican*, Sept. 25 and 30, 1876; the *St. Louis Globe-Democrat*, Sept. 25 and 30, 1876; the *Faribault Democrat*, Sept. 29, 1876; and the *State Journal*, Jefferson City, MO, Oct. 6, 1876.

254 Chief McDonough refers to Cal Carter as the "eighth man of the gang" in his letter to Governor Hardin of Sept. 22, 1876, cited above. Little information is available on Carter (possibly an alias), although the Youngers were acquainted with the outlaw. Jim Younger described Carter as six feet two, very slender, straight, and having red hair. Texas authorities named Carter as a participant in several Texas stagecoach robberies beginning in 1874, when he robbed a San Antonio & Austin mail coach with Jim Reed, a former member of Quantrill's guerrillas, and a John Boswell. Cole stated that Carter had died in 1875. A photograph of Carter, copied from a tintype, was sent to the St. Paul chief of police to aid in the identification of the Northfield robbers. See the *Pioneer Press and Tribune*, Sept. 26, 1876; the *St. Louis Republican*, Sept. 25, 1876; the *Galveston Daily News*, Aug. 9, 1874; the *Palo Alto Pilot*, Emmetsburg, Iowa, Oct. 28, 1876; and the *Minneapolis Tribune*, Oct. 5, 1876.

Cole's suggestion of a $1,000 bet that Jim was his brother is from the *Pioneer Press and Tribune*, Sept. 26, 1876; and the *Minneapolis Tribune*, Sept. 25, 1876.

255 The quote from the *Saint Paul Dispatch* reporter on McDonough's theory regarding Jim Younger's movements is from the issue of Sept. 27, 1876.

The vote by the train passengers on what should be done with the Youngers was reported in the *Saint Paul Dispatch*, Sept. 25, 1876.

Eight: The Pursuit of the James Boys

257 The Thomas Hughes letter to his family of Sept. 22, 1876, is in the Carleton Archives, Carleton College, Northfield, MN. Adelbert Ames's letter to his wife of Sept. 22, 1876, is quoted from Blanche Butler Ames, ed., *Chronicles from the Nineteenth Century: Family Letters of Blanche Butler and Adelbert Ames* (Clinton, MA: Privately printed, 1957), 2: 425.

The James brothers' appearance at the farm northwest of Madelia, which belonged to a man named Jackson, was reported in the *St. Paul and Minneapolis Pioneer Press and Tribune*, Sept. 16, 1876; and the *Faribault Democrat*, Sept. 22, 1876.

259 Frank and Jesse's overnight stay with the German farmer near Lamberton is from the *Pioneer Press and Tribune*, Sept. 19, 1876; the *Saint Paul Dispatch*, Sept. 18, 1876; the *Minneapolis Tribune*, Sept. 18, 1876; and the *Faribault Democrat*, Sept. 22, 1876. Because of the German farmer's information that both outlaws had wounds in their right legs, some newspapers speculated that both wounds came from the single shot of the guard at Lake Crystal. And because of Cole Younger's claim that neither Frank nor Jesse had wounds when the gang split, there has been a willingness to accept this theory. However, as will be seen in this chapter, Frank would tell Dr. Mosher that he received his wound in Northfield. And we have the account of farmer Jackson near Madelia, cited above, who observed one of the outlaws, whom I believe to have been Frank, dressing an "old" wound—Frank's

wound was more than a week old at that time. Years later, the Lake Crystal guard, Richard Roberts, would claim there was a bullet hole in the hat lost by one of the robbers (he believed the hat belonged to Jesse). Roberts assumed that the bullet hole had come from his gun, but it could just as easily have come from one of the Northfield citizens, and likely did. I believe, then, that Jesse's wound in the right leg came from Roberts. Roberts's reminiscence is in the *Mankato Free Press*, Feb. 16, 1931.

260 The events and route of Jesse and Frank's flight from near Lamberton to near Sioux City, IA, are at times most difficult to decipher. Various newspapers sometimes published contradictory or variant versions of the same incident, leading later writers to make one episode into two or three. There were also numerous false sightings and reports (like the one out of Yankton, Dakota Territory, claiming that 150 Indians were chasing Jesse and Frank). Reminiscences and local folklore usually add nothing but more confusion. I have drawn my narrative from the following sources: the *Pioneer Press and Tribune*, Sept. 19, 1876; the *Faribault Democrat*, Sept. 22, 1876; the *Sioux City Daily Journal*, Sept. 19, 21, and 24, 1876; the *Sioux Valley News*, Sept. 23, 1876; and the *St. Louis Globe-Democrat*, Sept. 25, 1876. An account supposedly written by a posse member who trailed the James brothers from Mankato to Dakota Territory appeared in the *St. Louis Globe-Democrat* of Dec. 5, 1876, under the title "A Ride for Life." Purporting

to correct many errors reported about the manhunt, this article commits a number of its own. I have also made extensive use of U.S. and state censuses to verify names and ages of some of the people Jesse and Frank encountered, as well as to confirm the locations of their residences.

261 An incident that caused much confusion at the time—and still does today—was the sighting of three suspicious men on foot on Sunday afternoon, Sept. 17, at Ocheda Lake, four miles southwest of Worthington, MN. The individual who spotted the men said one wore a rubber coat with a cape. One of the men appeared to be sick or wounded, for as the three fled, the wounded man fell several times and had to be helped up. When a posse traveled to the scene the next morning, they found tracks made by "the notorious square-toed boot with small heel." But that's all they found; the three suspicious men were not seen again. Many naturally suspected that these men were part of the James-Younger gang. They were not. The James brothers were at least forty miles away at the time, mounted on the noted iron-gray mares. The Youngers and Charlie Pitts were somewhere between Mankato and Linden Lake. The three mysterious men—if they were not the figment of someone's imagination—may very well have been nefarious characters with their own reasons for avoiding contact with strangers. See the *Saint Paul Dispatch*, Sept. 18, 1876; the *Mankato Review*, Sept. 19, 1876; and the *Worthington Advance*, Sept. 21, 1876.

263 Perhaps the most ludicrous tale connected with the James boys' flight is the story that Jesse, a posse close on his heels, jumped a chasm twenty feet wide called Devil's Gulch (today within Devil's Gulch Park, near Garretson, SD). Jesse is supposed to have performed the feat on horseback, of course, but the tale does not explain what happened to Frank. Nor does it explain how Jesse could have jumped the gulch when he and Frank actually passed several miles to the south. Another problem with the story—conveniently overlooked by writers—is that the iron-gray mares were completely used up by this time. Jesse would have been lucky to coax his exhausted mount over a small ditch, let alone a chasm of twenty feet. See Ried Holien, "Did Jesse James Jump?" *True West* (Jan.–Feb., 2009); and Charles A. Smith, "The James Brothers in Dakota," typescript, folder 1, Homer Croy Papers, Western Historical Manuscript Collection, Columbia, MO.

267 A good contemporary account of Dr. Mosher's encounter with the James brothers appeared in the *Sioux City Daily Journal*, Sept. 22, 1876. However, the best and most detailed account, and one previously unknown, is the story Mosher gave to a *Pioneer Press* reporter in 1878. The *Sedalia Weekly Bazoo* reprinted the story in its issue of May 28, 1878, and it is this *Bazoo* version that I have consulted. See also "Sioux City Family Treasures Bullet Pierced Trousers Worn by One of James Brothers," newspaper clipping, Northfield Public Library, Northfield, MN.

276 Richard S. Hall, a brother-in-law of the Youngers, met Dr. Mosher while on a trip to visit the Youngers in jail at Faribault. Mosher told Hall that Frank had a severe wound above his knee and that Jesse was wounded just above the heel. See the *Kansas City Times*, Oct. 10, 1876.

277 Several newspapers ran the story that Jesse and Frank paid a farmer, J. C. Thompson, to take them a distance away with his buggy and team, leaving their gray and bay horses in Thompson's barn. According to the story, nightfall had arrived and Thompson was still missing. I could find no follow-up reports to this incident, however, an incident that I do not believe to be true. At the same time the story placed Jesse and Frank with Thompson, the brothers were spotted miles away, still riding the gray and bay horses. See the *Sioux City Daily Journal*, Sept. 23, 1876; and the *Minneapolis Tribune*, Sept. 23, 1876.

For the James brothers' route from the West Fork of the Little Sioux to Ida Grove, see the *Sioux City Daily Journal*, Sept. 26, 1876. The quote from the posse member about letting "someone else" head off the Jameses is from the same issue.

278 The Iowa newspaper quote lamenting that more had not been done to capture the James brothers is from the *Iowa Liberal*, Le Mars, IA, Sept. 27, 1876.

280 Chief McDonough's boast to Governor Hardin about being able to capture the James boys is from his letter of Sept. 29, as quoted in Nancy B. Samuelson, "How

the James Boys Fled the Disaster at Northfield and the Capture of 'Frank James,'" *Western Outlaw-Lawman History Association Journal* 3 (Spring-Summer 1993): 4–9. Zerelda Samuel's experience with the detectives/ lighting rod salesmen is quoted from the *Kansas City Times*, Oct. 17, 1876.

282 The capture of John N. Goodin (also Goodwin) and the subsequent controversy over his identity were covered extensively in the press. See the *Kansas City Times*, Oct. 15, 17, and 18, 1876; the *St. Louis Globe-Democrat*, Oct. 15, 16, 17, 18, and 19, 1876, and Sept. 8, 1880; and the *State Journal,* Jefferson City, MO, Oct. 20, 1876. Chief McDonough's letter of Oct. 19 informing the Missouri governor that Goodin was innocent is in Records of Charles Henry Hardin, 1875–1877 (RG 3.22), Missouri State Archives, Jefferson City, MO.

286 John N. Goodin's lawsuit against Chief McDonough appears to have been unsuccessful. Goodin was reported to have sued Sergeant Boland, also unsuccessfully. See the *St. Louis Globe-Democrat*, Mar. 19, 1879, and Sept. 8, 1880.

287 The information on the James brothers' escape route provided by the unnamed Independence man appeared in the *Kansas City Times*, Oct. 15, 1876. This informant also stated that "Both were wounded, one in the leg and the other in the foot."

The Bob and Charley Ford interview appeared in the *St. Louis Globe-Democrat*, Apr. 8, 1882. Dick Liddil's comments on the James brothers' escape are from George Miller Jr., *The Trial of Frank James for Murder* (1898; reprint, New York: Jingle Bob/Crown Publishers, 1977), 329–330; and William H. Wallace, *Speeches and Writings of Wm. H. Wallace, with Autobiography* (Kansas City: The Western Baptist Publishing Co., 1914), 291–292.

288 The claim by the Sioux City newspaper editor that he helped the James brothers escape is from the *Sioux City Journal,* July 25, 1954. The reminiscence claiming the Jameses escaped through Wisconson is in L. B. Keene to Homer Croy, Seattle, WA, July 16, 1949, folder 746, Homer Croy Papers.

Jim Cummins is quoted from the *Interior Journal,* Stanford, KY, May 5, 1916. The story originally appeared in the *Kansas City Star.* The book he said he was writing on the James gang was never published and likely was never completed. Cummins died at Missouri's Confederate Soldiers Home in Higginsville in 1929.

289 In Dick Liddil's signed confession, he stated that "Ed Miller [Clell's brother] told me that Jesse and Frank a short time after the Northfield robbery went to Mrs. Samuels'. They were both wounded. Jesse told me that he was also at Gen. Jo. Shelby's in Lafayette county before he got well of his wounds." Liddil is quoted from the *Sedalia Weekly Bazoo,* Sept. 18, 1883. Clay County sheriff John S. Groom believed that Jesse and Frank had "been in Clay and Caldwell counties ever since the raid into Minnesota, and that they had been

harbored by citizens of those counties." As quoted in the *Liberty Tribune,* Jan. 19, 1877.

General Jo Shelby is quoted from the *Kansas City Journal,* Apr. 2, 1882. Shelby claimed that the James brothers and other guerrillas saved him from capture at the Battle of Prairie Grove, AK, in 1862. However, from everything we know, Jesse and Frank were not participants in that engagement.

290 The *St. Louis Globe-Democrat* on the breaking up of the James-Younger gang is from the issue for Sept. 25, 1876.

Nine: One Last Escape

292 The accidental shooting of Faribault policeman William Henry Kapernick is from the *Faribault Republican,* Oct. 4, 1876; and the *Faribault Democrat,* Oct. 6, 1876.

293 J. Newton Nind related the purpose of his daily visits to the Youngers in the Rice County jail in a letter to a Mr. Curtis dated Chicago, June 30, 1905. This letter is in the collection of Robert G. McCubbin, Santa Fe, NM.

294 Henrietta Younger's visit to her brothers was widely reported. See the *Minneapolis Tribune,* Oct. 4, 1876; the *Faribault Republican,* Oct. 4, 1876; and the *Saint Peter Tribune,* Oct. 4, 1876. Richard Hall mentioned Ira Sumner's offer of $500 for Henrietta's portrait in an interview given upon their return to Missouri. See the *Kansas City Times,* Oct. 10, 1876.

295 For the visit of Sam Hardwicke and Edward T. Miller to the Rice County jail, see the *Liberty Tribune*, Oct. 27, 1876. The interview with Zerelda Samuel, originally published in the *Chicago Times*, was carried in several newspapers, including the *Saint Paul Dispatch* of Oct. 19, 1876. The *Saint Paul Dispatch* reporter's interview with Sam Hardwicke is in the *Saint Peter Tribune*, Oct. 25, 1876. See also "Why It Was the James Boys Went to Minnesota," the *State Journal*, Oct. 27, 1876.

298 Hardwicke's letter urging that the Missouri governor pay the Rocky Cut rewards was written to Judge E. H. Norton, Platte City, MO, on Dec. 23, 1876. A transcription of the letter appears in Nancy B. Samuelson, "How the James Boys Fled the Disaster at Northfield and the Capture of 'Frank James.'" *Western Outlaw-Lawman History Association Journal* 3 (Spring-Summer 1993): 9.

The First National Bank of Northfield withdrew its reward offer for the capture of Jesse and Frank on Jan. 3, 1877. Bank circular from J. C. Nutting, Correspondence records file, Northfield Historical Society, Northfield, MN.

299 For the court proceedings connected to the Younger case and their appearances in the courtroom of Judge Samuel Lord, I have relied entirely on contemporary newspaper accounts. They are the *Faribault Democrat*, Nov. 17 and 24, 1876; the *Saint Paul Dispatch*, Nov. 1, 15, 17, 18, 20, and 21, 1876; and the *Minneapolis Tribune*, Nov. 14–21, 1876. For criticism of the

Minnesota law allowing the Youngers to escape capital punishment by pleading guilty, see the *Pioneer Press and Tribune,* Sept. 24 and 26, 1876. Jim Younger's refusal to reveal the names of the two robbers who escaped is quoted from the *Mankato Review,* Nov. 28, 1876.

305 Sheriff Groom's raid was reported in the *St. Louis Globe-Democrat,* Nov. 24 and 26, 1876; the *Liberty Tribune,* Dec. 1, 1876; and the *State Journal,* Dec. 8, 1876. The role of Jesse's cousin, Ed Samuel, in tipping off Sheriff Groom was revealed in an article published in the *San Francisco Daily Evening Bulletin,* Feb. 25, 1880, copied from the *Kansas City Times.*

307 The best reference for Jesse and Frank's time in Tennessee is Ted P. Yeatman, *Frank and Jesse James: The Story Behind the Legend* (Nashville, TN: Cumberland House, 2000). Frank recounted some of his Tennessee activities in an interview published in the *St. Louis Republican,* Oct. 6, 1882. See also the account of a close Tennessee acquaintance of the James brothers in Robertus Love, *The Rise and Fall of Jesse James* (New York: G. P. Putnam's Sons, 1926), 257–268.

308 For the Glendale train robbery, see the *St. Louis Globe-Democrat,* Oct. 10, 1879, and Sept. 24, 1881. For the Mammoth Cave stage robbery, see Yeatman, 220–221; and the *New York Tribune,* Sept. 5, 1880. For the Winston train robbery, see George Miller Jr., *The Trial of Frank James for Murder* (1898; reprint, New York: Jingle Bob/Crown Publishers, 1977), 43–44 and 311–312; the *St. Louis Globe-Democrat,* July 17, 1881,

and Sept. 1, 1882; and the *Sedalia Weekly Bazoo,* July 26, 1881.

310 Charley Ford said that his share from the Blue Cut robbery was $135 and a gold watch and chain. Clarence Hite said that each man got about $140. See the *Richmond Democrat,* Aug. 16, 1883; Miller, *The Trial of Frank James,* 318; and the *St. Louis Globe-Democrat,* Sept. 8 and 9, 1881.

311 Jesse's designs on the Platte City bank are from interviews with the Ford brothers that appeared in the *Western News,* St. Joseph, MO, Apr. 7, 1882; and the *Kansas City Daily Journal,* Apr. 4, 1882.

Ed Miller's death was reported in the *St. Louis Globe-Democrat,* Oct. 31, 1881. For various theories on Jesse's reason for killing Miller, see the *St. Louis Globe-Democrat,* issue cited above, and those for Apr. 1 and 8, 1882.

312 There is some confusion over the reward offered the Ford boys by Governor Crittenden. The figures I use are from an interview with Charley Ford that appeared in the *Richmond Democrat,* Aug. 16, 1883. However, the governor's July 28, 1881, proclamation offered $5,000 each for the "arrest and delivery" of Frank and Jesse and another $5,000 each upon conviction. The official proclamation did not offer a reward for the outlaws "dead or alive," and Crittenden would strongly deny that he offered the Ford boys such a provision. Yet in a newspaper interview from October 1882, Crittenden is quoted as saying, "I offered a reward of

$50,000 for the arrest and conviction of those bandits who belonged to the James gang, and $10,000 each for Jesse and Frank James, dead or alive." This statement is in line with the claim of Charley Ford. The Crittenden interview was published in the *Rocky Mountain News*, Oct. 4, 1882. See also H. C. Crittenden, ed., *The Crittenden Memoirs* (New York: G. P. Putnam's Sons, 1936), 224–225.

313 For contemporary accounts of Jesse's death, including interviews and testimony of the Ford brothers, see the *Western News*, Apr. 7, 1882; the *Daily Gazette*, St. Joseph, MO, Apr. 5, 1882 (extra edition); the *Kansas City Daily Journal*, Apr. 4, 1882; and the *Weekly Graphic*, Kirksville, MO, Apr. 7, 1882. The St. Joseph telegraph operator's recollections of Bob and Charley Ford are in the *Hickman Courier*, Hickman, KY, Dec. 1, 1901.

315 Frank's reaction to his brother's death is from his own account as published in the *St. Louis Globe-Democrat*, Sept. 1, 1883; and a statement by Frank's son, Robert, to Elmer Pigg. See Elmer Pigg to Homer Croy, Jefferson City, MO, Oct. 30, 1948, folder 742, Homer Croy Papers, Western Historical Manuscript Collection, Columbia, MO. The *New York Herald* reported Jesse's death in its issue of Apr. 4, 1882.

Annie James is as quoted in William H. Wallace, *Speeches and Writings of Wm. H. Wallace, with Autobiography* (Kansas City: The Western Baptist Publishing Co., 1914), 284.

316 For the visit of Annie James and Zerelda Samuel to Governor Crittenden, see the *St. Louis Globe-Democrat,* June 4, 1882. The surrender of Frank James is from Governor Crittenden's own account of the event in the *Rocky Mountain News,* Oct. 10, 1882. See also the *St. Louis Republican,* Oct. 6, 1882.

318 Several newspapers described Frank James's stay in the county jail in Independence and the steady stream of visitors he drew. See the *Kansas City Daily Journal,* Oct. 8 and 9, 1882; and the *Jefferson City Daily Tribune,* Feb. 11, 1883. The "darling of Missouri society" quote is from the *Winona Daily Republican,* Nov. 13, 1882.

319 John Newman Edwards letter of Oct. 26, 1882, to Frank James, written at Sedalia, MO, is in the collection of Robert G. McCubbin, Santa Fe, NM.

321 Students of the Northfield Raid and the James-Younger gang have been unaware that Governor Hubbard's requisition for Frank James still existed. After reading in the contemporary newspaper reports that Governor Crittenden returned the requisition to Hubbard, I asked my friend, Donna Tatting, of Forest Lake, MN, to check in the requisitions file of Hubbard's papers at the Minnesota Historical Society to see if it contained the James requisition. It did. She found it in box 29, folder 488 of the Records of Governor Lucius F. Hubbard, 1882–1891. The requisition is very significant because it contains the sworn complaint and affidavit of Frank Wilcox naming Frank James as the killer of

Joseph Lee Heywood. The complaint and affidavit are previously unknown to scholars.

The receipt and return of the Minnesota requisition was reported in the *St. Louis Globe-Democrat,* Feb. 8, 1883; and the *St. Paul Daily Globe,* Feb. 10, 1883. Frank James is quoted from the *St. Louis Globe-Democrat,* Feb. 9, 1883.

322 The Edwards letter to Frank James of Mar. 18, 1885, is as quoted in William A. Settle Jr., *Jesse James Was His Name, or Fact and Fiction Concerning the Careers of the Notorious James Brothers of Missouri* (Columbia: University of Missouri Press, 1966), 158.

Epilogue

324 I have not attempted to chronicle the Youngers' years at Stillwater, although because they were the prison's most famous inmates, there is considerable primary source material available. The best published account of their time as inmates is John Koblas, *When the Heavens Fell: The Youngers in Stillwater Prison* (St. Cloud, MN: North Star Press of St. Cloud, 2002).

325 Cole's account of the raid appeared in the *Saint Paul Globe,* July 4, 1897, as well as in several other newspapers.

327 The letters and petitions submitted in conjunction with the Younger application to the pardon board are in the collections of the Minnesota Historical Society. Many are available online at http://www.mnhs.org/library/

findaids/gr00277.xml. Several letters in support of the pardon are also published in W. C. Bronaugh, *The Youngers' Fight for Freedom* (Columbia, MO: E. W. Stephens Publishing Company, 1906). Warren C. Bronaugh, a Missouri Confederate veteran, was a driving force behind the efforts to secure the release of the Youngers.

There were some, including the Stillwater warden, who suspected that Horace Greeley Perry had more than platonic feelings for Cole. See Bronaugh, 285–290. Perry had a very interesting career as a journalist, eventually becoming a reporter for a newspaper in Mexico City. See "Is a Smart Woman: Miss Horace Greeley Perry and Her Work," the *Broad Ax*, Salt Lake City, Sept. 25, 1898; and "She Braved Indians and Bears and Got a Husband," the *Des Moines Daily News*, Aug. 19, 1906.

328 Northfield's reactions to Cole Younger's written account of the raid and the townspeople's objections to a pardon are chronicled in the *Saint Paul Globe*, July 7, 1897. Mayor A. D. Keyes is quoted from the *Northfield News*, July 17, 1897. See also "Youngers Are Denied a Pardon," the *Saint Paul Globe*, July 14, 1897.

329 For the parole of Cole and Jim Younger, see the *Minneapolis Journal*, Apr. 12 and July 10, 1901; the *Saint Paul Globe*, Mar. 8, 1901; and the *St. Louis Republic*, July 11, 1901.

330 For Jim Younger's life after his parole and his suicide, see the *Saint Paul Globe*, Oct. 20 and 21, 1902; the

Minneapolis Journal, Oct. 20, 1902; and the *St. Louis Republic*, Oct. 26, 1902. For Younger's relationship with Alix J. Muller, see the *Boston Globe*, Aug. 30, 1901; the *St. Louis Republic*, Oct. 21, 1902; the *St. Paul Globe*, Oct. 26, 1902; and "Tragic Romance in the Life of Jim Younger," the *Jennings Daily Record*, Jennings, LA, Dec. 8, 1902. Alix Muller died of tuberculosis two years after Jim's suicide. Her friends claimed her grief over the loss of Jim was "largely the cause" of her death. Her body was cremated, and the ashes reportedly spread over Jim's grave in Lee's Summit, Missouri. See the *Minneapolis Journal*, Apr. 9 and 11, 1904.

332 For Cole's conditional pardon and his return to Missouri, see the *Saint Paul Globe*, Feb. 5 and 10, 1903; and the *Minneapolis Journal*, Feb. 16, 18, and 23, 1903.

The distribution of the reward monies is detailed in the *Mankato Review*, Dec. 18 and 25, 1876. See also the *Madelia Times-Messenger*, Apr. 29, 1938. The legislation outlining how the state's reward offer was to be distributed is found in *General Laws of the State of Minnesota, Passed During the Nineteenth Session of the State Legislature* (St. Paul: Ramaley & Cunningham, 1877), 262–263.

333 Governor Pillsbury's wish that Oscar Sorbel be given an education at the University of Minnesota is from *Annual Message of Governor J. S. Pillsbury to the Legislature of Minnesota, Delivered January 4, 1877* (St. Paul: Pioneer Press Co., 1877), 34–35.

Oscar Sorbel's obituary is in the *Webster Journal*, Webster, SD, July 17, 1930; and the *Evening Tribune*, Albert Lea, MN, Aug. 5, 1930, reprinted from the *Northfield News*. The "rough old codger" quote is from Edith Olson's recollections of Oscar Sorbel, whom she first met in 1927, from the Oscar Sorbel collection of Oscar Lindholm and Myrna Wey, Green Mountain Falls, CO.

The Manning and Wheeler bill, No. 116, is in *House of Representatives of the Nineteenth Session of the Legislature of the State of Minnesota* (St. Paul: Ramaley & Cunningham, 1877), 149. The joint resolution thanking the heroes of Northfield is in *General Laws of the State of Minnesota, Passed During the Nineteenth Session of the State Legislature*, 271–272.

334 For John B. Bresette's later career and death, see the *Saint Paul Globe*, Mar. 18, 1892.

A long letter with several charges against Mike Hoy is in the *Saint Paul Globe*, Aug. 24, 1887. Hoy's obit is in the *Saint Paul Globe* of Mar. 21, 1895.

James McDonough's ouster as chief of police is covered in "The Chief Choked Off," *St. Louis Globe-Democrat*, June 9, 1881. The board of commissioners is quoted from Allen E. Wagner, *Good Order and Safety: A History of the St. Louis Metropolitan Police Department, 1861–1906* (St. Louis: Missouri History Museum, 2008), 193. McDonough's Kansas ranch operations are described in the *St. Louis Globe-*

Democrat, Sept. 27, 1883. His death was reported in the *Daily Inter-Ocean,* Chicago, Mar. 22, 1892.

335 The distribution of monies to Heywood's wife and child are from George Huntington, *Robber and Hero: The Story of the Northfield Raid on the First National Bank of Northfield, Minnesota, by the James-Younger Band of Robbers, in 1876* (1895; reprint, Minneapolis: Ross & Haines, 1962), 105. Details on Lizzie May's later life are from Huntington, 82; and John J. Koblas, *Faithful Unto Death: The James-Younger Raid on the First National Bank, Northfield, Minnesota, September 7, 1876* (Northfield, MN: Northfield Historical Society Press, 2001), 184.

For the legal squabbles of the Ames family and General Butler over the Northfield mill, see Blanche Butler Ames, ed., *Chronicles from the Nineteenth Century: Family Letters of Blanche Butler and Adelbert Ames* (Clinton, MA: Privately printed, 1957), 2: 550–594 passim; and the *Saint Paul Globe,* June 22, 1888. Adelbert Ames's obituary appears in the *New York Times,* Apr. 14, 1933.

336 The Minnesota Historical Society reported on its Northfield Raid acquisitions in *Sixth Biennial Report of the Minnesota Historical Society, St. Paul, to the Legislature of Minnesota, Session of 1891* (Minneapolis: Harrison & Smith, 1890), 19. See also the accession records of the Minnesota Historical Society.

337 The discovery of Pitts's skeleton in Como Lake and its subsequent identification by Dr. Murphy was reported

in the *Saint Paul Globe,* Dec. 13, 1878. The medical student who sank the bones in the lake was Murphy's nephew, Henry F. Hoyt. Hoyt gives his version of the incident in his *A Frontier Doctor,* ed. Doyce B. Nunis Jr. (Chicago: The Lakeside Press, 1979), 34 and 181–183.

338 The letter reporting the burial of Clell Miller's body in the Muddy Fork Cemetery appeared in the *Liberty Tribune,* Nov. 17, 1876.

The story of Elisha Stiles's visit to Dr. Wheeler's Grand Forks office is in "He Shot the Youngers," the *Macon Telegraph,* July 25, 1897. A much later newspaper article claimed that Clell Miller's father visited Wheeler to see the skeleton sometime after 1881. However, Moses Miller died in Missouri in 1879. See the *Waseca Journal,* Waseca, MN, Mar. 4, 1915.

339 That Wheeler claimed to have Miller's bones is revealed in "Survivor Recalls Part in Bank Raid of 1876," *Northfield News,* Sept. 9, 1926. The announcement of the preliminary results of the craniofacial superimposition study, headed by Dr. James Bailey, was reported in the *Northfield News,* Mar. 15, 2012. See also the *Kansas City Star,* June 11, Aug. 10, Sept. 13, and Sept. 24, 2012; and Motion to Exhume the Body of Clelland "Clell" D. Miller, Case No. 12CY-CV09153, Clay County Circuit Court, Liberty, MO.

340 Frank Wilcox's move to Yakima, WA, was reported in the *Yakima Herald,* Aug. 25, 1909. He is also found in the U.S. censuses of 1910 and 1920 living in Yakima County. The gift of the calendar clock to Wilcox is told

in "Old Clock Saw James Robbery," undated clipping, Northfield Public Library.

Sam Hardwicke's return to Clay County is mentioned in the *Liberty Tribune*, July 13, 1877. His reconciliation with Zerelda Samuel is in the *Daily Review*, Decatur, IL, Aug. 2, 1894. Hardwicke's obituary is in the *Liberty Advance*, July 19, 1895.

341 The Younger & James Wild West show is the subject of John J. Koblas's *The Great Cole Younger & Frank James Historical Wild West Show* (St. Cloud, MN: North Star Press of St. Cloud, 2002). See also the *Minneapolis Journal*, Feb. 18, 1903; and the *St. Louis Republic*, Feb. 19, 1903.

342 Governor Johnson is quoted from the *Minneapolis Journal*, June 25, 1906.

343 Harry Hoffman wrote many times of the deathbed conversation with Cole. Hoffman's account of the Northfield Raid, "The Younger Boys Last Stand," which he supposedly based on what Cole told him, is not very reliable. See Harry C. Hoffman, "The Fog Around the Rumors Cleared Away," typescript, Harry Hoffman Donations Accession File, Missouri State Museum, Jefferson City, MO; the Harry Hoffman letters in the Homer Croy and B. James George collections at the Western Historical Manuscript Collection, Columbia, MO; and the *Norborne Democrat and the Leader*, Missouri, Jan. 3, 1936

345 Frank James is as quoted in the *Pittsburgh Press*, Mar. 21, 1915.

Resources

ARCHIVAL MATERIAL

Carleton College Archives, Northfield, Minnesota
"Reminiscences of Carleton's first Dean of Women, Margaret Evans Huntington, made on June 19, 1916"

Milton F. Perry Library, James Farm, Kearney, Missouri
Samuel Hardwicke File
Clell Miller File
Charlie Pitts File
Jesse and Frank James Files

Minnesota Historical Society, St. Paul
Accession Files (Northfield artifacts)
Northfield Bank Robbery of 1876: Selected Manuscript Collections and Government Records (Microfilm M468)
Records of Governor Lucius F. Hubbard, 1882–1891
Rice County District Court Case Files and Miscellaneous Court Papers

Missouri State Archives, Jefferson City
Records of Charles Henry Hardin, 1875–1877 (RG 3.22)
Register of Inmates, Missouri State Penitentiary

Missouri State Museum, Jefferson City
Accession File, Harry Hoffman Donations

Missouri Valley Room, Kansas City Public Library
Newspaper clippings files for James brothers, Younger
    brothers, James-Younger gang

Northfield Historical Society, Northfield, Minnesota
John J. Koblas Collection
Asle Oscar Sorbel Collection
Younger Brothers Indictments File

Northfield Public Library, Northfield, Minnesota
Early Northfield history scrapbook

Rice County Historical Society, Faribault, Minnesota
Grace Sumner Northrop to Emith Buth, Sun City, Arizona,
    July 18, 1978
James-Younger Gang Posse Book
Rice County Jail Inmate Register

Watkins Woolen Mill State Historic Site, Lawson, Missouri
Culbertson Collection

Western Historical Manuscript Collection-Columbia, Missouri
Carland Carr Broadhead Papers, 1853–1908 (C1000)

Bronaugh-Bushnell Family Papers, 1852–1930 (C0079)
Homer Croy Papers, 1905–1965 (C2534)
B. James George Collection, 1832–1965 (C3361)
Missouri, Cooper County. Circuit Court Records, 1876–1884 (C1564)
John A. Rich Diaries, 1884–1943 (C0898)
Cole Younger Papers, 1915 (C1670)

Western History Collections, University of Oklahoma Library, Norman
Jennie (Wells) Lamar interview, #7631, Vol. 52, Indian-Pioneer Papers

PRIVATE COLLECTIONS
David Dary, Norman, Oklahoma
Oscar Lindholm and Myrna Wey, Green Mountain Falls, Colorado
Robert G. McCubbin, Santa Fe, New Mexico

THESIS AND DISSERTATIONS
Dary, David. "Alexander Black MacDonald: Reporter." M.S. Thesis. University of Kansas, Journalism, 1971.

PUBLISHED MATERIAL
Books and Articles
Ames, Blanche Butler, ed. *Chronicles from the Nineteenth Century: Family Letters of Blanche Butler and Adelbert Ames.* 2 vols. Clinton, MA: Privately printed, 1957.

Anderson, John Q. "Another Texas Variant of 'Cole Younger,' Ballad of a Badman." *Western Folklore* 31 (Apr. 1972): 103–115.

Andreas, A. T. *Illustrated Historical Atlas of the State of Iowa*. Chicago: Andreas Atlas Co., 1875.

———. *An Illustrated Historical Atlas of the State of Minnesota*. Chicago: A. T. Andreas, 1874.

Arthur, Anthony. *General Jo Shelby's March*. New York: Random House, 2010.

Bell, Bob Boze. "Classic Gunfights: The Battle of Northfield." *True West* 49 (Aug./Sept. 2002): 24–28.

Berry, C. B. *The Other Side, How It Struck Us*. London: Griffith and Farran, 1880.

Brant, Marley. *Jesse James: The Man and the Myth*. New York: Berkley Books, 1998.

———. *The Outlaw Youngers: A Confederate Brotherhood*. Lanham, MD: Madison Books, 1992.

———. *Outlaws: The Illustrated History of the James-Younger Gang*. Montgomery, AL: Elliott & Clark Publishing, 1997.

Breihan, Carl W. *The Complete and Authentic Life of Jesse James*. New York: Frederick Fell, Inc., 1953.

———. *The Man Who Shot Jesse James*. South Brunswick, NJ: A. S. Barnes and Co., 1979.

———. *Ride the Razor's Edge: The Younger Brothers Story*. Gretna, LA: Pelican Publishing Co., 1992.

———. *Saga of Jesse James*. Caldwell, ID: The Caxton Printers, 1991.

Bronaugh, W. C. *The Youngers' Fight for Freedom*. Columbia, MO: E. W. Stephens Publishing Company, 1906.

Buel, James W. *The Border Outlaws . . .* St. Louis: Historical Publishing Co., 1882.

Cantrell, Dallas. *Youngers' Fatal Blunder, Northfield Minnesota.* San Antonio: The Naylor Company, 1973.

Castel, Albert. "Kansas Jayhawking Raids into Western Missouri in 1861." *Missouri Historical Review* 54 (Oct. 1959): 1–11.

————, and Thomas Goodrich. *Bloody Bill Anderson: The Short, Savage Life of a Civil War Guerrilla.* Mechanicsburg, PA: Stackpole Books, 1998.

Crittenden, H. C., ed. *The Crittenden Memoirs.* New York: G. P. Putnam's Sons, 1936.

Croy, Homer. *Jesse James Was My Neighbor.* New York: Duell, Sloan and Pearce, 1949.

————. *Last of the Great Outlaws: The Story of Cole Younger.* New York: Duell, Sloan and Pearce, 1956.

Cummins, Jim. *Jim Cummins' Book, Written by Himself.* Denver: The Reed Publishing Company, 1903.

————. *Jim Cummins the Guerilla.* Excelsior Springs, MO: The Daily Journal, 1908.

Current, Richard Nelson. *Those Terrible Carpetbaggers: A Reinterpretation.* New York: Oxford University Press, 1988.

Dacus, J. A., and James W. Buel. *A Tour of St. Louis, or, the Inside Life of a Great City.* St. Louis: Western Publishing Co., 1878.

Duke, Thomas S. *Celebrated Criminal Cases of America.* San Francisco: The James H. Barry Company, 1910.

Edwards, Jennie, ed. *John N. Edwards: Biography, Memoirs, Reminiscences and Recollections.* Kansas City: Jennie Edwards, 1889.

Edwards, John N. *Noted Guerillas, or the Warfare on the Border.* St. Louis, MO: Bryan, Brand & Co., 1877.

Fitzgerald, Ruth Coder. *Clell and Ed Miller: Members of the James Gang.* Fredericksburg, VA: Privately printed, 1987.

Geiger, Mark W. *Financial Fraud and Guerrilla Violence in Missouri's Civil War, 1861–1865.* New Haven: Yale University Press, 2010.

George, Todd Menzies. *The Conversion of Cole Younger and the Battle of Lone Jack Early Day Stories.* Kansas City, MO: The Lowell Press, 1963.

Gordon, Welche. *Jesse James and his Band of Notorious Outlaws.* Chicago: Laird & Lee, 1891.

Harrigan, Stephen. "Metamorphosis of a Killer." *American History* 47 (June 2012): 54–61.

Harris, Charles F. "Catalyst for Terror: The Collapse of the Women's Prison in Kansas City." *Missouri Historical Review* 89 (Apr. 1995): 290–306.

Heilbron, W. C. *Convict Life at the Minnesota State Prison, Stillwater, Minnesota.* 1909. Reprint. Stillwater, MN: Valley History Press, 1996.

History of Clay and Platte Counties, Missouri. St. Louis: National Historical Company, 1885.

The History of Daviess County, Missouri. Kansas City: Birdsall & Dean, 1882.

The History of Henry and St. Clair Counties, Missouri. St. Joseph, MO: National Historical Company, 1883.

The History of Jackson County, Missouri. Kansas City, MO: Union Historical Company, 1881.

Horan, James D. Desperate Men: Revelations from the Sealed Pinkerton Files. New York: G. P. Putnam's Sons, 1949.

Hoyt, Henry F. A Frontier Doctor. Edited by Doyce B. Nunis Jr. Chicago: The Lakeside Press, 1979.

Huntington, George. Robber and Hero: The Story of the Northfield Raid on the First National Bank of Northfield, Minnesota, by the James-Younger Band of Robbers, in 1876. 1895. Reprint. Minneapolis: Ross & Haines, 1962.

James, Jesse Jr. Jesse James, My Father. Cleveland: The Arthur Westbrook Co., 1906.

Jesse James: The Life and Daring Adventures of This Bold Highwayman and Bank Robber, and His No Less Celebrated Brother, Frank James . . . Philadelphia: E. E. Barclay and Co., 1883.

Kildahl, Harold B. Westward We Came: A Norwegian Immigrant's Story, 1866–1898. Edited by Erlinge E. Kildahl. West Lafayette, IN: Purdue University Press, 2008.

Koblas, John J. "Charlie Pitts' Body May Have Been Dumped on a Golf Course." James-Younger Gang Journal 17 (Summer 2010): 8–9.

———. Faithful Unto Death: The James-Younger Raid on the First National Bank, Northfield, Minnesota, September 7, 1876. Northfield, MN: Northfield Historical Society Press, 2001.

———. The Great Cole Younger & Frank James Historical Wild West Show. St. Cloud, MN: North Star Press of St. Cloud, 2002.

———. *Jesse James Ate Here: An Outlaw Tour and History of Minnesota at the Time of the Northfield Raid.* St. Cloud, MN: North Star Press of St. Cloud, 2001.

———. *Minnesota Grit: The Men Who Defeated the James-Younger Gang.* St. Cloud, MN: North Star Press of St. Cloud, 2005.

———. *When the Heavens Fell: The Youngers in Stillwater Prison.* St. Cloud, MN: North Star Press of St. Cloud, 2002.

Leading Manufacturers and Merchants of Cincinnati and Environs. Boston: International Publishing Co., 1886.

Lemon, John Jay. *The Northfield Tragedy.* 1876. Reprint. London: Westerners Publications Ltd., 2001.

Leonard, Reverend Delavan L. *The History of Carleton College, Its Origin and Growth, Environment and Builders.* Chicago: Fleming H. Revell Co., 1904.

Leslie, Edward E. *The Devil Knows How to Ride: The True Story of William Clarke Quantrill and His Confederate Raiders.* New York: Random House, 1996.

Lord, Stuart B. "Adelbert Ames: Soldier & Politician, A Reevaluation." *Maine Historical Society Quarterly* 13 (Fall, 1973): 81–97.

Love, Robertus. *The Rise and Fall of Jesse James.* New York: G. P. Putnam's Sons, 1926.

McCorkle, John. *Three Years with Quantrill.* 1914. Reprint. Norman: University of Oklahoma Press, 1992.

McDougal, Henry Clay. *Recollections, 1844–1909.* Kansas City, MO: Franklin Hudson Publishing Co., 1910.

McKinney, Francis F. "The Northfield Raid, and Its Ann Arbor Sequel." *Michigan Alumnus: A Journal of University Perspectives* 61 (Dec. 1954): 38–45.

Mangum, William Preston. "The James-Younger Gang and Their Circle of Friends." *Wild West* 16 (Aug. 2003): 24–31.

Metz, Leon Claire. *The Encyclopedia of Lawmen, Outlaws, and Gunfighters.* New York: Facts on File, Inc., 2003.

Miller, George Jr. *The Trial of Frank James for Murder.* 1898. Reprint. New York: Jingle Bob/Crown Publishers, 1977.

Minnesota State Gazetteer and Business Directory, 1878–9. Detroit, MI: R. L. Polk & Co., 1878.

Morn, Frank. *"The Eye That Never Sleeps": A History of the Pinkerton National Detective Agency.* Bloomington: Indiana University Press, 1982.

Muehlberger, Jim. "Showdown with Jesse James." *Wild West* 22 (Feb. 2010): 50–53.

Neal, Robert J. and Roy G. Jinks. *Smith & Wesson, 1857–1945: A Handbook for Collectors.* Revised edition. New York: A. S. Barnes and Co., 1975.

Newson, T. M. *Pen Pictures of St. Paul, Minnesota, and Biographical Sketches of Old Settlers.* St. Paul, MN: Author, 1886.

The Northfield Bank Raid. Northfield, MN: The Northfield News, 2008.

Otis, Gerald D. *Joseph Lee Heywood: The Humble Hero.* Northfield, MN: Northfield Historical Society, 2006.

Peabody, Christine. "A Lady's Account of the Missouri Express Robbery. *Missouri Historical Review* 66 (July 1972): 671–672.

Pence, Samuel Anderson. *I Knew Frank . . . I Wish I Had Known Jesse.* Independence, MO: Two Trails Publishing, 2007.

Petersen, Paul R. *Quantrill at Lawrence: The Untold Story.* Gretna, LA: Pelican Publishing Co., 2011.

———. *Quantrill of Missouri: The Making of a Guerrilla Warrior, The Man, the Myth, the Soldier.* Nashville: Cumberland House, 2003.

Petrone, Gerard S. *Judgement at Gallatin: The Trial of Frank James.* Lubbock.: Texas Tech University Press, 1998.

Pinkerton, William A. "Highwaymen of the Railroad." *The North American Review* 157 (Nov. 1893): 530–540.

Probing a Mystery. Kearney, MO: The Kearney Courier, 1996.

Rattenbury, Richard C. *Packing Iron: Gunleather of the Frontier West.* Santa Fe, NM: Zon International Publishing Co., 1993.

"Robbery of the United States and Adams Express Companies on the Missouri and Pacific Railroad." *The Expressman's Monthly* (Aug. 1876): 249–252.

Ryan, William Summerfield. *A Biographical Sketch of Mr. James W. Buel, the Famous American Author.* 1889.

Samuelson, Nancy B. "How the James Boys Fled the Disaster at Northfield and the Capture of 'Frank

James.'" *Western Outlaw-Lawman History Association Journal* 3 (Spring-Summer 1993): 4–9.

Settle, William A., Jr. *Jesse James Was His Name, or Fact and Fiction Concerning the Careers of the Notorious James Brothers of Missouri*. Columbia: University of Missouri Press, 1966.

Smith, Robert Barr. *The Last Hurrah of the James-Younger Gang*. Norman: University of Oklahoma Press, 2001.

Spencer, Jake W. *An Authentic and Graphic Account of the Assassination of Jesse W. James, at St. Joseph, Mo., April 3, 1882*. St. Joseph, MO: John Combe, 1882.

Stevens, D. W. *The James Boys in Minnesota*. The Five Cent Wide Awake Library, No. 479. New York: Frank Tousey, 1882.

Stiles, T. J. *Jesse James: Last Rebel of the Civil War*. New York: Alfred A. Knopf, 2002.

Sutherland, Daniel E. *A Savage Conflict: The Decisive Role of Guerrillas in the American Civil War*. Chapel Hill: The University of North Carolina Press, 2009.

Trenerry, Walter N. *Murder in Minnesota: A Collection of True Cases*. St. Paul: Minnesota Historical Society Press, 1962.

Ventimiglia, Jack. *Jesse James in the County of Clay*. Liberty, MO: The Friends of the James Farm, 2001.

Wagner, Allen E. *Good Order and Safety: A History of the St. Louis Metropolitan Police Department, 1861–1906*. St. Louis: Missouri History Museum, 2008.

Wallace, William H. *Speeches and Writings of Wm. H. Wallace, with Autobiography*. Kansas City: The Western Baptist Publishing Co., 1914.

Weinmann, Earl, ed. *Caught in the Storm: A Field Guide to the James & Younger Gang Escape Trail.* Northfield, MN: Northfield Historical Society Press, 2008.

Wells, Shirley. "The Real 'Charlie Pitts.' " *James-Younger Gang Journal* 17 (Summer 2010): 6–7.

Wilde, Oscar. *The Complete Letters of Oscar Wilde.* Edited by Merlin Holland and Rupert Hart-Davis. New York: Henry Holt and Co., 2000.

Wood, Larry. *Ozarks Gunfights and Other Notorious Incidents.* Gretna, LA: Pelican Publishing Company, 2010.

Woodson, W. H. *History of Clay County, Missouri.* Topeka: Historical Publishing Co., 1920.

Wybrow, Robert J. *From the Pen of a Noble Robber: The Letters of Jesses Woodson James, 1847–1882.* London: The English Westerners' Society, 1987.

———. *"Horrid Murder & Heavy Robbery": The Liberty Bank Robbery, 13 February 1866.* London: The English Westerners' Society, 2003.

———. *"My Arm Was Hanging Loose": The Pinkerton Attack on the James' Family Home.* London: The English Westerners' Society, 2005.

———. *"Ravenous Monsters of Society": The Early Exploits of the James Gang.* London: The English Westerners' Society, 1990.

Yeatman, Ted P. *Frank and Jesse James: The Story Behind the Legend.* Nashville, TN: Cumberland House, 2000.

Younger, Thomas Coleman. *The Story of Cole Younger by Himself.* Chicago: The Henneberry Co., 1903.

Ytterboe, Elise. *Ole Voices No. 1, Reminiscenses.* Edited by Jeff M. Sauve. St. Olaf College: Shaw-Olson Center for College History, 2009.

Newspapers
The Atchison Daily Champion (KS)
Boonville Daily Advertiser (MO)
Boonville Weekly Advertiser (MO)
The Boston Globe
The Buckeye Informer (OH)
Cameron Daily Vindicator (MO)
Carrollton Journal
Chicago Tribune
Chillicothe Weekly Constitution (MO)
Colorado Chieftain (Pueblo, CO)
The Columbus Journal (NE)
The Commonwealth (Topeka, KS)
Daily Inter-Ocean (Chicago)
The Daily Review (IL)
The Daily Tribune (Salt Lake City)
The Dubuque Herald (IA)
Eau Claire Leader (WI)
The Evening Tribune (MN)
The Faribault Democrat (MN)
Faribault Republican (MN)
The Farmington Press (MN)
Freeport Journal (IL)
Galveston Daily News
The Hickman Courier (KY)
Indiana Progress (PA)
The Indianapolis Journal
Iola Register (KS)
Iowa Liberal
Ironwood News Record (MI)

Jefferson City Daily Tribune (MO)
Kansas City Daily Journal
Kansas City Daily Journal of Commerce
Kansas City Evening Star
Kansas City Times
Kansas City Weekly Journal
Kansas City Weekly Journal of Commerce
Leavenworth Weekly Times (KS)
Liberty Advance (MO)
Liberty Tribune (MO)
The Macon Telegraph (GA)
Mankato Free Press (MN)
Mankato Record (MN)
The Mankato Review (MN)
Milwaukee Daily Sentinel
The Minneapolis Journal
The Minneapolis Tribune
The New Ulm Herald (MN)
New York Times
The Norborne Democrat and the Leader (MO)
Northfield News (MN)
Oak Grove Banner (MO)
The Palo Alto Pilot (IA)
The Prison Mirror (MN)
Red Wing Argus (MN)
Rice County Journal (MN)
Richmond Conservator (MO)
Richmond Democrat (MO)
Rocky Mountain News
St. Joseph Daily Herald (MO)

St. Joseph Weekly Gazette (MO)
St. Louis Dispatch
St. Louis Globe-Democrat
St. Louis Missouri Republican
St. Louis Republic
St. Paul and Minneapolis Pioneer Press and Tribune
St. Paul Daily Globe
The St. Paul Daily News
Saint Paul Dispatch
Saint Peter Tribune (MN)
Sedalia Daily Democrat (MO)
Sedalia Weekly Bazoo (MO)
Stillwater Messenger (MN)
The Waseca Journal (MN)
The Webster Journal (SD)
Weekly Sedalia Times (MO)
Western News (MO)
Western Progress (MN)
Windom Reporter (MN)
Winona Daily Republican (MN)
Wright County Times (MN)
Troy Herald (MO)

HARPER LUXE

THE NEW LUXURY IN READING

We hope you enjoyed reading
our new, comfortable print size and found it
an experience you would like to repeat.

Well – you're in luck!

HarperLuxe offers the finest in fiction and
nonfiction books in this same larger print size and
paperback format. Light and easy to read, HarperLuxe
paperbacks are for book lovers who want to see
what they are reading without the strain.

For a full listing of titles and
new releases to come, please visit our website:

www.HarperLuxe.com

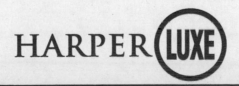